T0243609

ONE SIGNAL
PUBLISHERS

ATRIA

Mood Machine

The Rise of **Spotify** and the Costs of the Perfect Playlist

Liz Pelly

ONE SIGNAL
PUBLISHERS

ATRIA

New York   Amsterdam/Antwerp
London   Toronto   Sydney   New Delhi

ONE SIGNAL
PUBLISHERS

ATRIA

An Imprint of Simon & Schuster, LLC
1230 Avenue of the Americas
New York, NY 10020

First One Signal Publishers/Atria Books hardcover edition January 2025

ONE SIGNAL PUBLISHERS / ATRIA BOOKS
and colophon are trademarks of Simon & Schuster, LLC

For information about special discounts for bulk purchases,
please contact Simon & Schuster Special Sales at 1-866-506-1949
or business@simonandschuster.com.

The Simon & Schuster Speakers Bureau can bring authors to
your live event. For more information or to book an event,
contact the Simon & Schuster Speakers Bureau at 1-866-248-3049
or visit our website at www.simonspeakers.com.

Interior design by Kyle Kabel

Manufactured in the United States of America

1   3   5   7   9   10   8   6   4   2

Library of Congress Cataloging-in-Publication Data has been applied for.

ISBN 978-1-6680-8350-5
ISBN 978-1-6680-8352-9 (ebook)

Contents

Introduction

In the mid-2010s, I had been working as a freelance music journalist for about a decade, and like many other freelance music journalists, I of course had other jobs. One of them was at a DIY music venue in Brooklyn. If there was an indie rock or post-punk band playing in town at the time, I probably saw them, talked to them across the bar, or handed them an envelope of cash at the end of the night. As soon as I became interested in writing my first article about Spotify, the floodgates opened.

All I had to do was bring up the topic of music streaming, and everyone from entrepreneurial label owners to anti-industry punks had an opinion, some intel, or a story tip. In the summer of 2016, a friend who worked in the music industry suggested that I investigate how the major labels were influencing Spotify playlists. A musician I knew from the venue linked me with my first source. It was immediately clear that playlist politics only scratched the surface of streaming-related topics deserving investigation. What started as one blog post turned into almost a decade of researching, writing, and asking questions.

As it turned out, 2016 was a fascinating year to begin covering Spotify. It had been exactly ten years since the company was founded in Stockholm by two advertising industry men opportunistically capitalizing on the music industry's weak status in their home country, thanks to the seemingly unstoppable force that was digital music piracy in Sweden. And it would only be two more years until Spotify went public on the New York Stock Exchange, which meant that in those days, the company was doing everything to make itself attractive to future shareholders. "Everything was about shifting to profitability," a former employee told me. "Everything was about a good IPO, and good shareholder value."

Like other technology companies in the twenty-first century, Spotify spent its first decade claiming to disrupt an archaic industry, scaling as quickly as possible, and attracting venture capitalists to an unproven business model. But the product itself—stream all the world's music for $9.99 per month, or for free with ads—was not turning a profit, which investors would soon demand.

From the app's European launch in 2008, to its U.S. arrival in 2011, to the stock market listing in 2018, Spotify reinvented itself repeatedly: as a social platform in 2010, an apps marketplace in 2011, a hub for what it called "music for every moment" by the end of 2012. The next year came its big move into curation, hiring a staff of full-time editors to compile playlists themed to moods and activities, followed by its 2014 investment in algorithmic personalization tech. All of this so-called innovation was going to "level the playing field" for artists, Spotify obsessively promised.

What we actually got, though, were playlists heavily dominated by major label acts, endless feeds of neo-Muzak loaded with ghost artists—anonymous, stock music commissioned at a discount—and a series of pay-to-play schemes. Those include the controversial Discovery Mode program, which sells (mostly independent) artists and labels algorithmic promotion in exchange for reduced royalty rates, and frames it as an "opportunity." This cost-saving initiative is a move popularly regarded as a new type of payola, the term that emerged in the 1950s to describe the process of record labels making under-the-table cash payments to radio stations in exchange for airplay. For artists trying to figure out how to survive these shifts, there have for many years been more questions than answers.

I've long been confounded by the expectation that we simply accept the dealings of the powerful as unexplainable. It's a perspective informed by my background in DIY music spaces, where we try to live the reality that there are other ways to think about collective culture. Grassroots music communities often work directly to demystify the process of making, distributing, and sharing art. If you show up to a gig an hour before doors, someone might ask if you can help set up chairs or run to the store for some ice. At the end of the show, it's not uncommon to discuss what each band was paid and whether the splits were fair. When it comes to recordings and labels, transparency is held as a foundational ideal worth aspiring to.

With music streaming, it was jarring watching independent artists become convinced to accept a new system that no one could understand.

In my writing and reporting, I've been driven by a deep impulse toward demystification—toward shedding light on the inner workings of streaming companies and debunking the myths they perpetuate. Sometimes it feels more complicated and convoluted than I could have ever imagined. Other times it all just feels like music industry business as usual. The truth is somewhere in the middle: the story of streaming is as much about what's changed as it is about what's stayed the same.

By the mid-2010s, digital media platforms more broadly had been conflating themselves with democracy and self-expression for years, disingenuous claims comprising a defining propaganda project of the Web 2.0 era. Spotify was part of this. The music streaming service had worked tirelessly to position itself as a neutral platform, a data-driven meritocracy that was rewriting the rules of the music business through the power of its playlists and algorithms.

The now-normalized model of an every-song-in-the-world subscription service is a functional impossibility without the participation of the major label oligopoly of Universal, Sony, and Warner, though, who together control 70 percent of the recorded music market. That put the majors in a position of power when they started negotiating their initial deals with Spotify—which was not the first streaming service they all licensed—and by that time, their standard streaming contracts had come to require the labels getting equity, advances, free advertising, and influence over how the platform evolved. At the time Spotify launched, the majors together owned a nearly 18 percent stake in the company.

This is all to say, the very concept of music streaming was designed for the benefit of extremely popular, major label music. But independent musicians have also been expected to conform to its one-size-fits-all model. This is strange and new: independent music has historically maintained its own economies, with its own retail outlets and promotional ecosystem, with dedicated fanbases particularly likely to pay for records and downloads. And while it has become common rhetoric to discuss the algorithm-driven platform era in terms of its flattening of aesthetics, this is also part of the flattening that has occurred: the flattening of the winner-take-all pop star world and the working artists of the independent world. Flattening might really just be another way of thinking about media consolidation.

In her 2014 book *The People's Platform*, the writer and filmmaker Astra Taylor challenged the idea that the so-called digital revolution had democratized culture. In particular, she warned that the same problems of "consolidation, centralization, and commercialism" that defined our old media systems would continue to shape the digital world without a serious reckoning. "Networked technologies do not resolve the contradictions between art and commerce," she wrote, "but rather make commercialism less visible and more pervasive."[1]

There are evergreen lessons for the music world. Independent music—or underground, DIY, alternative, whatever imprecise word you prefer—is also the province of participation and experimentation. Many are drawn to these more subterranean musical worlds because they are places to get involved: start a band, create a radio show, book concerts. The platform era capitalized on people's impulses to want to participate in their own lives, to share their writing and photos and favorite songs, in pursuit of the human need for connection. Being able to participate does not mean that what you're participating in is fair, though. And platforms mostly only offered the illusion of togetherness. They are not public squares; they're corporate digital enclosures where your every move is tracked. Streaming, and Spotify in particular, created a music-themed version, where participation was captured, reduced to data points, and used to strengthen a commercial machine, to achieve the financial goals of Spotify and the majors.

It was not Spotify, or streaming for that matter, that first created the conditions that listeners and artists find themselves existing within today, where art is conflated with content. The roots of commercialism inflecting creativity predate even the era of recorded music. Interrogating the streaming status quo is just one way into that bigger story, at one of its contemporary front lines. And while Spotify's rise to power does not encompass the entire history of streaming, its scale and ubiquity make it a useful entry point to understanding the plights of listeners and musicians today.

In the story of Spotify is the story of a broken music industry desperate to keep existing after the era of digitally enabled file-sharing. Of ad-tech executives bringing the logic of their industry to music in new ways. Of an already highly consolidated industry growing ever more consolidated. It is the story of the twenty-first century's overeager and opportunistic tech solutionists, of billionaires and their overhyped machines, looking around for problems to solve, arrogantly disregarding the social problems left in their wake. It's a story of listeners being sold music more as a utility than an art form, and musicians starting to see themselves more as content creators than artists. It is a story of precarity, hyper-commercialization, individualism, and all of the above being obfuscated under the notion of "vibes." And it's the story of how those problems then played out over the span of many years, as music became personalized, playlisted, autoplayed, and algorithmic. It is the story of the social, cultural, and political issues that came with those changes.

As of this writing, streaming accounts for 84 percent of recorded music revenues, with Spotify, the largest of all services, capturing 30 percent of the market, with over 615 million users and 239 million paying subscribers. And as the public discourse on the relationship between AI and creative labor has taken hold, the whole streaming conversation now takes place under this looming cloud: how tracks created with generative AI software are flooding the streaming services and the effects this will have on working musicians and aspiring artists alike. And while the potential of generative AI feels urgent, it's also important to remember the less flashy ways that artists and listeners have been impacted by different systems of automation and machine learning over the past decade-plus, as artists' careers have become increasingly managed by algorithms, and listening has become more and more mechanized. At a moment when the very future of music can feel at stake, the time feels right to take a serious look both backward and forward.[2]

When I first started conceptualizing this book, I thought it had to be told in two parts. First, there would be unpacking how streaming has impacted listeners, watering down our musical relationships and discouraging adventurous listening via algorithmic homogenization. Second, there would be the story of streaming's impact on artists, with its minuscule payments and new types of pay-to-play. What I learned myself through the process is that these are not separate stories, but entirely connected. Over its first two decades of existence, as Spotify moved from in-house playlisting into its next act as a personalization engine, it became increasingly concerned with shaping user behavior on the platform—which is to say, influencing listening habits, because Spotify benefits when we stream content that's cheaper for them to provide. Internally, the company looks at a metric called "programmed streamshare"—the percentage of total listening influenced by its recommendations—and aims to make that metric increase. This should concern listeners for reasons that go beyond matters of personal taste and user experience, but also due to issues of power and labor. The goal is to hook us as users, of course, but also to divert overall streamshare toward discounted offerings—works that have been licensed to Spotify at a lower price point, both through its ghost artists program and its algorithmic payola-like practices. It might seem grim to realize that what makes culture less interesting for listeners is also what makes it less sustainable for artists. But knowing the opposite is also true—that working collectively to improve material conditions for musicians benefits all of us who love listening to music, too—is where there's power and possibility.

1

The Bureau of Piracy

I n June 2001, over fifteen thousand activists took to the streets of Gothenburg to protest that year's European Union summit, where political leaders would be meeting with then U.S. President George W. Bush. This was the height of the anti-globalization movement, which saw mass mobilizations swarming the private meetings of the power brokers of global capitalism. In those years, protesters regularly showed up by the thousands to disrupt meetings of groups like the World Bank, the World Trade Organization, and the G8, and to loudly condemn what they represented: the corporate privatization of everything.

In Sweden, the police response was brutal. Three protesters were shot in the street; hundreds were injured. "It was a kind of traumatic experience for many people," recalled Rasmus Fleischer, a Stockholm-based writer, academic researcher, and musician, who took part in the protests. "After 2001, for many of us, there was a search for how to find another kind of activism that was not so much about going with thousands of people to one city at a time, but building from everyday life."

Some Swedish anti-globalization activists turned to local projects. In Stockholm, they took on public transportation during a time when significant fare hikes were leading many to fare dodge. To promote riding for free, which they saw as a form of strike, and to simultaneously wage a campaign for accessible public transport, they organized a fund akin to DIY insurance: pay 100 krona per month, or about $10, and if you're caught fare dodging, we'll cover your ticket.

"The Bureau of Piracy was another one," Fleischer told me, referring to Piratbyrån, an activist group he co-created in 2003, promoting free music and information sharing. Piratbyrån would become best known for some of its members eventually creating the Pirate Bay, the world's largest website for downloading music and movies using peer-to-peer file-sharing, meaning its users could obtain items from each other's libraries without a central server.

Piratbyrån was a "hard to pin down group that tended to morph over time" with a membership of varying ideologies—there were left-wing political activists, but the loose collective also included hackers and musicians, punks and ravers. It was formed in response to Antipiratbyrån, or the Anti-Piracy Bureau, a local Hollywood-aligned, anti-piracy lobbying group. Piratbyrån's goal was to provide a counterweight in the public arena. They were taking on the big questions, Fleischer explained: "What are the alternative ways to think about power over networks? What counts as art and what counts as legitimate ways of using it? Or distributing money? We involved ourselves in these discussions."

The group was "trying to make something political from the already existing practice of file-sharing," he continued. "I guess it blew up more than anyone expected, and continued to morph in different ways."

When Spotify was born in 2006, the Swedish debates around piracy were reaching a fever pitch. By that year, the Swedish census had found that 1.2 million out of the country's 9 million citizens took part in file-sharing. The practice wasn't only incredibly popular in Sweden; it was also a regular topic of national media coverage. There was even an entire political party, called the Pirate Party, which was unaffiliated with Piratbyrån, but contributed to the urgency of the discourse.[1]

The Pirate Bay, which eventually split off from Piratbyrån, was the bane of the global entertainment industry's existence. When the website went live in 2003, the major labels had just spent four years trying to stop the unrelenting wave of digital piracy unleashed by Napster in 1999. Napster arrived at the height of the CD boom, an era when unprecedented profits—and corporate greed—defined the music business. On Napster, users could search for and download any track within minutes. Piracy had existed in different forms for generations among music enthusiasts, from the bootlegging of the early recorded music era to the tape trading that came with the rise of the cassette. Musicians always had varied feelings about it. "Home taping is killing record industry profits!" wrote the left-wing punks Dead Kennedys on the packaging of a 1981 cassette. "We left this side blank so you can help."[2]

But Napster took piracy mainstream. At its peak, in 2000, it had over 60 million users. Record execs were split on how to deal with Napster, and ultimately, the response from the music industry was incoherent. The major label lobbying group, the Recording Industry Association of America, began scheming ways that the labels and the pirates could strike a deal to legalize the app—and at the same time, they launched lawsuits to sue Napster out of existence. By late 2000, Thomas Middelhoff, the head of the German multimedia conglomerate Bertelsmann AG, had announced a $60 million deal with Napster, and plans to develop a paid platform—all while the major label that his company owned, BMG Records, was suing Napster for copyright violations. Months later, in the spring of 2001, Napster was shuttered in a $20 billion infringement lawsuit waged by another major label, *A&M Records, Inc. v. Napster, Inc.* The file-sharing company went bankrupt, and Middelhoff was fired.[3]

While some industry factions were spending money on TV commercials broadcasting the virtues of buying CDs to put money in artists' pockets, others were trying to figure out how they could launch all-you-can-eat subscription services that certain artists and managers, from the start, vehemently opposed. Two of the first streaming platforms both launched in 2001: PressPlay, a joint venture between Universal and Sony, and Music-Net, a creation of BMG, EMI, AOL Time Warner, and Real Networks. Both were categorical disasters, not just because of the reportedly clunky interfaces and complicated user terms, but because of the crumbs they were set to pay musicians. Some artists could quickly see that these efforts might be more about the majors capitalizing on consumer trends to boost label profits, rather than trying to figure out fair licensing deals for those who created the music. As one pop music manager told the *New York Times* in 2002: "All of my clients had their attorneys advise the labels that if they did use my clients' music on PressPlay or MusicNet, they would be in breach of contract. Some artists they took off, but some they didn't. It's becoming very obvious to me and my peers that we're becoming victims of what is a huge conspiracy." It should give readers pause that "a huge conspiracy" was one of the first phrases used to describe music streaming in the mainstream news media.[4]

The labels called musicians "ungrateful" for the work they were doing to launch "legitimate" responses to piracy, the article continued, while artist representatives presciently worried that a horrible precedent was being set for future subscription services drastically underpaying artists. The artist teams also accused the majors of breaking contracts, putting music on their new streaming services without permission, and then bullying artists into accepting the poor deal terms. Soon enough, the majors had added clauses to record contracts automatically allowing them to sell an artist's music through subscription services; take it or leave it.

And the services would continue to appear. Rhapsody also arrived in 2001—shortly before PressPlay and MusicNet, in fact—as a streaming offering launched by Listen.com, a directory for legal mp3 downloads. Another early streamer was imeem, a VC-funded, ad-supported service founded in 2003, attempting to offer a social music platform at a time when Apple and Amazon were launching their mp3 stores. In 2007, the press around imeem emphasized the licensing deals it struck with the labels: the majors were reportedly paid multimillion-dollar advances, given equity stakes, and were making flat rates of up to a penny per stream. Similar terms would be reported for other streaming start-ups throughout the mid-2000s. "By the time Spotify came along, there was a quite well-established business model for how we would license subscription services," one major label digital director, who was close to the first license negotiations, told me.[5]

But for all of the record industry's anti-piracy PSAs and failed streaming start-ups, file-sharing seemingly could not be stopped. The RIAA made a big show of directly taking legal action against music fans throughout the decade: it sued upward of eighteen thousand individuals for downloading songs in the U.S., levying fines, and even taking some listeners to court in cases that played out for years. But just a few months before Napster closed, Kazaa had already launched. And soon after, there were Lime-Wire, Grokster, Morpheus, and the Pirate Bay. And while the U.S. music industry was heavily reliant on the Apple iTunes store during this period (which launched in 2003 and gave labels seventy percent of money from downloads), it was never really embraced by Swedish music fans. The life of piracy was different in Sweden, on a cultural and political level, and thought to have been more pervasive than anywhere else.[6]

"It was not a coincidence that [Spotify] started in Sweden," said Fleischer, who in 2019 was also one of five coauthors of *Spotify Teardown:*

Inside the Black Box of Streaming Music. "The big record companies were very reluctant to license something like Spotify at the time, except maybe in a place like Sweden. At the time, the record companies talked about Sweden as a lost market."

If the activist scene's first turn to local work was a fare strike, Piratbyrån seemed to position file-sharing like a strike against the corporate culture industry, an argument for culture as a public good. But what was the then-popular ideological argument for free music? To Peter Sunde, one of the three Piratbyrån members who went on to create the Pirate Bay, it lies in understanding the meaning of free. "I don't mean *gratis*," he clarified on our phone call. "I mean more like *libre*. Actual free culture that is not based on financial incentive, or someone making money somewhere along the line, but on actual love for culture itself."

"We were people who were interested in culture and society, who found technology to be fascinating," Sunde continued. "We had an ideological goal, which is the opposite approach of what tech people usually do. I'm from the tech community. It's usually that someone accidentally bumps into some technology and then has this idea of okay, I know how to improve this, I can make this. But it's rare that they do it for ideological reasons."

Even some musicians supported Piratbyrån, for reasons that Fleischer put bluntly: "For them, it never really appeared that the official music economy was a working entity anyway."

One of those musicians was Dennis Lyxzén, the singer of the long-running Swedish hardcore band Refused, who at the time was playing with International Noise Conspiracy. Today, he continues to be a full-time musician playing in a handful of groups, including fronting a post-hardcore supergroup Fake Names (which includes former members of the germinal Dischord Records bands Minor Threat and Embrace). In Stockholm, we met up as his post-punk band INVSN was about to play a packed Saturday night show. "There was an idea that here comes a new sort of way of viewing music, an economy that might change, or at least challenge the capitalist infrastructures," he said, sitting outside the club between sound check and doors. "That we can share stuff with each other, help each other out, and sort of undermine the basis of capitalism. I thought that was super exciting."

"In the early days, I was very excited about the idea that this could challenge the rigid structures of the record industry," Lyxzén continued. "How wrong I turned out to be. I mean, 100 percent wrong. From this idea of 'let's challenge these power structures' came a paradigm shift that just became a new power structure that did not benefit musicians at all. It did not challenge capitalism at all, but became an ultra-capitalist sort of thing."

The messy reality was that multinational technology corporations and their extractive advertising models ultimately benefited greatly from the celebration of gratis music circulation online. Olaf Dreier of the Knife, who DJed at Piratbyrån's first party, likened it to a process of co-optation. "All of this piracy, somehow, had done the groundwork for all of this," he said. "It's like a gentrification." And while there's much discussion about the impact of technology on music, there has been less about the impact of music on technology; many of the most invasive developments of the platform era—YouTube and Facebook, for example—were popularized in part thanks to the free circulation of music. For musicians, there could be especially dire outcomes, considering the lack of labor protections for artists.

During the post-piracy but pre-streaming years, musicians around the world were deeply engaged in debates over whether or not the corporate-controlled copyright regime was working in the interests of artists. In 2007, a U.S. indie rocker and activist named Jenny Toomey undertook a research project for which she spoke to musicians from all around the world about copyright, finding that perspectives varied dramatically depending on the broader cultural circumstances artists found themselves within. "There was an extreme diversity around copyright," she said. "I have a very complex feeling about copyright because I do want artists to get paid. And I also don't want information to be locked up."

Toomey had been part of the Washington, DC, underground music scene in the nineties, fronting a popular band called Tsunami and running her own DIY label called Simple Machines. In addition to putting out records, Simple Machines also published an influential booklet called the *Mechanic's Guide*, which instructed musicians on every aspect of recording, producing, and distributing their own records. As the very first digital services of the late nineties and early aughts emerged, Toomey started to wonder what a *Mechanic's Guide* for the Web 2.0 era could look like, eventually leading her to cofound in 2000 an independent music advocacy group called Future of Music Coalition, which exists to this day.

The exploration of copyright felt endless to parse. "It was really scorched earth," she recalled, reflecting on how things had changed between 2000 and 2007. "In the early days, there was this kind of openness where nobody knew where anything was going to go. And you could have these really interesting, complicated conversations about how you might design systems in ways that were more transparent and accountable to artists and would remunerate more royalties to them. It felt like that world was possible."

"But by the end of it, the major labels tried their different platforms, and none of them competed with the tech company offerings," Toomey continued. "The new boss partnered pretty well with the old boss. Instead of having the world that we all thought we would have, where you'd have thousands of artists getting a larger portion of the royalties that they deserved directly, we ended up in an environment where the very value of the artists' work was greatly reduced. The power of gatekeeping got worse, the accountability got less transparent."

In that environment, the industry largely split into two factions, Toomey explained: "The people who wanted everything to be open got supported by the tech companies, and the people who wanted everything to be closed got supported by the traditional major labels, and it became like a religious war."

It can be a bit disorienting to remember just how complicated the pre-streaming discourses about file-sharing and copyright were, if only because so many of the questions that were being asked are ones that independent musicians and organizers are still asking today: questions of whether copyright—and an artist's ability to monetize their copyrights by selling plastic discs and downloads, or renting them out to media conglomerates in exchange for penny fractions—is actually an effective way to support arts and culture.

In attempting to make sense of it all—wanting artists to get paid, and wanting art and culture to be accessible—it can seem that there are convincing arguments on all sides. In the early 2000s, big ideas were in the air. In 2003, the U.S. Center for Economic and Policy Research proposed something called the "Artistic Freedom Voucher," which urged the federal government to dedicate $20 billion dollars to a fund that would give each taxpayer a $100 voucher in the form of a refundable tax credit, which they could voluntarily choose to allocate to a musician or group. "The copyright system is not working," read a pamphlet the organization made to promote its idea, which claimed to "cut out the corporate music industry" and "increase access to music."[7]

The debates about piracy were not just about whether artists should throw their hands up and let all of their music be gratis for all. They were also debates about whether it should be up to the corporate-controlled copyright system to adequately value music and culture. Spotify and streaming more broadly, in a sense, were like a Band-Aid over these debates for politicians and powerful labels. But for some, these debates have never really ended.

"For us, it never felt that there existed a working alternative, or that copyright was that alternative," said Fleischer. "We never claimed to have the definite solution. . . . But we also tried to turn it around and say that strict enforcement of copyright law also does not solve the problem. We tried to not generalize too much between the very different kinds of music . . . for certain music scenes, public support is definitely already very central for how it works. For other parts, it's more based on live music. . . . It has to do with what kind of music subcultures you're involved in yourself. But no, we never had a perfect answer for this, and I still don't have it."

Some researchers have connected the mainstreaming of piracy in Sweden directly to how the country treated the internet as a public good: starting in the nineties, the government provided high-quality public broadband for much of its population, allowing file-sharing and peer-to-peer technology to quickly take hold. And while Sweden had passed legislation discouraging piracy in 2005, it also had privacy laws preventing companies from easily attaching an IP address to a name in order to enforce penalties. Labels had trouble identifying downloaders. Another factor was simply that copyright laws were less rigid in European countries than in the U.S., which was largely considered to be the force exporting aggressive copyright penalties across the world at the time.[8]

In the spring of 2006, the U.S. government threatened to impose trade sanctions on Sweden through the World Trade Organization if it did not "effectively combat crimes against copyright law," a spokesperson for

Sweden's Justice Department said at the time. By the end of May, responding to pressure from the American entertainment industry, Swedish police raided the data center where the Pirate Bay was hosted.[9]

After the Pirate Bay police raid, file-sharing would be in the news every day. Music and media professionals were constantly looping on three words: *new business models, new business models, we need new business models.* "For people starting Spotify, it might have seemed obvious that there was some opportunity to hook into this discourse somehow," Fleischer said. That summer, Spotify would hire its first engineers.

It took until 2008 for the Pirate Bay's three cofounders to be charged with "promoting other people's infringements of copyright laws," and eventually sentenced to year-long prison terms. Infamously, the week after the police investigation concluded in 2008, the police officer leading the effort accepted a six-month job working for Warner Bros., a plaintiff in the case.[10]

When the Pirate Bay's second trial took place in 2009, it was sometimes happening at the exact same moment that Spotify was negotiating licenses for new markets and new product offerings. "The heated debates around file-sharing would be so high on the general agenda in Sweden in a way that might be hard to realize in retrospect," Fleischer recalled. "Anything that could present itself as a solution to this would be very attractive for politicians. . . . This tech solutionist appeal."

As recounted in *Spotify Teardown*, the book Fleischer coauthored, Spotify began as a "de facto pirate service"—because its beta product was made using pirated files—delegitimizing its stated mission of offering an alternative. But what's possibly more telling is Spotify's ambivalence about being grouped in with pirates. It simply aligned itself alternately with piracy or with industry interests when it was convenient to do so.[11]

According to Sunde, from the Pirate Bay, when the idea of Spotify first started spreading word of mouth through tech communities around Stockholm, those in the piracy scene initially thought it could be interesting. "They used torrents, like p2p file-sharing, and all of the music was downloaded from Pirate Bay," he recalled. "People we know worked there. But then we realized it was just people who were interested in selling ads using music. So that was kind of a sad realization."

"Daniel Ek and Martin Lorentzon were advertising dudes who wanted to sell more advertising and realized that music was cheap," Sunde went on.

(In fact, music would eventually prove to be quite expensive.) "That was the starting point for Spotify. It was not *we want to save the music industry*. It was more like *here is a business opportunity*. Every time I hear the story of Spotify, it's this dressed up version. And the record labels want to have that dressed up version, too, because they are storytellers more than anything else. If you start looking at Spotify as an advertising company rather than a culture company, a lot of things make more sense."

2

"Saving" the Music Industry

In the fall of 2005, while the major record labels were trying to figure out what to do about the Pirate Bay, Daniel Ek was on a considerably different journey: working as the twenty-two-year-old chief technical officer of a cartoon doll browser game for tween girls. Though young, Ek had been working in technology since high school. This was the season when Ek began pitching the thirty-six-year-old tech entrepreneur Martin Lorentzon—whose affiliate marketing company was soon to go public and make him a multimillionaire—on the idea that would become Spotify. The concept was not yet music-specific, but he wanted to build something that would combine advertising, streaming, and peer-to-peer technology (which also underpinned file-sharing).[1]

Ek and Lorentzon had some things in common: they both knew a lot about search engine optimization, metadata, and selling ads. But they were by no means music guys. The pair had met for the first time a few months earlier, when Ek unsuccessfully pitched Lorentzon's company on a search product. Ek was starting to make an impression, and Lorentzon decided his next venture would be a partnership with him. Before the end of 2005, they both established holding companies in the small Mediterranean country of Cyprus, a tax haven. In early 2006, Lorentzon sent Ek 10 million crowns, or around $1 million, overnight, to confirm his commitment. That was just the beginning: Lorentzon would eventually fund the first two years of Spotify operations with his own fortunes earned through ad-tech.[2]

Born in 1983 and raised by a single mom, Ek grew up in Rågsved, a working-class suburb of Stockholm. He took an interest in technology as a kid and, by fourteen, was running a website-making business. According to Ek's childhood neighbor, who I happened to meet while in Rågsved, by eighth or ninth grade, Ek was earning thousands of dollars per month this way: "He was making more money than his teachers," the neighbor recalled, with a laugh. In some media appearances, Ek has characterized himself as a musical teenager who liked to play guitar. Sources from Rågsved, though, explained to me that robust local public music education programs meant this was typical—it is common for young people there to play music. At sixteen, Ek unsuccessfully applied to a job at Google, who told him to try again when he had a college degree. Instead, he made his own open-source search engine, and after graduating high school got a job at a local SEO firm, Jajja, before landing at Stardoll. He also founded an ad-targeting business, Advertigo.[3]

Lorentzon was on a different path. Born in 1969, he hailed from Borås, a town in the west of Sweden, and worked in Gothenburg's early dot-com scene, before a stint at a Silicon Valley search engine, and eventually moving to Stockholm in the late nineties for an ad-tech job. In 1999, Lorentzon and a coworker launched Tradedoubler, which automated the sale of banner ads. It became one of Europe's largest affiliate sales networks.

In March of 2006, after Tradedoubler went public, the company bought Ek's Advertigo for $1.3 million. This reportedly added nothing much of value to Tradedoubler, but it allowed Ek to quit his cartoon doll job and focus on what would become Spotify. In his own mythmaking tours of the mainstream media, Ek shaped a grand tale of this brief period, explaining how he and Lorentzon would watch movies in Ek's mom's house and bond over shared feelings of emptiness, spurred on by wealth. Ek has often recounted the story of how after selling Advertigo, he retired at twenty-three, bought a Ferrari, and hit nightclubs, but was totally miserable and felt surrounded by fake people. In the *New Yorker* in 2014 he painted himself like a Swedish tech scene version of Bon Iver. The piece claimed that he'd "moved to a cabin near his parents' place" and "meditated about what to do with his life"; that he and Lorentzon did "soul searching" and reconnected with their authentic selves. But as some Swedish newspaper journalists have chronicled, the beginnings of what would become Spotify had been put in motion for months already.[4]

By the end of 2006, Ek and Lorentzon registered a number of companies in various countries. There was a software company called "Spotify AB"; an advertising company called "Spotify Sweden AB." A parent company, "Spotify Technology SA," was registered to a post office box in Luxembourg, where they wouldn't have to pay Swedish taxes. The purposes of these companies were not clear. Although Spotify has long claimed that Ek aimed to save the music business from the start, there is plenty of evidence against anything so specific. For example, its first U.S. patent application described a platform that would circulate "any kind of digital content, such as music, video, digital films or images."[5]

Lorentzon himself has explained that the early days of the company were about advertising, not music. "The revenue source was ads," he once said on stage at a conference. "Because I had knowledge [of] ads from Tradedoubler. But the traffic source we were debating. Should it be product search? Should it be movies, or audiobooks? And then we ended up with music. So we actually checked the biggest format and we went down to the smallest format. We had no clue about how hard it would be to get the record license agreements."[6]

Ultimately, that's what music was to Spotify in its early days: a traffic source for its advertising product.

Spotify's founders pin the company's official genesis to April 2006, at Lorentzon's thirty-seventh birthday dinner. (If Spotify was, indeed, the result of an existential search for purpose spurred on by the meaninglessness of wealth, it all could have lasted only a few weeks.) By the end of the month, the domain name was registered. The name allegedly had no meaning—it was a word that Ek misheard Lorentzon yell from another room. The company started coming together in earnest that spring, when Spotify recruited its first-ever employee, CTO Andreas Ehn, one of Ek's colleagues from Stardoll.[7]

"It wasn't even clear back then that we were going to do music at all, or that music would be the focus," Ehn once said at a conference appearance, further disproving Spotify's founders' longtime claims that they were driven by a mission to save music. "The initial conversations were around building a video streaming service. And even after the company had got started, we were still considering a video streaming service. It was only after we had recruited the team and started really building things, that we finally decided that we were going to do music."[8]

Ehn started putting together the first team of engineers in the summer of 2006. By some accounts, the eventual decision to focus on music was practical: the files were smaller and would require fewer resources to host. But in retrospect, music may have simply seemed easier because of the industry's then weak position in Sweden, as it struggled against piracy.

In August, the first office opened in Stockholm, and by the fall, Spotify had launched its first bare-bones website, which included a brief bio: "Spotify was founded in 2006 by serial entrepreneurs Daniel Ek and Martin Lorentzon. The company is privately held and has 15 employees. Spotify is based in Luxembourg." (In fact, Spotify was based in Sweden. Only the bank account was in Luxembourg.) Having decided to become a music company, they settled on a slogan printed under a lime-green logo: "Everyone Loves Music."[9]

"When we started, there were a few other commercial music services out there, but we didn't really look to them for inspiration because none of them were particularly successful," Ehn recalled, during the same conference talk. "At the time, a lot of people were already listening to music online, but 98 percent of that music was pirated. . . . The benchmark we set for ourselves wasn't existing music services. It was the file-sharing networks. Two music start-ups came out of Stockholm, Sweden. Spotify and the Pirate Bay. That's what we saw as our competition. And it wasn't because we were out to kill piracy. We didn't mind piracy particularly. But we did want to give users a better experience."[10]

In Spotify's quest to create a product that was "better than piracy," as Ek would often say, it aimed to have files load and stream as quickly as possible when a user pressed "play." The engineering team even gave themselves a specific metric: any song should begin within two hundred milliseconds of pressing the button. They wanted it to feel instant. In his own telling of Spotify's origins, Ek has described a "maniacal focus" that drove Spotify's early attention to "latency optimizations" and "speed of search." The goal was to create the effect that every file was already on the user's device, using learnings from BitTorrent, which would break files into small pieces before transferring and reassembling them on arrival. To achieve this, they hired a programmer named Ludvig Strigeus, who was known for creating uTorrent, a peer-to-peer software similar to Pirate Bay.

As part of the hiring, Spotify also purchased uTorrent, and named Ek the CEO for a season, before selling it to BitTorrent.[11]

As the engineers built Spotify's demo version, in lieu of licensed music, which would take over two years to secure, they instead filled the platform with tracks culled from their own personal music libraries, including many downloaded from the Pirate Bay.

Rasmus Fleischer, the writer and researcher who helped start Piratbyrån, noticed that music from one of his bands, which had only ever distributed music through Pirate Bay, appeared on the Spotify beta service. "I thought that was so funny," he told the website *TorrentFreak*. "So I emailed Spotify and asked how they obtained it. They said, 'Now, during the test period, we will use music that we find.'" (Some of the pirated files were reportedly still on the service until 2009, when the company completed something it called the "Big Clean," wiping all unlicensed music.)[12]

The first Spotify accounts were created in the spring of 2007, and employees hyped it up as an invite-only service to friends. Beta users and industry executives reportedly loved the app's instantaneous feel. What Spotify had really done was engineer a frictionless experience: the sense that the music just materialized from thin air. But similar to other app-enabled magic tricks of recent history, such as overnight packages and instant food delivery, frictionlessness is always an illusion.

Over the years, Daniel Ek has liked to suggest that getting the rights to the music was an afterthought. "When I started Spotify, I didn't actually know that I needed licenses from record labels," he once told a crowd at Stanford. "I was like, we'll figure it out."[13]

This nonchalance suggests an industry-averse position, a cool outsider shaking up the status quo; for one public appearance, around this time, he showed up wearing a T-shirt that said "SUITS SUCK." It all seemed like part of an elaborate branding exercise, as the company sometimes aimed to align itself with piracy (when trying to attract Swedish music listeners and talented engineers), and sometimes stood in staunch opposition to it (when appealing to the labels). They simultaneously had hired giants of the piracy scene and high-powered entertainment industry consultants.[14]

One of those industry consultants was a man who happened to be on the board of Stardoll: Fred Davis, the son of music mogul Clive Davis, and a seasoned entertainment lawyer representing the likes of Britney Spears. The VC-backed website, formerly known as Paperdoll Heaven, included a Spears doll. The junior Davis agreed to take Spotify on as a client in its early years (Spotify was "literally a PowerPoint" when they met, he'd later say), advising the music biz newcomers on best approaches to navigating relationships with the major record labels.[15]

Having previously consulted on negotiations for licenses with YouTube, Myspace, and Last.fm, Davis likely knew how Spotify needed to best position itself in those initial meetings: what words to avoid, what perks to offer early on. As *Billboard* would eventually report, for those first European deals, Davis "took Ek around to the labels" to pitch his business model of a service that would be free with ads. "Davis' credentials helped convince the biggest names in the business," *Billboard* wrote, including Universal Music Group (UMG) CEO Lucian Grainge, who was then based in London heading up UMG International. Today, UMG is the biggest of the major labels, and Grainge is considered one of the most powerful executives—if not the single most powerful executive—in the record business.[16]

"They had very good counsel in the way that they approached the majors, good people to advise them on how to structure the deal," Barney Wragg, the former head of digital at EMI, told me. Even just a few years earlier, labels hadn't really established protocols for granting licenses to online services, and as a result, he explained, "people didn't know how to talk to the labels to achieve a license." Another powerful consultant, former EMI exec Ken Parks, joined Spotify in 2007, and would lead negotiations in the U.S.

By the time Ek arrived for these meetings with the digital departments at major label offices, a lot of recent realities were working to his benefit. Among them were the destruction that piracy had inflicted on these companies and their bottom lines, the way in which the majors had started to consider Sweden a "lost market," and how desperate the private and public spheres alike were for something that would "solve" piracy. He had well-connected consultants, and a seemingly bottomless pit of Lorentzon's Tradedoubler money to spend. On top of that, many other streaming start-ups had tried and failed, and the industry was getting eager for something that would work.

In some ways, the music industry had been preparing for that moment for years. Even in those pre-Spotify years, there was already a semi-universal acceptance among some major label executives that music was becoming a more ubiquitous commodity. Industry insiders had long been predicting the imminent arrival of what they then called "the celestial jukebox," where all the songs in the world would be stored in the cloud somewhere. "At the time, as an industry, we knew subscription was going to be the savior," said Wragg. "The problem was, when would the subscription technology be ready? There were a lot of subscription services that came through before Spotify. A lot of them were quite clunky to use. The user interfaces were not great. They often were not intuitive, slow, and there was a lot of buffering." There were so many pre-Spotify music streaming options, that months before Spotify's final deal negotiations were ironed out, *Wired* ran a news piece outlining the top 20 most-visited music streaming websites of 2008. Imeem topped the list, followed by AOL Music, Myspace Music, Hype Machine, Last.fm, and Pandora. The relative abundance of streaming sites did not mean it was easy to get a music start-up off the ground in those days, though. According to some sources, the major labels actually made it quite difficult. "We were in this weird time where people couldn't really start digital music media products," Anthony Volodkin, founder of Hype Machine, told me. "Because you would show up at the label offices and they were not happy to see you. They were still making a lot of cash from selling CDs and were not ready to admit that a big transition was coming."[17]

Spotify was committed to its initial business model, which paired a free service with advertising, and paid rights-holders a percentage of ad revenue. But through 2007, as the negotiations carried on, a major sticking point arose between Spotify and the majors: Spotify wanted to pay them a percentage of advertising revenue, but the labels wanted to be paid per stream. Universal, for example, wanted 0.5–1.0 cents per stream, which had become standard for interactive streaming services (where a user could select and stream any song, as opposed to digital radio services like Pandora). As chronicled by Swedish journalists in the 2021 book *The Spotify Play*, Spotify's lawyers had to convince Ek that a paid version of the service would be the only way to appease the majors. By the end of 2007, the freemium business model—which included ad-supported and subscription-based tiers, with the goal of funneling users from free to paid—was created as a deep collaboration between Spotify and the labels. Launching in the

U.S., though, seemed further and further off, so the negotiations shifted to focus solely on Europe.[18]

Even then, one of the major disagreements was over the free tier. On one hand, some of those involved felt that an advertising-funded service would move users from illegal to legitimate products, and that they eventually could be converted to paid. On the other hand, there was a strong sense that if the free service was too high-quality, users would never pay. Spotify's business model eventually became upselling; they had to position the free tier as a funnel to getting customers onto the service, at which point they would work aggressively to convert them to paid. It created a situation where, for users of the freemium tier, the product they were most often hearing advertised was a premium Spotify account.[19]

In the end, the major labels got their preferred business model, enormous advances, guaranteed minimum payments per stream, and shares in the company. The details of streaming contracts are notoriously highly secretive, but in 2015, Spotify's initial U.S. contract with Sony was leaked to *The Verge*, revealing that the label had received a $25 million advance for its first two years, with no clarification of whether this had to be shared with artists; it received $9 million in free ad space, which it could either use or sell for cash, with no stipulations about whether that income had to be shared with artists. Sony had secured for itself a series of complicated negotiations regarding guaranteed per-stream minimums on the free tier and per-user minimums on the subscription tier. It is safe to assume that the other major label contracts were relatively similar in structure: each of the major label contracts reportedly included something known as a "most favored nation" clause, ensuring that they received terms at least as good as or more favorable than the other majors.[20]

Even before the label deals, Lorentzon had already been aggressively pursuing VC funding. By summer of 2008, a handshake deal between Spotify and the majors meant some were finally willing to invest. Though the deals wouldn't be signed until the fall, by August 2008, Spotify was worth $86 million. On October 7, 2008, a press release went out—"Spotify Announces Licensing Deals and Upcoming Launch"—explaining that the service would launch that day in the UK, Germany, France, Italy, Spain, Finland, Norway, and Sweden.

The first of Spotify's investors had included Lorentzon's former boss, a man named Pär-Jörgen Pärson of the venture capital firm Northzone.

When Spotify went public in 2018, Northzone owned 5 percent of the company. These were the people for whom streaming was made by and for: major label execs, consultants, ad men, and venture capitalists, all working to get their own share of the pie.[21]

The saga of how the major labels struck their first deals with Spotify has been widely recounted before, but the story of how the independent labels got involved is not as well known. In retrospect, it is a bit confounding, considering how poorly so many independent artists and small labels have fared with streaming. What convinced them to get on board at the very start?

While the major labels negotiated their licensing deals directly with Spotify, for independent labels, those conversations were largely happening through an organization called the Merlin Network. Back in 2008, Merlin was brand new, founded one year earlier to guide its members—independent labels and distributors—through the unfamiliar world of emerging commercial platforms online. As of this writing, Merlin represents tens of thousands of labels from sixty-eight countries and 15 percent of global recorded music market share, but in 2008, the organization was just finding its footing.[22]

The bigger independent labels prided themselves on being especially open to new technologies, which then were succeeding somewhat in branding themselves as rebellious disruptors to the archaic and out-of-touch old-school music business (despite the fact that it was often affiliates of the old-school music business consulting on and helping shape the so-called new models).

But in its early days, Merlin struggled to get digital services to take it as seriously as the majors. In some ways, Spotify benefited from this: around the same time it was seeking to license Merlin content, other services, like Myspace Music and Nokia Comes With Music (yes, the service's real name), were in the process of disastrously fumbling their relationships with the indies. For example, when Myspace Music was rebranding as an ad-supported streaming site, despite the fact that Myspace had made its name on its association with independent and DIY artists, the new service did not seek to arrange licenses or equity with independents to the same extent they did with the majors. Right around the dawn of Spotify, another service that the independent sector had come to rely on, eMusic, had also similarly let some of the independent labels down when it signed special, privileged deals with major labels.[23]

Merlin's very first commercial deal was the 2008 Spotify license, after eighteen months of negotiations. A press release at the time described the deal as a "vindication" of what Merlin had created. Perhaps this move doesn't signal as much about Spotify's friendliness to the independents as it tells us about how the very concept of independent music was changing during this time: Spotify refers to Merlin sincerely as "the fourth major." Merlin got equity, which it eventually cashed out, passing the value earned along to its members.[24]

While Merlin celebrated the deal, some of its member labels struggled to muster the same excitement. "There was a lot of confusion about how the business model worked," said one independent label manager. "And a lot of independent labels realistically should have done more to explain that to artists and ask what they thought. Looking back, that's one of the bigger regrets of my career." It was a complicated time to be an independent label or artist. On one hand, independent labels were definitely still feeling the hit from piracy: CD sales were tanking, vinyl hadn't really made a comeback yet, Bandcamp wasn't popular yet. They were often looking for whatever life raft they could find.

On the other hand, some independent artists were really making the most of the internet in a time before the consolidated social web had taken hold. Just a few months before Merlin signed that first Spotify deal on behalf of much of the independent sector, there was a presentation at the 2008 Future of Music Coalition (FMC) conference on the "vitality" of the emerging online marketplace for independent artists, painting a somewhat rosy picture. "We hear a lot from the major record labels that things aren't going so well, that the music industry isn't managing this transition very well, that the old business model is failing, that no one has really figured out how to make things work," said musician Jean Cook, who was then the policy director for FMC, at the conference. "But in this context we can look at the independent sector and not the major labels. Independent sales were up almost five percent in the past couple years." It was still years before Spotify would launch in the U.S., but the sales and download numbers for independent music were both pointing upward. Did independent music need to be "saved" after all?[25]

For some, there was still a sense that maybe the internet would live up to its potential as a liberating force for culture. But more importantly, this was a time when the independent music world still had its own thriving media ecosystem, before so much of the music press was swallowed by the shifting digital ad landscape and streaming services. In 2009, there were more alt-weekly newspapers in the U.S. than ever before—135 of them—and these papers tended to cover local music in a way that to date has never really been replaced.[26]

At the same time, the music blog era was blooming: a whole constellation of small-scale community-oriented media outlets sharing free mp3s, connecting dots throughout scenes, and injecting a lot of enthusiasm into homespun DIY music culture online. "The mp3 blogs were great because the majors weren't playing in that world," one independent label director told me. "Because they wouldn't dare to give away mp3s. They hated us for doing it. But it was great for us, and we met so many great people that way."

It does not seem coincidental that the DIY blog era started winding down around 2012, a year after Spotify launched in the U.S. "It was connected," said Jessi Frick, owner of the independent label Father/Daughter Records, which grew out of the "golden age of music blogging" in 2010, when a wave of small music blogs started releasing seven-inch singles. From Frick's perspective, the convenience culture pushed by streaming was part of the shift away from blogs, but also the way that Spotify specifically hyped up discovery. "Spotify kept pushing the discovery angle, so we thought, okay, this is going to be perfect for independent music. But we didn't know that nobody was going to make any money off of it. And that was before everybody knew that the majors were the puppet master behind the scenes."

When the independent music sector embraced Spotify in 2008, something else was lost, too. It was part of independent music losing its own media ecosystem—or at the very least, it was drained of significant energy reserves. Indeed, a lot of the problems of the streaming era begin coming into focus when considered as issues of media consolidation.

In January 2009, a perplexing illustration appeared in the pages of the UK music mag *NME*: a parody of the supposed image of human evolution, where man emerges from ape to Homo sapiens, slowly standing and straightening his hunched back. But instead of advancing to hold clubs and arrows, this depicted the civilization of music listening as an act of progress: from gramophone to jukebox, boombox to iPod to laptop. It landed on a guy at a laptop perusing a streaming service, all under the headline, "The Day the Music Evolved"—the letter "O" stylized like the Spotify logo. Fans were "going crazy" over the new web service, *NME* wrote, before urging readers to "download it now"![27]

At this point, Spotify had been launched in parts of Europe for months, and was live as an invite-only beta in the UK; it was still over two years away from launching in the U.S. But the press hype was already building: "Unlike most new technologies, Spotify has been greeted with a virtual ticker-tape parade from the notoriously critical tech blogs," wrote *NME*. The same year, *Rolling Stone* wrote that Spotify was the "slickest" free legal music service and "the best argument yet for getting rid of your CDs." Gawker called it "everything iTunes should be."[28]

Music in the cloud was the future, and Spotify was going to deliver it, the press seemed to suggest. The company was characterized as a beacon of progress, in line with the general air of Obama-era tech solutionism. Just like journalists were writing puff pieces about Facebook and Twitter, a bevy of pieces in the popular press were helping build buzz for Spotify by inciting FOMO, a tactic that has helped sell all sorts of technological myths for decades: don't miss out, don't get left behind.

Soon enough, Spotify started attracting press attention for very different reasons. By the end of 2010, the biggest daily newspaper in Sweden, *Dagens Nyheter* (*DN*), ran a report under a headline that simply said, "Spotify's Money Is Distributed Unevenly." The piece documented the experience of Naxos, a big independent classical label, which was threatening to pull its catalog of over one hundred thousand tracks. The paper reported that the majors were getting paid a rate up to six times higher than independents. So, while Universal, EMI, Sony, and Warner, which together at the time owned 18 percent of Spotify, were reporting that streaming had become their single biggest source of income, independents were left wondering when some of the wealth might trickle down to them—a question some have never stopped asking.[29]

Another column ran in the *Guardian* in early 2011 under the head-line, "Spotify Should Give Indies a Fair Deal on Royalties." The piece, by Helienne Lindvall, explained how independent labels were increasingly threatening to leave Spotify over low rates. Lindvall warned of the unfairness of the pro rata business model, which endures to this day, where artists are paid not on a set rate per stream but a share of the total revenue according to "usage reports." She reflected on how unlikely it was that this would work out well for independents: a system where the biggest labels were shareholders, where the majors were getting advances that no one else could command, where NDAs prevented even major label artists from understanding the rates they were paid. "It is well known in music industry circles that Universal was able to secure a minimum streaming rate for the ad-funded version of the site—something, it is understood, not even the other majors have been able to accomplish," Lindvall wrote. "This is not only a Spotify issue: it is a growing problem for smaller labels and unsigned artists with most new digital music services."[30]

Spotify had not even launched in the U.S. yet, and it was already becoming clear that saving the major record labels was not exactly the same as saving music.

3

Selling Lean-Back Listening

In the beginning, the experience of being a Spotify user revolved around the search bar. Daniel Ek especially was initially quite opposed to the idea of an overly curated service. The company's first discovery features didn't go much further than some Pandora-esque autoplay "Radio" stations. "We're essentially the Google of music," Ek said on stage at the 2009 Future of Music Coalition conference. If that all seems somehow more egalitarian than a selection of premade, gatekeeper-controlled playlists, remember that Ek's advertising background included an interest in search engine optimization: gaming the results. Search algorithms are often embedded with all sorts of bias. The UCLA professor Safiya Umoja Noble, an expert on how racism and sexism are embedded into commercial search engines, has noted that "one of the most important factors that enables a link to rise to the top of the rankings is the amount of capital you have."[1]

By the turn of the decade, Spotify was getting ready to launch in the U.S., but it was going to be challenging. Ek had someone new helping him out: Sean Parker, the cofounder of Napster and former president of Facebook, who invested $15 million for a five percent stake in the company in 2010. Despite its growing venture capital investments, Spotify had lost $26.5 million the previous year, and, as ever, needed to figure out its path to profitability. There was much more pre-existing competition in the U.S., though, so the company would need to find new ways to stand out and attract subscribers. That same year, in Europe, it tested out selling itself as a social platform, hyping up a partnership with Facebook. Then, just after its 2011 U.S. arrival, the company reintroduced itself as a global marketplace for music apps, or "new and exciting music experiences built around your music taste."[2]

The music press had contributed significantly to the pre-launch hype for Spotify in the U.S., and some of those same outlets were its partners on the apps marketplace. Apps from *Rolling Stone* and *Pitchfork* featured playlists and album suggestions, while the Last.fm app offered personalized recommendations. In an ad, Spotify highlighted an app called Moodagent, which let users create playlists and then adjust their tracklists according to preset moods like "sensual," "tender," "happy," and "angry."

"We have to turn ourselves into the OS of music," Spotify's director of platform said at the time, using the shorthand for operating system. "We are in the middle of a transformation from being an app ourselves to being a platform."[3]

The app platform was ultimately a doomed bet, to use Spotify's internal language; according to several employees, the company's "bets board" is an ever-changing list of the high-priority goals and projects getting significant resources at any given time, and it changes quite frequently. But another bet they made, in 2012, had more of an impact.

By mid-2012, Spotify needed to grow—to get past the early adopters and reach a more mainstream audience in the U.S. They needed some kind of new ad campaign, and wanting to figure out how people actually used the app, they commissioned a research agency. According to a source close to the company at the time, the researchers identified about forty participants in major cities who were tasked with keeping detailed listening diaries, mapping out how they actually engaged with music throughout the day. The study revealed people listened to music across a range of "moments": cleaning, driving to work, at the gym, at a house party, to name a few. "It highlighted that there are a bunch of different functional and emotional roles that music serves," the source told me; there was later a bigger study aimed at "market sizing" each "moment," trying to estimate the demand for each category.

"At first, Spotify really thought they were competing with iTunes," the source went on. "Rather than having the music on your hard drive, it was streaming. But having done the study they realized active listening was a smaller part of the experience. There were way more listening hours using music as a background experience—people who wanted to lean back and let Spotify choose things. I think that was a real breakthrough. They started to think about how to optimize for that experience, for a less engaged user . . . [to] make music consumption even more seamless."

This was the beginning of a strategic shift, and one that grew out of marketing conversations—not conversations about how to market music, but how to market Spotify. At a New York City press event in late 2012, Ek announced that big changes were afoot. He acknowledged that he'd been overly precious about the no-curation approach, and claimed that while Spotify was working well for users who knew what they wanted to hear, it wasn't working so well for anyone else. He announced that there were officially 1 billion user-generated playlists on the platform, which he called the "lifeblood of Spotify"; he also announced the addition of a "Follow" button where users could follow playlist influencers. More recommendation systems would be coming soon. "We're punks," Ek proclaimed, at the press event. "Not the punks that are up to no good. The punks that are against the establishment. We want to bring music to every person on the face of the planet." Playlists would surely be the way.[4]

By the end of the year, Spotify's website had been drastically reimagined for the first time. Where it previously focused on slogans like "Instant, simple and free" and "Play music now," that December, its new identity was unveiled: "Music for every moment." The splash page was overtaken with a full-page video that cycled through a series of moody images that looked straight from a Tumblr or Pinterest board: sun flares reflecting off a window on a city drive, a hammock rocking slowly side to side, a free-spirited hitchhiker walking by the side of a road, all soundtracked by a generic, sentimental acoustic folk tune that auto-played in the background. Like stock photos in a not-yet-used picture frame, waiting to be replaced by real life, the montage seemed less about explaining the technology to users, and more about getting users to imagine themselves as Spotify customers.

This all signaled what the coming years had in store. But even then, in late 2012, there was still no in-house Spotify playlist curation strategy. Before officially sanctioned "editorial programming" arrived, the playlist scene brewing on Spotify was dominated by the third-party apps as well as user-generated playlists. It was generally more of what some called a "Wild West" in playlisting, as one major label digital marketer once explained to me. Anyone could theoretically become a playlist influencer, but that also meant that anyone could theoretically try to invest money and resources into owning the visual real estate. The major labels took advantage of this, building and buying up playlist companies to "seed important tracks" in playlists and "juice SEO," early major label playlist strategists told me. Sony created a playlist company called Filtr, and put two of its Swedish digital employees in charge, and Universal created one named Digster. Warner bought a website called ShareMyPlaylists.com, which later rebranded to Playlists.net and had itself already bought a popular playlist page called Topsify. "We were building this playlist ecosystem before Spotify were," Kieron Donoghue, the founder of ShareMyPlaylists.com, told me. Before getting involved in playlisting, he had worked in affiliate marketing.

Owning these playlist brands also gave the major labels something other than their own records to advertise on Spotify's home page, since the initial contracts that the majors brokered with Spotify included gratis ad space. In the mid-2010s, for example, a premium subscriber might see a banner across the home page labeled "announcements," advertising a bunch of generic-looking Filtr playlists themed to different times of the day (naturally filled with lots of Sony artists). When users would select the most immediately visible "dinner playlist" or "workout mix," they might have unknowingly clicked through to a list owned and operated by a major label.[5]

The sprawling "Wild West" of playlisting didn't last long though. The streaming company was entering a new phase, one where it would seek more influence over the listening experience. Things would become considerably more streamlined starting in 2013, when Spotify built on its "Music for every moment" strategy with more tightly controlled pages titled "Home" and "Browse," featuring playlists sorted by context and mood. "Contexts" were activities and times of day, like "party" and "commute," while "moods" were more emotional and psychological states like "chill," "focus," and "romance." These new curated selections included lists made by users, as well as ones made by Spotify's latest addition to its staff: a team of in-house, professional playlist editors.[6]

The first of the curators came from Tunigo, a Swedish app for "readymade" playlists that Spotify acquired in May 2013. Tunigo had been making a name for itself on Spotify for a couple of years as a third-party app. In the press, it was compared to the U.S. playlisting app Songza, which had been offering streaming mood playlists since 2007 and would soon be bought by Google. But Tunigo's founders had a few advantages: they were based in Sweden, run by a company with ties to the music business, and they built their product directly within Spotify. According to a former Spotify employee who worked close to the playlist operation at the time, there were other similar playlisting companies, but "they just happened to be the one that Daniel was friends with, so they bought Tunigo."[7]

Tunigo had quietly launched in 2011 as a subsidiary of a music industry–connected social media platform called Snowfish. Collaborations with Spotify began in 2010, when Snowfish held an online competition called "The Next Big Thing," an *Idol*-type talent contest where musicians could upload tracks and users could vote on their favorites. Three thousand votes would win the musicians something called the "Spotify Award," where their songs would be serviced to the platform and given free promo and ad space. It's telling that one of the first collaborations between people from Tunigo and Spotify involved this sort of gamification, and the idea that playlist promo was something that could be "won" by those with the most online engagement; in time, this would become a theme of the early curation strategy.[8]

Snowfish's transition from social media network to playlisting company was partially motivated by work it had been doing with Telia, a Swedish multinational telecommunications company that was also an early partner to Spotify. As Tunigo founder Nick Holmstén recounted years later in a podcast, Telia wanted to "create new functions and services and features" to build on its relationship with Spotify. "That's what led us in to start exploring the whole kind of playlist world," he said.[9]

When Tunigo was acquired, Spotify absorbed thousands of its playlists, including what are now still popular titles like "Today's Top Hits," "Mood Booster," and "Your Favorite Coffeehouse," rebranding them as some of the first official Spotify editorial playlists. Tunigo's roughly twenty employees became Spotify's first editorial team. The Tunigo app's landing page became the new Spotify home page, and its mood and moment taxonomy became Spotify's new playlist categories. Spotify brought over Tunigo's style guide for "visually merchandising" playlists through covers, titles, and taglines. Soon, the sounds of "Mellow Morning," "Acoustic Covers" or "Evening Chill" would be a few clicks away.

The moods and moments playlists were Tunigo's core product at the time, but even in the early 2010s, its founders had a vision for more data, more optimization, more personalization. According to a 2013 story in *TechCrunch*, by the time of the acquisition, Tunigo had raised about 2.4 million euro from investors with a staff split between Stockholm and New York and a stated long-term mission to "provide a single button that users could hit to get the perfect playlist based on real-time data." This was a goal repeated by Tunigo execs over the years in various interviews.[10]

By the time the concept of the official Spotify editorial playlist emerged—a playlist curated and gatekept by Spotify employees—the digital era had already seen a number of music curation services come and go with different ideas about why people liked what they liked, and different justifications for the levels of science and creativity that ought to inform the whole process. Start-up founders claimed that users were overwhelmed by choice and needed recommendations to guide them. And they all claimed to have a solution. They knew what the future of music looked like, and it involved their proprietary apps, playlists, and algorithms.

There are a few different ways to contextualize the history of the streaming playlist. One place to start is with the lineage of technologies enabling the reordering of songs, including the arrival of the compact cassette tape in 1963, popularized in the 1980s with the rise of the Walkman. The handmade, analog mixtape culture of the late 1970s and 1980s is now synonymous with a type of pre-internet person-to-person intimacy via songs that is anathema to much of what we think of when we think of algorithmic corporate music culture.

But Spotify went to great lengths to position playlists as mixtapes, as it attempted to evolve and grow its new playlist system. Its first-ever advertising campaign, in 2013, featured a photograph of two hip young music lovers with their mouths awkwardly agape, inching toward an uncomfortable first kiss. To the left of the screen the banner read: "Because mixtapes still work." And while users could surely approximate the feeling of tape-trading through making their own playlists, the history of the mixtape—as one-to-one musical transmission, an expression of a fixed idea through song and sound collage, as an enemy of the industrialized record industry—actually serves as a useful foil to the data-tuned, ultra-surveilled ways music circulates on streaming playlists today. Under the gaze of streaming surveillance, the exchange is never truly one-to-one.[11]

Then there's the term "playlist" itself, which originates in the history of commercial radio, as Top 40 programmers moved to hook listeners, appease major labels, and control the soundtrack of daily life. In the introduction to *Listen to Lists*, a collection of essays about how playlists have shaped listening, German editors Lina Brion and Detlef Diederichsen write about how after the 1960s, playlists were pushed in order to rein in unpredictable radio disc jockeys and smooth out a more homogenous experience; the radio playlist's "main purpose was to make it difficult for listeners to switch to another station," they writes. Journalist Kristoffer Cornils puts the playlist more broadly into the history of lists in music, such as radio charts, writing that they "not only ascertain and communicate what is currently popular, but also define what popularity is." Cornils points to Jacques Attali's idea in *Noise: The Political Economy of Music* that "the music industry is not devoted to the production of supply, but rather to the production of demand itself." Playlists don't just respond to users' musical interests, but manufacture them, too.[12]

It's tempting to want to say that streaming playlists have nothing to do with mixtapes, and that the history lies more squarely with the monotony of pop radio. The truth is messier though: what has actually crystallized is a new commercial curation logic entirely, one that professionalizes the creative and often deeply personal act of mixtape-making and drags it into the hyper-commercial space of the modern music industry—that takes the traditions and emotional appeals of mixtapes and reshapes them to exist more like market-responsive radio playlists.

In *Selling Digital Music, Formatting Culture*, Jeremy Wade Morris chronicles a similar commodification process in recounting another corporate playlist history, one that existed within iTunes. In its early years, the iTunes Store sold its own playlists—greatest hits collections, seasonal mixes, yearly roundups—that were more like the commercial various-artists compilations that children of the nineties used to see TV infomercials for late at night. But iTunes eventually also unveiled a purchasable type of user-generated playlist called iMix. Users could make iMix playlists available for other iTunes users to listen to, vote on, and buy, and by early 2010, there were around 2 million iMixes for sale. Morris points to author Rob Drew, who describes how this new form of mix commodified "a practice that music fans have enjoyed on an informal, one-to-one basis for three decades," turning iMix-makers into "laborers on behalf of music retailers and record labels" while confining the practice of mixing to "the limited repertoires of particular music retailers."[13]

As playlist logics have grown more omnipresent, streamed surfaces have turned the don't-touch-that-dial strategy from a big-media playbook to a self-inflicted imperative: What if your whole life could feel like that?

As the Tunigo folks set up shop from their new positions of power and influence within Spotify's nascent editorial programming operation, they too were bringing curation practices that were both very new and very old. The playlist editors reported to Tunigo founder Nick Holmstén, who was named the global head of programming, and Tunigo director Doug Ford, who was now the global head of curation. Holmstén was a former pop songwriter with a background in marketing; Ford previously worked for a company called HitPredictor, doing "online song testing" to help labels and managers pinpoint which song from a record was most likely to become a hit single on commercial radio. This bears underscoring, as its implications would shape the essence of Spotify playlist culture: Ford's roots saw music entered into popularity contests, testing songs for pop potential. HitPredictor claimed each song would be heard by half a million testers, all offering feedback on its stickiness. "It took us a week or two to get the data," Ford later recalled in a conference appearance. "We get that on every single song on Spotify in literally twenty-four hours."[14]

The early Spotify playlist strategy was based on a broadcast model called the "Syndicate," a "hierarchy built very much on a radio network philosophy," Ford noted. This included a heavily marketed lineup of big, flagship playlists tailored to the major genre categories—playlists like "RapCaviar," "Rock This," and "Hot Country," for example—as well as a sprawling series of niche and regional "feeder" and "early bets" playlists, which each pointed upward to bigger counterparts. The idea was that Spotify could test out new songs on smaller playlists and "graduate" them up based on data. It sounded like the rules to a game show. In the early days, a major label digital strategist told me about the tight relationships that were being forged between major labels and Spotify curators—their weekly meetings, Excel spreadsheets of priority releases, dedicated label reps—and how they helped him market an up-and-coming hip-hop artist. "They were like, 'Okay, we'll put him on a playlist called "Most Necessary,"' which is a feeder playlist. They'll see how the song performs. They'll look at stuff like skip rate. If someone listens for fifteen seconds and then skips, that means the song isn't really reacting. But if it has a high completion rate, or a low skip rate, then maybe they'll test it in 'RapCaviar' and see if people like it."

The curators would also look at data from user-generated playlists, or "mass consumption data," as Ford explained at the same conference, to "super-inform the curation team, which then amplifies that through Spotify, drives more taste profiling and user consumption habits, which then in turn informs Discover Weekly and algorithmic programming. The cycle just starts all over again." They literally called this "the cycle of data." Spotify aspired to apply the HitPredictor model at scale, every day, across all types of playlists, from massive Top 40 heavy-hitters to playlists for sleeping, coffeeshop vibes, or other lean-back purposes. In the streaming era, the industry had identified a new type of target consumer: the lean-back listener, who was less concerned with seeking out artists and albums, and was happy to simply double click on a playlist for focusing, working out, or winding down. In this environment, what it meant to have a "hit" was changing: it didn't necessarily mean a mainstream breakthrough, but a viral streaming moment, or a data-driven playlist-ladder climb.[15]

Over the years, Spotify curators would repeatedly describe the "Syndicate" model as part of the grand democratization of music that was playing out across the streaming landscape. "We are not gatekeepers," Ford proclaimed on the panel. "We do not want to be the judge and jury over whether to give up on a song." And yet, the very decision to follow the data was, in and of itself, a process of judgment and jurying. Data is never neutral—it reflects the biases of the culture and business logics from which it is generated. And there was nothing inherently neutral about setting up a system that wrapped up all of a song's worth in its *replay value*. To do so is to suggest that a song's potential to ignite mass enthusiasm, and thus mass streams—or its capacity as background fodder, streaming endlessly, unnoticed—should determine its worth. Part of Spotify's earliest mythmaking involved shaping narratives around the ways it would abolish the gatekeeper power long held by radio, but in the end, it just emerged as a new type of gatekeeper, one bolstered by playlist data dashboards and automated systems.[16]

By 2016, Spotify had fifty in-house playlist curators, among which seven were "genre leads" and dozens were "junior curators." They'd made over 4,500 playlists (that number is now closer to 10,000) and 30 of those playlists had amassed over 1 million followers (as of this writing, the most popular playlist, "Today's Top Hits," has over 34 million followers). It was the dawn of what one former Spotify playlist editor described to me as "the peak playlist era," a span of time that the editor estimated lasted from 2016 until 2019, when these playlists were considered "the top of the discovery funnel" among many in the music industry.[17]

The early editors would tinker away at their "hypos," as they're called internally, or playlist hypotheses: the baseline idea of a playlist's premise, target audience, name, songs. Eventually the company built out special tooling for building, testing, tracking, and optimizing the playlist process. A 2016 *BuzzFeed* report described how the editors would use an app called PUMA, short for Playlist Usage Monitoring and Analysis, to track plays, skips, saves, and demographic data on listeners.[18]

"Songs live or die in playlists based on this information," Ford said, on that same panel. "We live or die, and those playlists live or die, based on what the audience thinks. It's not us, it's the audience that drives it." This was part of a bigger project of the platform era, one that suggested data-driven success was a meritocracy, that virality reflected the will of the people, and that social media had somehow empowered fans to nominate pop stars to power. It's present, too, in how Spotify's official "Charts" website claims that "hundreds of millions of listeners shape today's streaming charts, every day." Truthfully, though, success was also influenced by contracts, connections, and streaming-friendly music.[19]

"We call ourselves, on the curation team, the elected officials of the Spotify user base," said Ford. No one elected these people, though, and streams are, in fact, not votes. Especially not when the streams are most earned by music just inoffensive enough to not get shut off. This wasn't democracy, it was technocracy.[20]

In order to pitch their music to a Spotify playlist curator, in the early years labels would need to go through the Artists and Label Relations team. And while Spotify employed several dedicated reps for each major label, there were only a small handful of reps handling the whole of independent music, and at one point, those positions were eliminated entirely. The system for small independent labels could be a labyrinth: they would often have to talk to their distributor, who maintained a relationship with a Spotify label rep, who could hopefully talk to a curator. One independent label owner described the reps to me as "the gatekeeper to the gatekeeper." Eventually, Spotify added a form to its Spotify for Artists app so artists and labels could pitch tracks directly to the curators, but several sources report that the most effective way to get playlisted today is still an ever-elusive direct connection.

Spotify obsessively talked about how it was *leveling the playing field*, but there were plenty of anecdotes suggesting otherwise. Certainly something was being *leveled*—flattened, smoothed out, homogenized. Beneath *leveling the playing field* is a deeper assumption, too, that artists should want to be operating in a one-size-fits-all model—or that independent artists should want to conform to the norms of the winner-take-all pop star system. Data-driven hit-predicting was previously reserved for the stars; now, it was being presented as an *opportunity* for artists of all scopes.[21]

So much of the disconnection at the heart of streaming lies in this contradiction: that independent musicians have been convinced to make their livings in a system that was not only designed by the major labels but also prioritizes the type of music engineered and roundtabled for mass-scale success. But not all artists have mass-scale success in mind when they write, record, and release music. Not everyone who wants a music career also wants to be a pop star.

This was not a neutral way to think about curating music, and according to some artists and label workers who interacted with the playlist system at the time, most artists were not experiencing the magic of the "Syndicate." Instead, it was just a frustratingly powerful but mystifying system. It seemed like the order of business had become: editorial consideration for artists with well-connected labels and management, algorithmic mysteriousness for everyone else. Artists not only had no idea how to land coveted spots on "Morning Commute," "Weekend Buzz," or "Totally Alt," but also saw that when they happened to luck into a placement, it was re-contextualizing their work in bewildering ways. Why was this random B-side from three years ago so popular? Why was this instrumental deep cut suddenly a most-played track?

Still, the data democracy narrative that Spotify championed stuck. "Data drives the business," wrote one *Forbes* columnist in a 2017 story. "There's almost no chance for funny business because there are so many people involved in the decision-making process and because data is such a huge part of determining which songs make the cut."

The same year, a story in *Wired* claimed that "by the time a song lands on Today's Top Hits or other equally popular sets, Spotify has so relentlessly tested it that it almost can't fail." The piece likened the process to Facebook's A/B tests, where they served new features to small subsets of users, keeping some and abandoning others depending on engagement. "Think of it as the moneyball of music," the *Wired* journalist wrote. "Spotify considers every track a beta test." The article claimed that listeners were spending half of their time on Spotify listening to playlists, split between ones made by users and editors. Tunigo founder Nick Holmstén insisted to *Wired* that unlike with radio DJs of the past, since Spotify relied so much on data, there was no way for artists to sway their editors. "There's absolutely no way to push our team," Holmstén said, in the article. "It's no one person's feeling that matters." It was a myth that would eventually be disproven many times over.[22]

Some independent labels, in the later half of the 2010s, were starting to feel dependent on Spotify. "Playlisting is becoming a huge portion of revenue even for the smallest of labels," one independent record label owner told me in 2017. "I've been on two meetings at the Spotify office the past year and tried to stay really proactive because just from a pure numbers game they're about 73 percent of my label's entire digital revenue, and physical has been declining so rapidly for the label that they make up about 45 percent of total revenue. That's a huge cut." He told me that in 2016, eighteen of his label's tracks had been added to official playlists, and it was functionally keeping the label afloat. "A huge number of listeners, no matter what their taste may be, are using the platform—and in a lot of cases exclusively—and a majority just listen to playlists. There's a term thrown around called 'passive listeners.' That's pretty depressing."

Streams, for better or worse, add up equally. Users passively streaming music all day in the background meant just as much to Spotify as any other kind of listening, and it was easier to encourage. "We really want to soundtrack every moment of your life," Daniel Ek said in 2016. "So what excites us [is] when we are able to do that in moments which may seem counterintuitive at first. Take sleep as an example. Millions of people every day (or night!) now go to sleep listening to Spotify. This is a behavior that is brand new for a huge chunk of that same audience. So as we think about Spotify in the future, it's really all about bringing music (and other media) to more moments in your life. In order to do that, we need better recommendations, better partnerships, and the right content for those moments." It was corporate puffery, but in time, Spotify's supposed search for "better partnerships" and "the right content" would prove to be quite consequential.[23]

Of course, variations of this archetypal lean-back listener also existed in the radio era, but streaming wasn't just aiming to replace radio—it was being sold as a replacement for the record store, too. In time, the lean-back dynamic would infiltrate not just streaming, but a lot of the experience of being an internet user. One former Spotify engineer I spoke with described the TikTok feed, and Spotify's eventual attempts at approximating it, as an ultimate distillation of lean-back listening: "You're not putting any input in. You're just being shown things. You're giving it input based on which things you linger on longer, or what you skip. But it's not like you're choosing what you want."

If the streaming economy has contributed to any major cultural shift in recent history, it might be that it has helped champion this dynamic of passivity. And while listeners can—and many do—use the service without engaging the recommendations at all, what the interface nudges is more of a reactive mode: its model listener would just simply hit play or skip. Often, conversations about the streaming era center the way music has been financially devalued, but there is also a broader, harder-to-pin-down cultural devaluation that comes with streaming: the relegation of music to something passable, just filling the air to drown out the office worker's inner thoughts as spreadsheets get finalized and emails get circled up on.

To what degree does this constitute listening? The groundbreaking electronic music composer and educator Pauline Oliveros certainly would not have considered this to be listening at all. Oliveros dedicated a great deal of her life's work to spreading her philosophy of Deep Listening, a series of practices and writings teaching the core differences between *hearing* and *listening*. Oliveros long meditated on the concept that hearing is involuntary in nature, while listening requires consciousness. This is to say, she made a strong case that the act of listening was virtually incompatible with multitasking. In the Oliveros tradition, listening is something that requires focused attention on *the act of listening*, to music or sound or the natural world or the person next to you.[24]

This isn't to say that using music as a background accent for everyday activities is somehow always inherently meaningless. The compulsion to soundtrack the mundane moments of everyday life feels eternal, an extension of what the academic researcher Tia DeNora meant when she called music a "technology of the self" in her widely cited 2000 book *Music in Everyday Life*, built on fieldwork exploring the ways that people actually interact with music on a day-to-day basis. Choosing the music that soundtracks our lives can be part of how we process who we are. But Spotify's ideal mode of lean-back listening feels different, less an act of choosing than testing one's tolerance, how much one prefers the sound of "Deep Focus" or "Brain Food" to nothing at all. It follows that a population paying so little conscious attention to music would also believe it deserving of so little financial remuneration. Plus, passively *soundtracking your everyday moments* through song is not the only reason people listen, and the escalation of this single listening mode in service of boosting engagement is a disservice to artists, listeners, and music as an art form; it disregards the many different reasons why someone might listen to music.[25]

Surely Spotify is not alone in normalizing the non-listening pervading culture today, which perhaps has a longer history in tying the act of listening to personal computers or mobile devices, pieces of listening hardware that almost ensure a listener will be splitting their attention between music and some other activity. But it's all bolstered by a data-optimized system where success is determined simply by whatever moves the needle or fills the background. Taken to its logical endpoint, that's a mode of engagement that becomes hostile to art.

Unsurprisingly, by the mid-2010s, as the increasingly passive listening environment commanded less and less attention of users, an appropriate trend emerged: sleep playlists were absolutely crushing it on Spotify. One former employee recalled a specific all-hands meeting that reflected on and celebrated the success of these sleep playlists. "They were very proud of this," the former employee recalled. "It proved to them that they're not a music company. They're a time filler for boredom."

"There was a moment where it all started to feel Orwellian," the employee continued, reflecting on a different, later meeting. In his estimation, based on data observed while at the company, there was really only a tiny percent of lean-*in* listeners. "The vast majority of music listeners, they're not really interested in listening to music per se. They just need a soundtrack to a moment in their day. I think Daniel Ek was the first person to really exploit that. I honestly think that the core of the company's success was recognizing that they're not selling music. They're not providing music. They're filling people's time. And he said at a company meeting, I remember he was like, 'Apple Music, Amazon, these aren't our competitors. Our only competitor is silence.'"[26]

The ex-employee stared off and nodded. "I definitely think people are afraid of silence," he told me. "And Spotify has capitalized on that pretty well."

4

The Conquest of Chill

As playlists became more central to the Spotify experience in the mid-2010s, they also became stages of power struggles on the platform. Granular details were becoming political: where a playlist sat on the "Browse" page, what the cover looked like, how the title was stylized, and what songs ranked toward the top of the list. There were also the big picture quandaries: What ideas were these playlists putting forth about how music ought to be contextualized? What types of musical connections—or, more often, disconnections—were being normalized?

"Our initial growth was with music enthusiasts," a Spotify marketing executive told the *New York Times* in 2013, surrounding the "music for every moment" advertising campaign. "[Now] we're looking for that next group ready to experience music in a new way . . . a mass, mainstream audience." Spotify's rebrand was about selling its product to as many people as possible by targeting them on an *emotional* level, the article explained. To turn profits, Spotify needed to grow its user base, and organizing music by moods and moments was going to be part of attracting them.[1]

Moods and emotions are mysterious. AI accountability scholars today deeply oppose using technology to interpret and target people's emotions in part simply due to a lack of scientific consensus about what emotions even are. This has never stopped the advertising industry, though, from making emotions central to its playbooks. What sells a product better than an appeal to the emotions? Buy this soda and you'll be happy. Buy this makeup and you'll be loved. Choose one of these playlists—"Ambient

Relaxation," "Calming Classical," "Chill Vibes," "self-care vibes"—and you'll be at peace.[2]

Organizing music by mood is a way to transform it into a new type of media product. It is about selling users not just on moods, but on the promise of the very concept that mood stabilization is something within their control. It's a tactic for luring users to double click and start streaming. It's a form of "streambait"—like sonic clickbait, content created for the sake of engagement—to keep the data-generating wheels turning, to make the process of opening the app and finding something suitable more seamless. Like Facebook and Twitter before it, Spotify was after whatever kept people on the platform, whether they were paying attention or not. A former Spotify playlist editor explained to me that a goal of its editorial apparatus is "trying to reduce friction and cognitive work" that a user has to do when they open the app: "You get to the platform, you get what you want." Over time, though, the quest for a frictionless user experience resulted in a deluge of frictionless music: an ease of use that, in turn, facilitated easy listening.

For almost as long as recorded music marketing has existed, record companies and snake oil salesmen have been trying to shill new music technologies using mood. In 1921, Thomas A. Edison, Incorporated, the eponymous umbrella company for the proto-Musk serial entrepreneur's many ventures, issued a curious thirty-one-page publication titled *Mood Music: A compilation of 112 Edison Re-Creations according to 'what they will do for you.'* Edison famously invented the phonograph in the late nineteenth century, and by the twenties, the original tech giant was selling some of the first commercially available home record players and what he called "diamond discs," a signature type of vinyl record. This guidebook was his company's scheme to make customers out of people who were unsure what to listen to. It was a multipage marketing pamphlet disguised as science. Two years earlier, Edison's marketing firm had sponsored research on the emotional impact of music, using its own catalog as source material, conducted by the applied psychology department at the Carnegie Institute of Technology (now known as Carnegie Mellon). According to research by the historian and professor Alexandra Hui, in the margins of one letter about the project, Edison himself wrote: "This will be good propaganda."[3]

For part of the research, the Edison corporation distributed "Mood Change Charts" to customers, asking them to track their emotional states before and after listening to a record, and the company also promoted "Mood Change Parties," where the charts could be distributed. Over twenty-seven thousand charts were collected and used to create the booklet. Each page was dedicated to a different mood, with an illustration depicting how music could help one to overcome or experience said mood, along with information on how to purchase corresponding records from the Edison catalog. "See what music can be made to do for you," the copy urged. "Begin to utilize its power." These were the moods in question:

> To Stimulate and Enrich Your Imagination
>
> To Bring You Peace of Mind
>
> To Make You Joyous
>
> In Moods of Wistfulness
>
> Jolly Moods and Good Fellowship
>
> For More Energy!
>
> Love—and Its Mood
>
> Moods of Dignity and Grandeur
>
> The Mood for Tender Memory
>
> Devotion Is Also a Mood
>
> Stirring
>
> For the Children[4]

Although written almost a century before the rise of Spotify's "Study Beats" and "Peaceful Piano" playlists, Edison's marketing pamphlet carried a similar goal of generating mass interest in a new type of technology through mood music. As it turns out, Spotify was not the first company to pitch mood as an avenue of musical exploration—nor was it the first to prescribe a one-dimensional way of engaging with music as a method of inner self-regulation. As Hui explained in a 2014 research paper, *Mood Music* promoted the liberated listener's individual control, but by limiting the choices to a set number, it offered a very circumscribed form of control. Thus, by standardizing and limiting the choice of categories, it was [Edison staff] who ultimately tried to control the moods of phonograph listeners." There are lessons for the streaming-playlist era to be found in that observation. Those little boxes of emotional clichés that pepper streaming home screens have become so omnipresent that their very existence is hardly processed. And while they may not necessarily be determining the scope of possible emotional connections with music, they certainly work to narrow a horizon of possibility for the target user. "You're boxing people into a context and saying, we're only going to let you know this much, so you want this, based on what we're allowing you to know," a former Spotify playlist editor told me. "If we gave people more context and awareness, then what they want would change."[5]

When Edison published its catalog in 1921, mood music's most infamous chapter was just beginning. The same decade, a U.S. military general named George Squier created a way to transmit sound through physical wires rather than radio. He later sold his patents to a utility conglomerate, and together they created a music subscription service in 1934: Muzak. It would eventually become the world's most famous brand of "piped music"—generic, easy-listening background tracks for workplaces, shopping malls, and homes. And it helped introduce the idea of "elevator music," intended to calm down anxious riders when elevators were first popularized.[6]

In the beginning, though, Squier faced a problem that was pretty similar to the one Daniel Ek would face seventy-three years later: he had a patent for a distribution technology, but he didn't own the rights to any music. And like Ek, Squier couldn't just ring up the record companies to pick up licenses for whatever tunes he pleased. Instead, Muzak opened a recording studio in New York to crank out original tracks—an interesting precedent for the direction Spotify would eventually take commissioning ghost artists—and for $1.50 per month, a subscriber could have three channels of background music and news piped into their home.[7]

Muzak's ownership changed hands many times in the years that followed, eventually landing under the guidance of an advertising executive turned university vice president, who, like the tech overlords before and after him, turned to pseudoscientific research as a marketing tactic. By the 1940s, there had been a surge of university research on topics like workplace productivity and music therapy, and it had a surprising role in bolstering the military-industrial complex, lulling the makers of war materials: the BBC radio program *Music While You Work* was meant to boost the moods of workers in weapons factories, and soon enough the U.S. had thousands of war factories wired for Muzak, too.[8]

The new research-driven direction of Muzak led the company to eventually claim that its peppy, anonymous orchestral tracks could help increase workplace productivity by more than 10 percent. The company "was no longer regarded as background music, but functional music," reads a biography on its website today. "Muzak had finally found its niche." During the 1940s, Muzak started selling workplaces on programming packages called "Stimulus Progression," sequencing blocks of music and silence for maximum productivity; its marketing materials included in-house research studies, charts, and diagrams. "It was pseudoscience," noted David Owen of the *New Yorker* in 2006. "But it remained alive at the company until the late nineties, partly because it was a useful marketing tool and partly because it seemed so plausible: most people really were happier and more productive when there was something humming along in the background." Muzak was not actually controlling the minds of the masses through music, but its aspirations and successes illuminate the ways people in power have long bought into simply the very idea of mood manipulation. Eventually even the White House would pipe this stuff into its halls.[9]

Through the 1960s, Muzak moved away from background music and expanded to include instrumental pop covers. And in the 1980s, it merged with a Seattle-based competitor, Yesco, which had taken a different approach to background music, licensing soft-rock singles from the majors and sorting them into playlists; it called itself a "foreground" music company, but the objectives were aligned. In 1982, one-third of the U.S. population heard Muzak on a daily basis, according to one report. When Muzak made its HQ move from New York City to Seattle in 1987, against all odds, the office's employees included grunge-scene staples like Bruce Pavitt of Sub Pop Records and Mark Arm of the band Mudhoney (who both originally worked at Yesco and were folded into Muzak). As Pavitt remembered it, this whole crew of local indie rockers would be spooling easy-listening tapes and processing dinner soundtrack returns from restaurants, all while listening to and critiquing the latest Nirvana demos. At one point, Pavitt kept a stock of his label's catalog under his desk, and was basically running Sub Pop mail order out of Muzak on the low. "When someone called me with an order, I'd take a box, walk over to shipping, and just ship it out of their warehouse," Pavitt told me. "I had a parasitic relationship with the company. The receptionist was in on it." Sometimes he'd even see marketing materials for the 1940s Stimulus Progression program still kicking around.

"I remember reading that literature and thinking, that's pretty twisted. It was like a psychological operation."

By the end of the eighties, Muzak was being heard by over 80 million people in nineteen countries every day, and the company survived, somehow, until 2011, when it was rebranded into Mood Media. To this day it handles music playlists, in-store signage, and even scent marketing for a wide range of global corporations spanning Burger Kings, 7-Eleven stores, and Capital One banks. In 2021, it was acquired by the San Francisco–based Vector Capital Management, which describes itself as a "global private equity and credit investment firm focused on transformative investments in technology and technology-enabled businesses." It seems there couldn't be a more appropriate place for capital-M Muzak to go to die, but it was a foreboding tale for the tech-enabled lowercase-m muzak that would pervade culture in the years to come.

According to some of its employees, Spotify tends to throw a lot of things at the wall to see what sticks, and when something gains traction, quickly change strategy to follow what's moving the needle, without consideration for long-term consequences. Embracing "moods and moments" probably didn't seem like a big deal when it was a home page redesign and a press release. But there were ramifications for culture.

By championing the lean-back listener, Spotify helped popularize a resurgence of interest in "functional music," the industry's current preferred way to describe music for sleeping, studying, chilling, focusing, etcetera. Today, functional music is a defining phenomenon of the streaming era, especially mood music for wellness and productivity, which self-improvement culture increasingly renders the same. In the peak playlist era, the most popular mood-based commodities were ones offering self-regulation to burnt out millennials working on their laptops. "If you looked at the biggest playlists, it was things like 'Mood Booster,' 'Relax and Unwind,' and 'Songs to Sing in the Shower,'" a former playlist editor told me. The chill-vibes playlists, in particular, became popular at the same time as other tropes of late 2010s wellness culture, like CBD sodas and skincare routines. "Chill" became such a hot topic because of how it spoke to a generation that was anxious and overworked, engaged in cycles of trying to focus hard and chill hard. Similar to how Muzak's core marketing bid had more to do with selling the idea of being able to control workers and shoppers, what gets called "functional music" today is also more about selling a promise than offering a panacea.

Like other functional descriptors of the streaming era, what exactly amounts to "chill" music can be hard to pinpoint. Sometimes it is used as shorthand for the millennial reimagining of the "easy listening" title, a designation used since the 1940s to describe pop radio programming that was soft on the ears. Sometimes "chill" was used to describe motionless, ambient soundscapes claiming to regulate the nervous system, like music one might hear in a spa. Other times "chilled" was used as a type of filter, evoking a lighter take on any genre: "Chilled Dance Hits," "Chilled R&B," and "Chilled Reggae" were all among Spotify's official playlist offerings, alongside collections like "Chillin' on a Dirt Road," "lofi chill," and "Calm."

The ambiguity of the term is perhaps by design, similar to how the industry use of the phrase "functional music" obscures how it usually just means soporific, playlist-friendly music, which is to say smoothed-out background music. For some musicians, chill-vibes playlists were becoming new goalposts to hit in their songwriting. But more often, what happened was that the mellowest moments in their discographies were unexpectedly plucked—by editors or algorithms—for the purposes of a mood mix, taking on new life as playlist fodder. What was playlist friendly was proving to often just be what was most smoothed out.

Music industry defenders of streaming muzak like to point out that artists themselves have been making functional music for decades. The argument usually begins by pointing to Brian Eno's 1978 *Ambient 1: Music for Airports*, widely considered the first ambient record, which came with a manifesto outlining how ambient "must be able to accommodate many levels of listening attention without enforcing one in particular; it must be as ignorable as it is interesting." For example, the cofounder of Endel, a German app that builds on the logic of the functional playlist boom by generating "personalized functional soundscapes," cites Eno as his biggest influence.[10]

Today's functional music front-runners seem to miss something essential about the history of ambient, though, and the traditions it draws from and helped shape. For his part, Eno claims to have conceptualized ambient as a direct response to the cultural pervasiveness of Muzak, rather than a recreation of it. He called ambient music "an atmosphere or a surrounding influence: a tint," which he created to suit "a wide variety of moods and atmospheres." In Eno's explanation of it, consummate artists were not supposed to make background music, and he asked, why not? "I use it to make the space that I want to live in."[11]

But he was firm in the differences between his project and Muzak. In his *Airports* manifesto, Eno asserted that the very reason for creating the term "ambient" was to emphasize these distinctions: "Whereas the extant canned music companies proceed from the basis of regularizing environments by blanketing their acoustic and atmospheric idiosyncrasies, Ambient Music is intended to enhance these. Whereas conventional background music is produced by stripping away all sense of doubt and uncertainty (and thus genuine interest) from the music, Ambient Music retains these qualities." Muzak was intended for mood boosterism, but ambient was meant to induce reflection, and to help foster a relationship between the artist, the listener, and their surroundings. In the airport, Eno wanted listeners to confront their own mortality; his record had "something to do with where you are and what you're there for—flying, floating, and secretly flirting with death."

In other words, it wasn't pure escapism. From the start, ambient was less like functional music and more indebted to the rich histories of meditative ritualistic music or minimalist classical composition. It was akin to what the French composer and pianist Erik Satie, in 1917, called furniture music ("music that would be a part of the surrounding noises") and what the Satie-inspired seventies Japanese avant-garde called *kankyō ongaku*, or environmental music. The latter was meant to "drift like smoke and become part of the environment surrounding the listener's activity," said the Japanese composer Satoshi Ashikawa.

Spencer Doran, an electronic musician who performs as Visible Cloaks, and curator of a critically acclaimed 2019 kankyō ongaku compilation for the Light in the Attic label, noted in an interview once that its original architects similarly imagined their work "in direct opposition" to Muzak. Composer Kuniharu Akiyama, for example, was early to write about Muzak (before Eno, even) as the "generic music of the crowd," coming from no one person's artistic impulse, and instead poorly aspiring for generalized moods and styles. "In designing music that can be modularly organized for anyplace, for anyone, you end up with music for no place, for no one," Doran told me. The airports, lobbies, and chain stores known for playing Muzak were "non-places," he explained, using a term coined by Marc Augé. In Doran's explanation, environmental music was composed for "specific, exact" places, opening a "possibility space" for a new type of artistic expression and subtle connections, one that played with attention in new ways. And while streaming muzak-ification has worked to flatten musical difference, "the ideas behind kankyō ongaku teach that ambience can be redirected to a state of abstract communication, a way not of designing desired emotional states but expressing new ones that are as of yet inarticulable."[12]

When a Spotify user clicks through the "Browse" page to the "Ambient" hub, though, all of this history and context is easily missed. There is one editor-curated playlist that attempts to highlight some big names in ambient history, "Ambient Essentials," but the much more popular offerings are pure vibe wallpaper. "Peaceful Meditation," for example, is filled with homogenous stock tracks supplied by music libraries, but has ten times as many followers. "Stress Relief" and "Ambient Relaxation" are also followed by millions of users, and filled with library music. By muzak-ing ambient into utilitarian self-help content, tech companies have contributed to ambient going the way of punk and folk—traditions that started out rooted in philosophies of musical relationships, now flattened to the point that many listeners hear them solely as aesthetics.

As times changed, even Eno grew disillusioned with his own coinage. "I don't think I understand what that term stands for anymore," he wrote, of ambient music, in 2016. "It seems to have swollen to accommodate some quite unexpected bedfellows." By that point, the algorithmic re-rendering of ambient by streaming was underway. It was a peculiar process, and one that many genres, styles, and scenes would eventually fall prey to—jazz, lofi beats, and neoclassical first, and later practically everything else—as streaming curation grew more dependent on automated systems. Reflecting on how this played out with ambient is especially curious: a genre that was purportedly established to offer a more compelling response to capital-M Muzak, reimagined by corporate playlist machinations as lowercase-m muzak. In the streaming era, this is what happens; it's muzak as a verb, as a thing that could happen to anyone. And while there remains limitless music from inspired independent ambient artists and labels to be discovered these days, they are up against an endless sea of data-tuned fodder optimized for playlist success, as streaming platforms contribute to turbocharging cycles of commodification in culture.[13]

One streaming-era subculture reflected the rise of streaming neo-Muzak better than any other: "lofi beats." Since the late 2010s, most listeners have first encountered it through 24/7 YouTube streams like "lofi hiphop radio—beats to relax/study to." These endless feeds of lean-back cozy vibes are essentially Muzak for zillennials, to use the word for those on the Gen Z–millennial cusp. And they are often found through the YouTube or Spotify pages of curators-turned-labels with names like Chillhop, College Music, or most popularly, Lofi Girl (which rebranded from Chilled Cow in 2021).

But before it was all about studying and snoozing, and before it hit YouTube, lofi was largely just a bunch of musicians—many of them teenagers—in chat rooms talking about J Dilla and Madlib, the legendary boundary-pushing hip-hop producers who were among their biggest influences. Inspired by Dilla's iconic time-shifting drumbeats and dusty low-fidelity approach, these early-2010s revivalists posted their home recordings to SoundCloud, but also in a bare-bones browser-based chat room called "lofi.hiphop," where musicians would trade home recordings and try to outdo each other by flipping samples on their SP404 beat machines; it was a reportedly fun and supportive internet hang, devoid of commercialism.

For better or for worse, streaming services brought a new financial dimension. According to three lofi hip-hop beat makers I spoke with, as lofi beats culture moved from SoundCloud to YouTube to Spotify—and as lofi turned into playlist fare—the culture changed.

"Once Spotify popped in the game, that's also kind of when you started noticing the sound of lofi changing into this more easy-to-forget, study-oriented thing," said Graham Jonson, a Portland-based producer who records under the moniker quickly, quickly and is signed to the electronic label Ghostly International. Jonson's relationship with the genre is fraught: after a few of his songs went viral as a teenager, he paid his rent with lofi money for years before he abandoned the sound to follow new inspirations. "There were people doing crazy stuff within these genre boundaries, but as soon as the bigwigs started getting involved . . . it was like, okay, well, it is no longer the J Dilla and Madlib sound, it's now sad piano ballads with weird drums."

To Jonson's ears, the 2010s lofi culture really changed once streaming became normalized. The pre-streaming sound was about tape hiss and grit. "It didn't start out as background music," he said. "It's kind of like what happened with ambient music. . . . [Lofi] became this thing that started being engineered for people to just put on and tune out, rather than to be this kind of impressive showcasing of drums or a crazy sample chop."

As lofi became a totally lean-back trend, label-curators like Lofi Girl became more influential than the artists themselves, both on YouTube and Spotify; as of this writing, the Lofi Girl flagship Spotify playlist has over 7 million followers. A specific business model took hold: beatmakers would record new tracks, and then pitch them around to the lofi labels. If a label decided to accept a track, they would strike a deal that typically granted the label ownership of the track in exchange for a share of streaming royalties.

Most artists struggled to develop fanbases in a culture where they were essentially rendered anonymous. One producer who has released music with Lofi Girl, and landed on some of Spotify's official lofi playlists, told me that despite his three hundred thousand monthly listeners, if he "played a show in L.A. and promoted it really hard, maybe twenty people would come." He also noted that as the lofi scene became more dominated by a small group of curators and data-driven platforms, all of the tracks just started to sound the same. The lofi labels became less concerned with artists' careers and more focused on offering a seamless study playlist. "They curate their music so that it all sounds like the same product," the producer told me. "They curate all of the artwork to look the same. To the point where on YouTube, you'll see people commenting on a Lofi Girl upload saying, 'Thanks Lofi Girl, I love your music.' They really do think that Lofi Girl is the artist. And that's what Lofi Girl wants, as does every other big lofi label. That's where we're at now. There isn't such thing as a lofi artist. There's only such thing as a person who is a part of the lofi machine."

Similar dynamics played out with Spotify playlists more generally. "Editorial playlists work for consumption," one former Spotify playlist editor told me. "They don't work for creating fans. Because that's not what they are for. It's just tangential to the system. Algorithmic stuff doesn't create fans either. Playlisting was a lot of lean-back passive consumption that was an end in and of itself. You had people, like, buying houses and staying completely independent, just because of playlist consumption. But that didn't help them fill a one-hundred-fifty-cap venue or sell merch."

The rise of streaming muzak also contributed to the gamification of music-making for young producers coming up in this environment; it spawned a whole web of sketchy new labels and playlist companies, and attracted all sorts of investment companies. It also drew the attention of the major labels, who launched their own chill-vibes imprints, and projects releasing lofi remixes of back catalog. "It's a ridiculous cottage industry," said another longtime lofi beats producer. "If you're trying to succeed in lofi, you're barking up the wrong tree. It's a sinking ship. . . . It's such a race to the bottom. You can try to hustle as many low-ish quality uninspired beats as you can to as many labels as you can. But it's really a numbers game at this point because it's so saturated."

The same producer emphasized how the scene's extreme fixation on metrics had created seriously unhealthy dynamics among aspiring producers. "I've seen so much mental illness," he added. "There's so much money in those playlists. It's really like kind of sickening, how much money can be made by having that level of influence. It's just a lot of streams. You see so many businesspeople now buying up playlists, like, it's just money, because the royalty payouts are crazy." One producer told me that getting prime playlist placements could mean the difference between earning six figures or earning nothing. But another, in 2023, told me that for his peers, it wasn't so simple: "I think a lot of people are struggling with this right now. They can release music to a wide audience, but no one will care about it. Because it's not set up for anyone to care about it. It's really hard to reach people in a meaningful way."

Jonson (of quickly, quickly) described it all relatively similarly. "I could tell that at a certain point, nobody really cared about the music. It became this very passive listening experience, which is not generally how I listen to music, or not really what I make music for. I felt like it was just time to move on. I became really disillusioned with lofi as a concept."

He moved forward with conviction and released an album of more adventurous electronic productions, which also included him singing for the first time. "Sure enough, as soon as I released my album, you know, with all the singing and all that, the streams just completely plummeted, like cut in half. But it was weirdly like, freeing. Because I didn't have to check my monthly listeners, or wonder, did my song get put on the playlist? Where's it in the playlist? I kind of stopped caring about the algorithm and checking on my Spotify for Artists page and just got to focus on making stuff that really made me happy, which was very, very fulfilling. I'm so, so glad I did that." He pauses, and laughs. "But sometimes I do think about the money because that shit was kind of crazy."

Something unusual started happening with the lofi Spotify playlists after 2016. The second anonymous producer recalled watching, in real time, as musicians he knew were removed and replaced by stock music. "There was one drop in streaming that was felt pretty much across my group of friends and my network, when Firefly came on the scene," he said, referring to a mysterious Swedish stock music company, Firefly Entertainment. "They really took over a ton of playlists. A lot of people had a lot of questions." This was the season when some musicians and listeners first started noticing generic tracks from Firefly, and another Swedish background music company, Epidemic Sound, filling up dozens upon dozens of popular lean-back mood playlists. It was all very peculiar. "The Firefly playlist takeover was a big moment for a lot of people who felt it worse than I did. For what it's worth, I've never known anyone affiliated with Firefly. I know a lot of people affiliated with Epidemic Sound. Firefly is weirdly opaque," the producer continued. "It always confused me, like, how the fuck did this happen?"

With so many different industry players trying to get in on the lofi gold rush, this much was becoming clear: the easy-listening paradigm that took over music in the streaming era wasn't about delighting the user. It was about neither discovery nor democracy. It was about profit.

"It's just so fucking soulless," the same anonymous producer went on. "I've watched it happen while participating from within. My natural conclusion was: damn, yeah, I want to make music, but I don't really want to be involved in this. It's really upsetting. And I don't have to care. If I align my life differently, I don't have to care about making money off of this. I'm in the very beginning of that existential shift. Everyone I talk to who is getting into this, I want to tell to just do this for fun, and not worry about the numbers, because you'll just lose unless you're a ruthless capitalist. And I don't want more ruthless capitalists determining the music we all listen to. That's not the vibe, you know?"

During the first pandemic spring, in 2020, Ek gave a CNBC interview where he raved to finance TV personality Jim Cramer about the "wellness" trends Spotify was capitalizing on amid a year of global suffering.

Cramer proclaimed: "A lot of people don't realize it, but I'm a chill guy! I heard what you said about a lot of people listening to chill music. There is a mindfulness wave that is somehow being captured by the people who work at home. Are you able to detect that from artificial intelligence?" Yes, Ek replied, exactly; the personalization algorithms were observing "a lot of people turning to wellness" who wanted to "de-stress" and "focus on health." The interaction was a prime example of how Spotify attempted to sell its brand to Wall Street: overhyping its use of AI, conflating "chill" and "wellness."[14]

In this sense, the conquest of chill reflects an industry content to profit from a world of disconnection; capitalism both alienates us and sells us tools to distract us from the loneliness of nonstop alienated labor, sickens us and then sells us the cure. The Norwegian avant-garde songwriter Jenny Hval—who in 2018 debuted a performance piece where she projected visuals of chill playlists and an automated voice read their names—described it to me in these terms of simultaneous manipulation and medication: "I feel it speaks to a world of anxiety. It's a Band-Aid. But what's underneath the Band-Aid is not just the wound of the listener but the wound of the system."

Indeed, today's chill-out ambience feels less attuned to Eno's atmospheres, which were intended to create "musical experiences" that the listener could enter and leave as they wished, and more like personalized pseudoscientific therapeutics. If the Muzak of the 1940s was about disciplining workers in factories—or selling to employers the idea that this was possible—then today's mood music boom, in the age of being your own boss, might be more about the streaming user disciplining themselves, or being sold on that possibility, under the guise of self-improvement and empowerment, like an integral part of any self-care routine.

There's a playlist called "Musical Therapy," made by Spotify, filled with generic ambient tracks by artists that don't actually exist. In a sea of similar playlists and personalization feeds positioning themselves as musical tinctures, this one felt especially harmful. What were the stakes of streaming services passing this off as "music therapy"? For perspective, I turned to a certified music therapist with a master's from the SUNY New Paltz Music Therapy graduate program, Dan Goldberg (also an artist I met many years ago through the DIY music scene).

"This sort of playlist is belittling to the scope of practice of music therapists and the goals they work to achieve, as they are significantly wider than just 'soothing your mind' as the playlist states in the description," he told me. "There is no prescriptive music that works for everyone. It's pretty reasonable to expect that the music from these playlists (or the associations that come along with it) might get on some people's nerves and have the opposite effect of relaxation. Music therapists accept that someone might feel more relaxed from nu metal or hardcore punk than from easy listening."

Goldberg said that music therapy is generally not a "passive experience" and playlists like these are a growing concern for practitioners in the field. "A lot of music therapists receive training on improvisation techniques that welcome and empower the people they work with to play, express themselves, and take the lead. This certainly isn't possible from an online playlist."

One former Spotify playlist editor told me that the reason they all create so many chill playlists is straightforward. "Chill was successful," the editor said. "All of the playlist editors wanted to be successful and have their playlists be successful. So everyone made chill playlists. It was less that everyone was being told, 'make chill playlists,' and more like a new genre editor comes in, he sees that chill is successful, he wants to have big playlists, he makes ten chill playlists."

Anything can be chilled and repurposed in the economy of passive listening. And once a song is taken from its intended context and jumbled together with a bunch of unrelated music under the banner of a vibe, it enters the recommendation machine under those terms. (And generally not in the fun chaotic way.)

It's a self-fulfilling cycle. If a user sees that an editor added a specific track to "Sunset Chill," "Chilled Dance Hits," or "Indie Chillout," maybe they'll then add it to their own chill-vibes wake-up playlist. And if they listen to it enough, maybe it will later be suggested again and again on algorithmically generated "niche mixes" like "Chill Morning Mix," "Chill Morning Relaxing Mix," "Morning Chill Instrumental Mix," "Chill Morning Beats Mix," and "Chill Morning House Mix." These were all titles available to me during a recent search, along with even one advertising "Chill Morning Alternative Rock music picked just for you." Another source told me that no one internally could agree on what "chill" meant— that it was so ambiguous, it had "no definition that is meaningful."

Recently, some variation of this ambiguous data-tuning process led a very unchill track by the singer and songwriter Anohni called "Why Am I Alive Now?" to appear near the top of my "Chill Vibes" playlist on Spotify. The playlist is "algotorial," meaning that it was created using a mix of editorial and algorithmic input. When I delivered the news to Anohni on a video call—that her song had been absorbed into this chill-vibes playlist—she appeared visibly perplexed. "That song is so despairing," she said, deadpan, before reflecting on the dangers of the current climate of decontextualization.

Anohni released her first full-length album in February 2000. Her first three decades in the industry have offered her an up-front view to twenty-first-century tech power's corrupting influence on music's already quite corrupt economy. "There used to be a system where harder music had a place within the pantheon of the economy of music," she told me. "If we're going to just accept the economy of music for a second as a paradigm, within that there were complex conversations happening. Even within capitalism, there were smaller economies, smaller worlds where smaller musicians were thriving. And people were able to support themselves selling complicated records. Records that you wouldn't listen to hundreds and hundreds of times. Losing the physical object of the record, and instead leaning on monetization based on plays, really upends the transaction of music between songwriter and listener. It is a very, very politically astute maneuver that favors a narcotic relationship to music over a complex, meditative relationship to music."

Before streaming, Anohni saw more opportunities for non-pop music. "I'm not saying it was a noble economy, but there was more of an ecology to it. There were so many ways of approaching listening to a song. There was an innate integrity to paying a person for a record, whether you listened to it five times or five thousand times. Sometimes a record only needed to be listened to five times in order for a profound transaction to have taken place."

Shortly after speaking with Anohni, I met up with Darius Van Arman, one of the cofounders of Secretly Group, a big independent label group that includes Anohni's label, Secretly Canadian, and the label Van Arman started in 1996, Jagjaguwar. These days, Secretly is one of the most financially successful independent label groups, releasing records by the likes of Mitski, Phoebe Bridgers, and Bon Iver. But when he started, Van Arman was releasing considerably more obscure music. One of the first albums that his label ever released was by the Brooklyn noise band Oneida. "It was good business to work with Oneida, who made challenging, beautiful records and were a great live band," he said. The label could sell a few thousand CDs, cover the manufacturing and promotion costs, and have $25,000 left to split with the band. No one was quitting their jobs, but it kept them all going. People would buy the CDs at shows, or because they read a good review, and even if they only listened to it once and put it on a shelf, it had value.

How about now? "Monetization is shaped differently," Van Arman told me. "It's based on what gets repeat listens. It didn't take long for artists and labels to make that connection. It's not sustainable to put out challenging records. To be sustainable, you have to put out records that are going to get repeat listens in coffee shops. That people are going to want to listen to over and over again, and that are going to be playlist friendly and easier on the ears."

That's not to say that his and other independent labels are no longer willing to take those risks. But the considerations of running a label, for some, seem to have shifted. I asked him if he thought a label like his could ever get started in the streaming era, in the same way that he was able to start putting out bands like Oneida.

"I don't know," he said. "Probably not."

When I initially started to research the topic of streaming-era mood music, one of the first things I did was go to Discogs, an online marketplace for used records, to mail-order a copy of *Pure Moods*, the nineties CD compilation of Enya, Eno, and other new age music, immortalized in its late-night infomercial that promised to whisk listeners away to a world of no worries. I perched the CD compilation on a shelf above my desk as an omnipresent reminder: chill-out mood muzak is not new, and in fact, is a phenomenon with a whole history and many subplots. (*Pure Moods* was yet again another example of how mood music was used, in part, to usher in a new way of marketing and selling music—this time through TV commercials.)

Part of what is new is that everything can be part of a data-optimized *Pure Moods* compilation now. It's plausible to assume that the process of licensing tracks for *Pure Moods* involved phone calls, meetings, contract negotiations, and most importantly, the consent of each artist or one of their representatives. Now, by virtue of servicing one's music to a streaming platform, anyone's work can be used to create the new popular music commodity that is the official streaming editorial playlist. And while some might consider that empowering, others might not want to lend their work to the broader project of muzak-ing culture. The suggestion that the businesses of pop music, mood-enhancing background sounds, and independent art-making ought to all live on the same platform, under the same economic arrangements, and the same tools of engagement, is a recipe for everything being flattened out into one ceaseless chill-out stream.

Shaping user behaviors around its own discovery tools put Spotify in an outsized position of power; it shifted value away from the musicians and labels that supplied the material it relied on, and toward its own brand. This was, in part, the goal: if Spotify could shape user behavior around coming to the platform for certain playlists, certain moods, certain vibes, then it would maintain control over the user experience. If a user comes to the platform every night for a playlist called "Chill Vibes," "Ibiza Lounge," or "Fresh & Chill," it matters very little what is actually found on those playlists. If a musician decides to protest over unfair royalties? It's not hard to imagine a situation where a streaming service might just replace them with someone else. Or better yet, maybe just a ghost artist who doesn't actually exist.

5

Ghost Artists for Hire

I n 2015, the major labels had a reason to celebrate. Their revenues were finally on the upswing. For at least a decade prior, the record business had been in free fall. At the peak of the CD era, in 1999, recordings brought in more money than ever: an estimated $39 billion dollars globally. But between 2000 and 2010, physical music sales declined by over 60 percent. By 2014, the record companies were taking in a measly $14 billion. "The Music Industry Has Hit Its Rock Bottom," read a *Quartz* headline the next year. But hope, it seemed, was on the way. In 2015, for the first time in over a decade, the industry earned more revenue than it had the previous year. The charts were starting to trend upward again. The labels and the press declared a savior: Spotify.[1]

By the mid-2010s, the accidental music streaming app had cemented itself as the most important source of revenue for the major labels, which were raking in cash from Spotify's millions of paying subscribers. But while Ek's company was giving labels and publishers a *lot* of money—70 percent of its revenue, as contractually mandated—it had yet to turn a profit for itself, which shareholders would soon demand.

There were several possible routes the company could take: raising prices, cutting costs, attracting new subscribers. In those pre-IPO years, the higher-ups had a lightbulb moment. They knew that the vast majority of users were not coming to Spotify for specific artists and albums. They just needed something—anything—to soundtrack their days. They were coming for a passive experience, where they could press one button and hear some appropriate music. They were coming for a study playlist, background chill vibes, or maybe a dinner soundtrack. In the lean-back listening environment that streaming had helped champion, listeners often weren't even aware of what song or artist they were hearing.

How did it come to this? That might be a question that leaves musicians and devotees up at night, but Spotify's questions were different: Why were they paying full-price royalties if users were only half-listening? So its music programming execs tried something new: they developed a scheme to lower royalty costs by populating the most-followed mood playlists with low-budget filler tracks; stock music from background music studios to fit certain moods and genres, licensed by Spotify under what former employees and a review of internal records confirmed were special, cheaper deal terms. The songs were often made by anonymous session musicians—one of them, a jazz musician for hire, told me he would crank out dozens of tracks at a time, assigning them one-off monikers.

If people were mostly coming to the platform for lean-back playlists, would they even notice if top-shelf tracks disappeared from them? When listeners form regular behaviors around platform-controlled playlists, didn't that make the artists disposable and interchangeable? Spotify was about to test out just how interchangeable they were.

Journalists started covering this bizarre phenomenon, describing the ghost music-makers as "fake artists." That was technically correct, but it was also more complicated; there was a whole web of power and money behind this. Internally, the program had a name: perfect fit content, or PFC. Spotify's official definition for this material was "music commissioned to fit a certain playlist/mood with improved margins."

For the musicians whose tracks were being replaced by these ghost artists, it could be devastating; the difference between making a humble living and not. Watching it all play out, some of Spotify's full-time in-house playlist editors were crushed, too. They were watching the playlists they'd built up with pride get turned into budget content farms. "There were a lot of tears over this project internally at Spotify," a former employee told me.

In the years before the IPO, sources say the long-abstracted PFC program was introduced to playlist editors as a cost-saving initiative. "It was one of the company's new bets to help with profitability," another source said. "It started with only certain types of music." By 2023, according to a review of charts and messages shared on the company Slack, over 100 official playlists were made almost entirely of PFC, and a process of determining "search result overrides" was used to prioritize pushing that cheaper content when users went looking for certain moods. And Spotify went to great lengths to keep it all hidden.

It was first reported in 2016 by *Music Business Worldwide.* Spotify had allegedly been directly sourcing prefab instrumentals to "fit certain genres and themes, including jazz, chill, and peaceful piano playing," which producers would make in bulk and release under one-off monikers. According to that early investigation, Spotify had licensed these tracks directly from production companies for a cheaper royalty rate, and thus would promote them on its relaxing editorial mood playlists (with millions of followers) to protect its bottom line. The company responded by vehemently denying that these were "fake artists," but not the existence of the broader, hidden arrangement. Spotify claimed they had "found a need for content" and were simply looking for suppliers to help give listeners what they wanted. But were listeners creating that need, or had Spotify created it?[2]

In my early days of reporting on the streaming economy, I received more emails about the so-called "fake artist" issue than any other related topic. Initially, the owner of a long-running NYC independent record label dropped me a line, letting me know about a mysterious phenomenon that was "in the air" and of growing concern in the indie label scene. "Is it majors hiring studio musicians to make ambient tracks to collect a windfall of streaming cash, or Spotify themselves?" he wondered. "Maybe just a payola scenario but either way alarming." Spotify wanted these no-name ambient tracks to float on by in the background, but to those actually listening, they stuck right out.

A second independent record label staffer, who worked as a digital strategist, expressed some similar concerns to me at the time. "I'm not naive enough to believe that streaming is a meritocracy," he said. "Far from it. But at some point there's a trend of interventionism toward these producers, which isn't getting extended to 'actual' independent artists as often anymore, and isn't being acknowledged or explained. . . . The concept of Spotify or streaming as the pragmatic marketplace where artists will profit from their work in itself is perverted by this practice."

"So far it's happening within a genre that mostly affects artists at labels like the ones I work for, or Kranky, or Constellation," the staffer said, referring to long-running indie labels. "But I doubt that it'll be unique to our corner of the music world for long."

At first, I simply referred to them as "mystery viral artists"—they often had millions of plays, prime placements on mood lists, but no bio, no website, no digital footprint anywhere else. You could not Google these artists. Trusty citizen investigators on Reddit dug up example after example of artist pages that were clearly fake, but had Spotify's equivalent to blue-check verification. There were red flags all over the platform—something weird was going on.

For years, there were more questions than answers—until a 2022 investigation by the Swedish daily newspaper *Dagens Nyheter* (*DN*) brought new weight to the allegations. By corroborating scraped streaming data with documents retrieved from the Swedish collection society STIM, the newspaper revealed that around twenty songwriters were behind over five hundred artist names, and that between them, Spotify was flooded with thousands of their tracks streamed millions of times.[3]

On a summer afternoon in the lobby of the paper's Stockholm office, I met with technology editor Linus Larsson, who pulled up the Spotify bio of a supposed artist named Ekfat. Since 2019, a handful of tracks had been released under this moniker, mostly with Firefly Entertainment listed as the label. They appeared on official Spotify editorial playlists like "Lofi House" and "Chill Instrumental Beats." One of the tracks had over 3 million streams; at the time of this writing, the number has surpassed 4 million. But Larsson was particularly amused by the fairly elaborate artist bio, which he started to read out loud. It called Ekfat a classically trained Icelandic beatmaker who graduated from the Reykjavik "music conservatory," joined the "Lo-Fi Rockers Crew" in 2017, and released music only on limited-edition cassettes until 2019.

"*Completely* made up," Larsson said. "These are three Swedish guys [who make songs] in different constellations. This is probably the most absurd example because they really tried to make him into the coolest music producer that you can find." In retrospect, the bio sort of sounds like it could have been written using generative AI. It was just one example of what was all over Spotify at that point, in 2023: "A range of artists, in genres such as hip-hop beats, anonymous jazz and low-key piano music, are simply not real," explained the *DN* exposé. "What there is, however, is a hidden million-dollar industry with an anonymous Karlstad company at the center, where the management has close personal connections to a former Spotify manager."

Firefly Entertainment was so enmeshed in the scheme, it had grown its revenue tenfold in just a few years, fueled by streaming royalties. Later, in my own reporting, former Spotify employees would characterize Firefly as a "PFC provider."

While former employees gave conflicting reports on the exact managers that created the PFC program, the Spotify-Firefly connection emerged largely thanks to a longtime personal relationship between Nick Holmstén, the founder of Tunigo who would eventually become Spotify's global head of music, and Fredrik Hult, the founder of Firefly Entertainment. Hult and Holmstén grew up in the same town in the west of Sweden, and their many years of close friendship are documented across Hult's Instagram page: family vacations, dinners out on the town, visits to the Spotify office. In one of Hult's photos, he poses with some Firefly producers at Spotify's 2018 Best New Artist Grammy party.

"It wasn't a coincidence that this company had all these spots on the popular playlists," said Larsson, who uncovered the link with co-reporter Hugo Lindkvist. Rummaging through the depths of Discogs one day, I stumbled upon an even deeper connection between Holmstén and Hult: they had played together in a late-nineties powerpop band called Apple Brown Betty, releasing a couple of studio records. There's a video on You-Tube: Spotify's once global head of music on vocals, founder of the most mysterious fake-artist company on drums.

Besides the journalists at *DN*, music and media people in Sweden did not really want to talk about all this fake-artist stuff. In Stockholm, I found the address of one of the Swedish ghost labels and tried to knock on the door—no luck. I met someone who knew a guy who maybe ran one of these production companies, but he didn't want to talk. A local businessman would only reveal that he worked in the "functional music space," and got so cagey when I told him about this book, that I just had to laugh.

Despite the obvious signs, Spotify had gone to great lengths to down-play its formal relationships with the production music companies fueling its PFC program. And the licensees, too, seem to have been sworn to secrecy. It made sense. Because once you started pulling, the whole web of Spotify's curation universe unraveled.

Song selectors at Spotify now have access to an internal playlist monitoring tool, through which they can view various stats: plays, likes, bans, skips, saves, BPM. But right at the top of the page, editors can see another figure: the playlist's current percentage of PFC.

PFC was being piloted in 2016, but it wasn't until the next year that the program was officially presented to editors as one of the company's new bets to help with profitability. According to a former employee, the internal PFC-monitoring column appeared just a few months after that formal introduction. Playlist editors were soon encouraged, with increasing persistence, to add the cheaper songs. "Initially they would give us links to stuff, like, *Oh, it's no pressure for you to add it, but if you can, that would be great*," the former employee recalled. "But then that column came up. And then after that, the people who orchestrated the program would look through our playlists, and see, *How many songs does so and so have that are PFC? And Oh, so and so is not adding them, let's suggest some lightly*. And then it became more aggressive, like, *Oh, this is the style of music in your playlist, if you try it and it works, then why not? Why not?*"

Some editors were hesitant to partake. Because if the tracks performed well, the higher-ups would nudge them: *Why don't you move it up? Why don't you add more?* Executives argued that the average streaming service user would not notice or care whether the songs on their playlists were made by "real" or "fake" artists.

A former playlist editor told me that internally, employees were quite concerned that the company was not being transparent with users about the reality of this material. Another former playlist editor told me that in those early days, he started adding the tracks to his playlists but wasn't totally clear on the details. "I wasn't really sure who was making the music or where it came from," he told me. "But I understood that it was music that we benefited from financially, and that we wanted to incorporate it into certain playlists that were more of what we would call a lean-back experience than a lean-forward one. Sleep playlists would be the best example of a lean-back playlist. I just took it for what it was. Maybe I should have asked more questions, but I was just kind of like, *Okay, how do I mix this music with artists that I like and not have them stand out?"*

Internally, some employees felt that those responsible for pushing the PFC strategy onto editors had no knowledge of the instrumental traditions that were being impacted by the broader strategy. These executives were well versed in the business of pop hit-making, not necessarily the cultures or histories of jazz, classical, ambient, and lofi hip-hop beats—music that tended to do well on playlists for relaxing, sleeping, or focusing.

Someone familiar with the program told me that it was initiated by an employee who came from the major label system. "This person, he knows the pop hits and stuff, but he does not give a shit about these genres that are impacted—or listen to them, or know anything about the culture or the history of them," the source said. "He just sees it as *Oh well, no one actually goes to these people's concerts, most people aren't going to notice anyways."*

Like many other corners of the Spotify operation, it was all about metrics. If users weren't skipping tracks, the higher-ups didn't see a problem. The attitude was "if the metrics went up, then let's just keep replacing more and more, because if the user doesn't notice, then it's fine," the source continued. "They were trying to almost insert their own morality. Like, *Oh well, if the user reacts to it bad, then we'll change it, but if the metrics are fine, then it's fine."*

Eventually, it became clear internally that many of the playlist editors were uninterested in participating in the scheme. The company brought on new editors who were unbothered by the PFC model, a source told me, and whose job was specifically to look after mood and activity lists, "to do the stuff that other editors didn't want to do anymore."

These editors did not understand music culture, the source continued, "so they don't feel bad about what they're doing. There's no moral dilemma for these people. They're happy to do it, because to them it's just music in the background, too."

"Ambient Relaxation." "Deep Focus." "100% Lounge." "Bossa Nova Dinner." "Cocktail Jazz." According to internal communications reviewed in 2023, these official Spotify playlists were just a few of the many comprised of over 90 percent PFC tracks. At that point, several hundred playlists were being monitored by the PFC team, and over 150 of them were almost entirely made of this cheaper music.

The managers found ways to defend the PFC program internally. They would claim that it was only for background music, so listeners wouldn't mind, and that there was a "low supply" of music for these types of playlists. The background part was true: a glimpse at the "PFC dashboard," shared over Slack, showed how PFC streamshare was broken up according to activity types like sleep, mindfulness, unwinding, lounging, meditation, calming down, concentrating, studying, pampering, and others. But what types of songs were filling out those categories? That's what makes the "low supply" line so unbelievable—they were talking about ambient, classical, electronic, jazz, lofi beats, or in other words, genres with certainly no shortage across Spotify.

At some point, PFC had come to be handled by a team of ten employees called "Strategic Programming," or "StraP" for short. In the broader corporate structure, they operated underneath the Editorial team. StraP also handled something called "strategic genres," a term Spotify created to classify background-friendly mood playlist fodder and differentiate it all from "editorial genres," a term which referred to popular music with flagship playlists.

In one internal presentation slide, "strategic genres" were described as "underserved" styles on Spotify, and while it wasn't totally clear exactly what that word meant in that context, it was an oddly manipulative description: Wasn't this program also contributing to underserving actual ambient, jazz, and lofi artists? The same slide framed strategic genres as missed opportunities for "growth/programmed streams" that required innovative "back-end improvements" in order to better follow the metrics. It seemed they'd just created an umbrella term for sounds that could be exploited by finding new ways to strategically manipulate listeners into spending a greater percentage of their streaming hours on music it cost Spotify less to provide.

The strategic programming team regularly had conversations about how to make sure PFC streamshare was increasing. But, as was at times becoming more common for playlist editors in the 2020s, their job also involved labeling and sorting: tagging tracks with descriptors relevant to the PFC universe, so that they would ultimately end up in the appropriate content pools for algorithmic, algotorial, or otherwise PFC-heavy playlists. Rather than exclusively curating playlists, they also seemed to be curating data.

When new PFC providers were onboarded, senior staff would chime in on Slack to make sure attention was paid to their offerings. "We've now onboarded Myndstream," a StraP staffer wrote in one message. "Please prioritize adding from these as this is a new partner so they can get some live feedback." The employee shared a series of sublists from the new licensee, sorted into collections titled "ambient piano covers," "relax and breathe," and "lofi originals." A couple of months later, another team member posted a similar message: "Our new partner Slumber Group LLC is ready for their first releases. . . . Make sure to have them set up in your Reverb filters for more snoozy content :)." "Reverb" referred to an internal tool for managing tracks and playlists.

For years, Firefly Entertainment and Epidemic Sound dominated the media's speculation about shady playlist practices, but they weren't the only companies secretly collaborating with Spotify; internal messages revealed that this only scratched the surface. Firefly and Epidemic were just two names on a long list of at least a dozen PFC providers that Spotify employees discussed internally. That list also included companies with names like Hush Hush LLC and Catfarm Music AB. There was Queenstreet Content AB, the production company of Swedish pop songwriting duo Andreas Romdhane and Josef Svedlund, who it turns out also owned a bigger streaming mood-muzak operation, Audiowell, with investments from mega-producer Max Martin (who has shaped the sound of global pop music since the nineties) and private equity firm Altor. In 2022, the Swedish press reported that Queenstreet was bringing in over $10 million per year. Another company listed was Industria Works, a subsidiary of which is Mood Works, a functional music distributor whose website shows it also services its streaming-friendly tracks to Apple Music and Amazon Music. Spotify, it appeared, wasn't alone in this practice.[4]

On Slack, the employees of Strategic Programming chattered about metadata tagging issues. One day, the conversation turned to some recently reported "quarterly loyalty learnings": How often did users return to "Morning Study"? Did increasing PFC share on "Binaural Beats Deeper Sleep" help or hurt user engagement? The goal, it seemed, was building user habits around these playlists. In another thread, employees voted on new covers for sleep playlists. They pondered an eternal lean-back listening dilemma: Should the "Sweet Lullabies" playlist be tagged "mood" or "activity"? They shared a doc for brainstorming a "wishlist for PFC partners," seeming to answer the question of whether Spotify actively commissioned specific content from these ghost labels.

One day, the PFC team was mulling over whether it was realistic to aim for a billion streams on sleep playlists in Q1. "Let's do it," someone said, before the flexed bicep emojis trickled in. A particularly enthusiastic coworker hyped up the team: "ONE BILLY LET'S DO THIS."

The quest for PFC growth seemed to know no bounds, and yet, Spotify had gone to some great lengths to avoid owning up to the whole scheme. I want to say it's because they knew the stakes—that these were real music cultures being replaced, actual traditions within which artists were trying to make a living. But maybe it was just that this platform-wide project to cheapen music contradicted so many of the talking points upon which the company's brand had been built. Spotify had long sold itself as the ultimate platform for discovery—and who was going to get excited about "discovering" a bunch of stock music? Artists had been sold the idea that streaming was the ultimate meritocracy—that whatever rose to the top was simply the best music, because the people had voted with their streams! But here was a single program that disproved all of those lies. PFC was not the only way in which Spotify would deliberately manipulate programming to favor content with better margins, without making it clear to the listeners, but it was the most immediately galling.

It was not simply a matter of that mostly meaningless A-word—authenticity—or trying to draw boundaries around "fakeness" or "realness" in music. It was a matter of survival for actual artists and scenes, a matter of musicians actually having the ability to earn a living, on one of the main platforms where music is heard. It was irrefutable proof that Spotify had gamed its system against any musician who knew their worth.

And, as I noticed all of the places where these ghost artists would pop up—in my home page recommendations, personalized search results, algotorial mood mixes—and I read their made-up names, made-up bio pages (often touting the "healing" and "wellness" properties of their generic drones), even sometimes fake social media pages, it also just started to feel like a straight-up problem of misinformation and media degradation, issues that were only going to grow more insidious as the functional music trend opened the door for generative AI music makers to walk right in.

"When you are a DSP and you have that much power and influence over people's education about music, it's such a great responsibility," a

Spotify affiliate familiar with the PFC initiative told me. DSP stands for "digital service provider" and is typically used as music industry shorthand to refer to streaming services. "Spotify is a cultural force right now," the affiliate went on. "If I have a kid and I'm trying to teach them about the history of ambient music, and go to Spotify . . . more often than not, what you'll find is PFC artists. I can't teach my kid about jazz if they're listening to, like, 'Soft Jazz in the Background.'"

The same source also pointed out that there was a problematic racial dimension to the unfairness of the program, when stock music tracks started commonly being used in playlists historically dominated by artists of color: "Because what started happening was—spots for Black and brown artists making this music started getting cut down to make room for a few of these white Swedish guys in a studio."

When employees expressed concern that the music didn't feel culturally attuned to the traditions it was purporting to replace, and that it felt more like Muzak, the higher-ups suggested providing feedback to the PFC makers on how to make it better. Some who expressed criticism internally were "gaslit" and told that they were wrong for suggesting that these faceless, nameless producers were any less real than other artists. "It's a disease in Spotify recommendations and what they are doing to culture," one source told me. "Some of us really didn't feel good about what was happening. We didn't like that it was [sometimes] these two guys that normally write pop songs replacing swaths of artists across the board. It's just not fair. But it was like trying to stop a train that was already leaving."

The "fake artist" narrative, in some ways, might have diminished the issue. Yes, there were often fabricated monikers involved, but the musicians were real. The ghost labels that hired them were real. The direct licensing deals between those ghost labels and the streaming services were real. In a sense, the "fake artist" label oversimplified and obfuscated a whole apparatus of power, control, and deception. This was not just a laundry list of faceless scam artists trying to game the system, or a series of bad actors operating in isolation. This was a program created by Spotify, involving a web of individuals and organizations complicit in their scheme for cheap content: production companies, background-music licensing firms, record labels. And an endless flow of musicians with no better prospects than to create it for them.

6

The Background Music Makers

On a summer afternoon in Brooklyn, I met up with a local jazz musician on a couple of rocks at a park. Our conversation circled through all of the usual topics: recent shows we had been to, our current favorite and least favorite venues, our different respective pockets of the NYC scene. They spoke passionately about their friends' music and their most cherished small-scale spaces.

But our talk soon turned to something else: their most recent side gig, making PFC jazz.

They weren't familiar with that term, but had been working for a company that is on Spotify's internal list of PFC providers. As with many musicians in their situation, there was a lot they admittedly did not know about the whole arrangement. They had just agreed to talk to me about what they called their "Spotify playlist gig," a commitment they also called "brain numbing" and "pretty much completely joyless." The musician had signed a one-year contract that they got through a friend, to make anonymous tracks for a production music company. And while they didn't quite understand the details of the relationship with Spotify, they did know that many of their tracks had landed on official playlists with millions of followers. "I just record stuff and submit it and I'm not really sure what happens from there," they told me.

This wasn't a professional scam artist, or someone with a master plan to steal prime playlist real estate from anyone. This was just someone who, like other working musicians, was cobbling together a living from a long list of revenue streams. "There are so many things in music that you treat as grunt work," they said. "This kind of felt like the same category as wedding gigs, or corporate gigs." In their early twenties, the jazz musician often played what they called "background gigs" at restaurants around the city, and this felt sort of similar. "It's made very explicit on Spotify that these are background playlists, so it didn't necessarily strike me as any different from that."

There is a lot that is not made explicit, though, like the fact that when the rights-holders (in this case, the production music company) service the tracks to Spotify, they accept a lower royalty rate in exchange for a greater promise of prime playlist placements.

The jazz musician asked me not to identify the name of the company they work for, because they didn't want to risk losing the gig. Throughout our conversation, though, they repeatedly emphasized their reservations about the entire system, calling it "shameful." Another PFC maker in a similar position told me about how "the creative process was more about replicating playlist styles and vibes than looking inward." A third musician, a professional audio engineer making ambient recordings, told me he ultimately stopped making these stock music tracks because "it felt unethical, like some kind of money laundering scheme."

As the jazz musician told me, making new PFC starts with studying old PFC: a feedback loop of playlist fodder imitated over and over again. A typical session starts with the production company sending along links to target playlists as reference points; in their experience, these are often Spotify's in-house chill-jazz playlists. Their task is to then write out charts for new songs that could stream well alongside the ones on the reference playlists, or in other words, songs that have already done well on Spotify. "Honestly, for most of this stuff, I just write out charts while lying on my back on the couch," they explained. "And then once we have [enough material], they organize a session, and we play them. And it's usually just like, one take, one take, one take, one take. You knock out like fifteen in an hour or two."

With this particular group, the session typically includes a pianist, bassist, and drummer. An engineer from the studio will be there, and usually someone from the PFC company will come along, too—acting as a producer, giving light feedback, at times inching the musicians in more playlist-friendly directions. The most common feedback: play simpler. "That's definitely the thing: nothing that could be even remotely challenging or offensive, really," the jazz musician told me that day in the park. "The goal for sure is to be as milquetoast as possible. And that's made pretty explicit. They try to leave enough leeway for musicians to sort of not feel like they're completely losing their minds, but the agenda is play simply and inoffensively. And keep it short. Because obviously, if we were really playing, we would explore and improvise. Time wouldn't be an issue."

According to a former employee, the managers of the PFC program would justify its existence, in part, by saying that these were artists like any other, they had simply chosen to engage with the business side of their work in a different way. But all of the PFC musicians I spoke to told a different story, likening it much more to the process of making stock music or an advertisement score than making art. One composer I spoke with compared it to the shady practice of "soundalikes" in the advertising business, where a production company will ask an artist to write and record a cheaper version of a popular song.

"It's kind of like taking a standardized test, where there's a range of right answers and a far larger range of wrong answers," the jazz musician continued. "It feels like someone is giving you a prompt or a question, and you're just answering it, whether it's actually your conviction or not. Nobody I know would ever go into the studio and record music this way. And yet, hundreds of songs are being made and going on these playlists all the time that are exactly like this."

As they spoke about the process of making these monotonous recordings, I couldn't help but think about how the whole formula seemed distinctly algorithmic: "This work definitely takes advantage of certain skills that you get through working as a musician for a while, like learning music really quickly, learning a lot of different kinds of music, playing gigs a lot," the jazz musician explained. "Whether consciously or subconsciously, you develop the skills to get to the heart of this music and find patterns."

"I don't think about the music that I actually really love, and want to do right by, in this way," they continued. "But for rote gigs, you sort of become good at that. Like for wedding gigs, you have to learn hundreds of songs, and you have to find a way to do that quickly. Those skills transfer really well to doing this kind of work."

Commercial background music is its own industry. It's a somewhat open-ended term that could refer to the sounds passively heard in physical spaces, like retail stores, or the music heard in the background of commercials. It overlaps with the world of composing scores for TV and movies, but also increasingly means the sounds we hear in passing in virtual space, like the bland beats and generic synth beds that often soundtrack influencers monologuing on YouTube or Instagram. Much of the background music market has long been the domain of what gets called "production music"—music often made in bulk for libraries accessed by music supervisors for ads, in-store soundtracks, and film scores. It varies in quality; while scoring for film or TV is an art in and of itself, some production music is essentially the audio equivalent of stock photography. In any case, when musicians and songwriters pursue careers in production music, those musicians are undertaking a specialized entertainment industry task, often responding to client-provided prompts rather than following their own artistic or idealistic impulses. Music made-for-sync generally aspires to serve a scene, composed with the assumption that some other dialogue will play out, or there will be some other image or words on screen. It is meant to not be overly distracting.

The production music industry is booming right now, thanks to a digital environment where 70 percent of internet traffic comes from video and audio streaming—and a whole generation of YouTube and TikTok influencers aiming to soundtrack their videos without navigating the complicated world of sync (short for music synchronization licensing, the process of acquiring rights to play music in the background of audiovisual content) and without the fear of their videos being removed for copyright violations. In response, a whole crop of services has popped up to capitalize on it all, purporting to "disrupt" the process, buying out huge swaths of rights from aspiring producers looking for whatever work they can find, with what music advocates call horrible deals—offering flat-fee buyouts and taking over most of the royalty rights.

This dynamic might be best exemplified by Epidemic Sound, the Stockholm-based stock music giant that launched in 2009 and has long found itself at the center of the "fake artists" debate in the music press. Epidemic says it aims to "simplify" sync licensing. The company offers a library of pre-cleared, royalty-free production music for a monthly or yearly subscription fee. They also license in-store music for retail outlets, in the tradition of Muzak. And thousands upon thousands of those stock music tracks are released on Spotify with prime placements across its mood playlist ecosystem. While it's true that the business of sync is complicated, musicians from the Ivors Academy, a British advocacy organization for songwriters and composers, say that those "frictions" companies like Epidemic seek to smooth out are actually hard-won industry protections. "Simplicity is overrated when it comes to your rights," Kevin Sargent, a UK-based composer of television and film scores, told me. "The same could be said about union legislation and workers' rights," added Mat Andasun, a production music composer. "They're a pain in the neck if you're an employer, but they're pretty important if you're an employee."

In claiming to "simplify" the mechanics of the background music industry, Epidemic has championed a flat-fee buyout system, where it pays a set amount to retain all rights to the song. One musician I spoke with, who made electronic compositions for Epidemic Sound, said his payments were routinely around $1,700. "All tracks I made for Epidemic are purchased by them as a complete buyout," he told me. "They own the master." But he still received royalties from every streaming service that played those tracks. Epidemic's selling point is that the music is royalty-free, but it does collect royalties from streaming services, which it splits with artists fifty-fifty. The royalties collected are, of course, smaller than what non-PFC tracks would generate, due to Epidemic's discount deal with Spotify. But that deal also means the tracks are boosted on the platform: the company says its catalog gets 40 million streams per day. Still, the composer I spoke with said his streaming royalties from Epidemic tracks were always smaller than royalties from non-Epidemic tracks. And there are certain royalties artists are not entitled to at all: to refine its exploitative model, Epidemic also mandates that its composers resign from their performance rights organizations (PROs), the groups that collect performance royalties for songwriters when compositions are played on TV, radio, online, or even publicly, in a cafe or a retail shop.[1]

Ivors Academy previously led the "Composers Against Buyouts" campaign, which specifically targeted movie streaming apps, at a time when Netflix and Discovery were reportedly opting for royalty-free buyout deals, to avoid paying performance royalties. But Ivors members say that the overarching message applies here: when streaming companies try to buy out rights in order to exploit their own IP more freely, songwriters miss out on long-term earning potential. "Companies like Epidemic present themselves as disruptors, as new and exciting, when actually they're just taking advantage of people's ignorance and desperation," said Andasun. "In effect, all they're doing is building up an asset class to sell on. They have no interest in music. They have no interest in what's going to be left behind of the rights environment when they've sold their company and gone off to live in tax havens. I think that's reprehensible."[2]

As Sargent and Andasun explained it, writing production music often means creating a great deal of work and never being quite sure what tracks are going to take on a life of their own. Part of making it sustainable is holding on to the rights to generate royalties on the work. "Composers are entitled to their luck," said Sargent. "And I think trying to buy out composers' luck is a bit grubby."

"It's essentially a race to the bottom," Andasun adds. Unsurprisingly, one of the first venture capital firms to invest in Spotify, called Creandum, also invested early in Epidemic. In 2021, Epidemic raised $450 million from Blackstone Growth and EQT Growth, bringing the company to a $1.4 billion valuation. It is striking, even now, to think these venture capitalists saw so much potential profit in background music subscriptions. "This is at the end of the day, a data business," said a Blackstone executive at the time.[3]

Spotify and Epidemic launched just a year apart, two Swedish unicorns working together to flood the music market with dull production muzak. And as Epidemic grew, it started to carry itself like a record label. "Similar to any label, we were doing licenses with DSPs," one former Epidemic Sound employee told me. "Epidemic's content is primarily being made for sync, so it's primarily non-lyrical. This includes ambient content, lofi beats, classical compositions. Things a YouTube creator might put over a landscape video. And this content tends to also do well in playlists such as 'Deep Focus,' for example, on Spotify."

As the ex–Epidemic employee explained, this well suited Spotify's financial goals: "The bottom line is, Spotify wants content for as cheap as possible. Ideally they'd want to own content, like Netflix—hence their podcasting investment. If I'm Spotify and there's a lot of people making this type of functional music content, and there's AI now also making this type of content, you're going to want to find a way to supply that content to users at the lowest price possible."

The Spotify-Epidemic corporate synergies reflect—yet again—just another example of how streaming has flattened difference across musical purpose, another way in which it has contributed to a massive wave of consolidation: different music-adjacent industries and ecosystems that previously operated more in isolation, all suddenly now generating royalties from the same pots on the same platforms. As streaming has organized everyone into its lean-back-vibes economy, in the quest for a frictionless experience, musicians coming from historically separate corners of the music business have begun to operate within the same landscapes. That's true of the fact that major label pop stars and independent artists alike now rely on the same tools. But it's also true in this new reality where these other two distinct industries—the business of being an artist and the business of generating background sounds—are folding in on each other.

The business of buying and selling production music is very different from the business of being a recording artist who makes LPs and tours, and yet here we are. The Epidemic Sound musician, who ended up on many PFC-heavy playlists, told me he was actually required to release the tracks under his "real" artist name, on his pre-existing Spotify page. It came with its pros and cons. "My profile on Spotify picked up a lot once my Epidemic compositions found their way onto playlists," he said. "The sad thing is that rarely results in playlist listeners digging deeper into the artist of a track they hear or like."

The Epidemic artist explained how, like in the advertising industry, each month starts with Epidemic presenting a new playlist they've created. "You are then to compose however many tracks you and Epidemic agree on, drawing 'inspiration' from said playlist," he told me. "Ninety-five percent of the time, these playlists had very little to do with my own artistic vision and vibe, but rather focused on what Epidemic felt its subscribers were after. So essentially I was composing bespoke music. This annoyed the fuck outta me because I knew that these tracks would be released [on my personal Spotify page] but ultimately had very little to do with my own creative vision."

But at the end of the day, he said, it was a check: "I did it because I needed a job real bad and the money was better than any money I could make from even successful indie labels, many of which I worked with."

Again, this artist was unaware of the PFC program at Spotify, through which Epidemic was licensing his music. But he spoke to how confusing the whole arrangement was. "Honestly, I had no idea which tracks I made would end up doing well," he told me. "Every track I made for Epidemic was based on their curated playlist." The playlists weren't often specifically themed, but "mood [was] always a strong element to the curated playlist meant to inspire us."

During our correspondence, my Epidemic source brought up some wisdom that David Bowie once shared in an interview about staying true to yourself as an artist. "Never play to the gallery," Bowie offered, in a 1997 interview. "Never work for other people. Always remember that the reason you initially started working is that there was something inside yourself that you felt if you could manifest it in some way, you would understand more about yourself and how you co-exist with the rest of society. I think it's terribly dangerous for an artist to fulfill other people's expectations. I think they generally produce their worst work when they do that."[4]

Making PFC, the Epidemic artist told me, was just playing to the gallery: "That's what I was doing constantly while working for Epidemic."

The working conditions that PFC-generating musicians operate under vary, especially in regard to what types and percentages of royalties are returned to the musicians, but all three of the ones I spoke with were operating under some version of a buyout model. And while those terms are largely determined by the PFC-licensing production company or ghost label, as I spoke with the musicians it became clear that streaming services might have more wide-ranging incentives to shape user behavior around this content. It's not just that a lower royalty is required, but also that a whole other level of commitment is involved. When musicians sign up to make a stock track, they're essentially signing up for a day's work. It degrades the ability for musicians to have agency in how their songs circulate, and the ability to share in potential successes. The proliferation of stock music is part of a broader project of the streaming era, one that strives to disempower artists by propping up an ecosystem where the ball is always in the streaming service's court. Pesky protests for higher royalty rates aren't an issue when your playlists are filled with artists who don't exist. The relentless promotion of anonymous producers seems to be part of a larger effort that aims to disconnect listeners from the makers of the music they're consuming, laying the groundwork for users to accept the hyper-normalization of music made using generative AI software.

The reality of this power imbalance was ultimately why another musician, who made ambient tracks for a different, non-Epidemic PFC licensor, ended up ceasing his relationship with the company. "There was a fee paid up front," he explained to me. "It was like, *We'll give you a couple hundred bucks. You don't own the master. We'll give you a percentage of publishing.* And it was basically pitched to me that I could do as many of these tracks as I wanted."

In the end, he made only a small handful of tracks for the company, released under different aliases, and made a couple thousand dollars. It seemed pretty good at first, since each track only took a few hours. Eventually, though, as a couple of the tracks took off on Spotify, with one getting millions upon millions of streams, he started to see how unfair the deal was long-term; the tracks were generating far more revenue for Spotify and the ghost label than he would ever see, since he owned no part of the master and none of the publishing rights. "I'm selling my intellectual property for essentially peanuts," he said.

He quickly conceded to the creeping feeling that something was wrong with the whole situation. "I'm aware that the master recording is generating much more than I'm getting. Maybe that's just business, but . . . it's so related to being able to get that amount of plays. Whoever can actually get you generating that amount of plays, they hold the power," the musician reflected. "And if that entity that's generating the plays also owns your master, or owns the streaming services, or owns the means of distribution . . . that's some antitrust levels of collusion."

"It feels pretty weird," he continued. "My name is not on it. There's no crediting. There's not a label on it. It's really like, there's nothing, no composer information. There's a layer of smoke screen. They're not trying to have it be traceable."

The odd side effects of the burgeoning ghost-artist wallpaper-music streaming bonanza continued. One musician I spoke with wasn't in the PFC business, but had been making advertising-oriented library music for a boutique music licensing agency for years. This is someone who fronts an underground pop band, but has also found this to be a fulfilling day job. She explained that since roughly 2016, it had become "almost imperative" that all of the songs the agency made were released to DSPs under made-up one-off monikers. Not because the agency wanted them there, but because their advertising clients did. The company has ended up creating upward of one hundred new monikers, along with quick-generated album art, and serving them to Spotify. That's nothing compared to the likes of Epidemic, but also shows how much overlap exists between PFC and ad sync practices. And also how the trick-mirror effects of the digital environment currently have created a weird new authenticity imperative.

"When you're making music in-house for sync licensing, if you don't put it on DSPs, everyone knows it's quote 'fake,'" the musician told me. "Because oh, no artist would ever not put their music on DSPs. We have to have all of the music on DSPs because we have to make it seem as 'real' as possible—I can't ever say real without using quotes because I don't even know what 'real' is anymore."

This echoed some of the reasons why Spotify seemed to find it important for ghost artists to maintain fake biographies and profile photos. "I struggle every time I talk about 'real' and 'fake,'" she continued. "There's so much gray area. Stock music and production music is made for a purpose that goes beyond just the act of making art. The music exists to either license well or stream well or something. That's what stock music is in my mind."

The same source said that, on an artistic level, she struggles with the idea that stock music is always bad, period, and finds some of it to actually be "really interesting," like older Italian library music. "I don't think you could ever say stock music is bad, period. I just think it's worth noting that it's written for a purpose that's beyond only art," she said. "It has to do with making money in some way." Of course, the same could be said of the pop music machine, but PFC seemed specifically positioned to deceive listeners in new ways.

"I think casual listeners might have a much harder time telling the difference," the production musician continued. "I think people in the business, we don't really have a hard time. We can hear how the music itself is crafted and how it builds and grows, like, *Oh, this was so written to a brief.* I can even guess which reference song this was written for. And like, you can look at the album art. There's so many tells. The album art looks very Canva 1.0. It's never that good. If you scroll down and look at what, quote, label released it. Sometimes it's just such an obvious tell."

"I have found a song or two here or there where I'm like, *I think this is tight.* It will be on my playlist for a month or two, and I'll be like, *Wait, this album art looks fishy.* But then I have that moment. Does it matter?

I like this song. It may have some weird random name and some Canva art. But do I hate this producer? I mean not really, I think they're making kind of interesting music. So I'm confronted by these moments of like, should I delete this off my playlist by principle? Or should I just be like, I like it, whatever, it doesn't matter. I mostly delete them," the musician explained. "But not always. It does require a little bit of extra thought from me. What do I like about this? Does it matter that this was made for the sheer reason that I would stream it?"

It feels fitting that Spotify was originally imagined as an advertising platform, because in many cases, when you press "play" on a calm-down, wellness-vibes, or whatever mood playlist, what you're hearing is something that was cranked out by someone making music for an advertising library. It makes sense that as the digital world has grown to feel more like a shopping mall, it is also sometimes the very companies making music for shopping malls that are flooding its soundtrack.

7

Streambait Pop

In 2013, Spotify launched its artist-facing marketing operation called Spotify for Artists, first as a stand-alone website and then, by 2016, with an app. Through Spotify for Artists, which is internally referred to as S4A, artists are encouraged to view their work through a data-oriented lens. The app notifies artists of their latest streaming stats and playlist adds—left open, it will buzz whenever the numbers increase—while the editorial Spotify for Artists website produces how-to content and celebrity career-advice interviews. Among its earliest efforts was a video series called *The Game Plan*, billed as a blueprint for "everything [artists] need to get the most out of Spotify," and urging them to remember: "There's no rule book," and "It's about hustle!"[1]

One of these videos was titled "How to Read Your Data," a telling encapsulation of how the company subtly planted its data-driven doctrine into the minds of musicians. In the video, an upbeat employee explains how these detailed stat reports can help artists "understand which songs listeners are liking most" and see when a song "might be added to a playlist that's super unexpected for you." Maybe you made a polka song, but it has surprisingly been added to a hip-hop playlist—well, maybe it's time to think about leaning into hip-hop. The video then shifts to a soft-spoken white male artist duo named Slenderbodies. The pair previously considered themselves an indie-pop band, but through the magic of Spotify data they've learned they are often classified as an electronic group. After checking out their stats, they ponder whether instead of focusing on full-band setups, maybe they'll explore a more electronic route, maybe add some DJ sets to the mix.[2]

The video's tenor is light and goofy, but its message is serious: follow the data if you want to make more streaming-friendly music. The video narrator proclaims that "data can help you learn things that maybe you hadn't even thought about before!" But the undertone is: study the data, see what is generating mass enthusiasm, and let the stats influence your sound.

In doing so, Spotify is not just selling artists on data. It is selling them on optimization. The writer Rob Horning once argued in his newsletter that datafication, or the process of rendering our lives as data, is "first and foremost . . . a kind of surveillance designed to impose classifications and norms on the surveilled while devaluing whatever ways they understand themselves." It's a way to encourage artists to minimize their own conception of their work, and maximize its machine-legibility.[3]

This is partly what's unfolding when Spotify encourages musicians to understand themselves in terms of their data. The "How to Read Your Data" testimonials were not just demonstrating how to retrieve data from an app—data points that Spotify had decided were important enough to collect—they were subtly nudging musicians in directions more profitable for Spotify. They were sending a strong message about Spotify's vision of the ideal creator-consumer, an artist generating exploitable content while also participating as a customer of the artist-facing promotional products, one who didn't just seek to read data but to act on it according to what would generate streams. This was part of the grand promise of the so-called level playing field: now DIY artists, too, could data-test and roundtable their art the way a major label exec might.

As the Spotify model took hold, its platform values were manifesting not just in how music was classified, but in the music itself, too; in the ways artists were thinking about their own work, and in what rose to the top simply by serving the system well. Similar to how digital advertising incentives have filled our newsfeeds with clickbait, the streaming era encouraged its own data-driven sounds and styles tailored to the playlist listener: streambait.

Music journalists began taking note of how streaming was changing the sound of pop music around 2017. In terms of song structure, because streams were only monetized after thirty seconds, there was a particular emphasis placed on perfecting song intros. Sometimes, streaming-conscious songwriters would just dive directly into the chorus. "On a playlist, it's just so easy to click *next*," a pop songwriter once told me. "The chorus should always be the best bit, so if you're taking a minute to get there, you've got a good chance of losing people. . . . Even more so now with Spotify, those first few seconds, you've got to give them something good." Take Post Malone's "rockstar," featuring 21 Savage, for example, which became the breakthrough hit in 2017 that catapulted him to streambait royalty; it not only began right with the chorus, but the label also released a version on YouTube where the chorus just looped for three-and-a-half minutes. It was considered a controversial chart-manipulating tactic at the time, but would have hardly registered as a blip just a few years later, when TikTok spawned a pop culture soundscape defined by sticky snippets looping ad nauseam.

The 2017-2018-era pop landscape rewarded music that did well across playlist categories. "Location" by the chill-pop singer Khalid is exemplary of that moment. It opens right with the chorus, and its success was in part due to its playlist adaptability—it was the kind of song that could work on playlists for hanging out, exercising, winding down, and so on, smooth enough for the background but emotional enough for the isolated headphones listener. In the spring of 2017, "Location" journeyed through lists like "Fresh & Chill" and "Soul Lounge" before it was boosted by the even bigger "Mellow Bars" and "Chill Hits"; Khalid's streaming-friendly catalog has since earned him nine different tracks with over 1 billion plays, putting him alongside the likes of The Weeknd, Bad Bunny, Drake, and Taylor Swift on Spotify's "BILLIONS CLUB" playlist.[4]

Another artist synonymous with this time was Billie Eilish, whose career took off after her brother sent her Soundcloud-trending 2015 "Ocean Eyes" single to a pair of well-connected managers. *Billboard* eventually wrote that a similar strategy of "chameleonic" playlist adaptability helped boost Eilish on streaming, with one of her managers explaining that this allowed her to "be everywhere at once." The same article noted that it wasn't until her collaboration with Khalid, "Lovely," that her "whole catalog exploded," with Spotify's head of global genre groups comparing her success to that of Post Malone's. "This is what true reactivity looks like in an attention economy," he said.[5]

In those years, every major streaming service was clamoring to claim credit for Eilish's rise. The music journalist David Turner once wrote in his newsletter *Penny Fractions* that Eilish's story was "one of an industry desperate to make a broken model appear well-functioning." In general, industry actors have made a point to champion artists who represent the ability to blow up via streaming; it makes the system look effective. Another example was Lauv, whose first single, "The Other," went viral on Spotify in 2015; the success of his made-for-streaming music has been so tied up with Spotify that the company dedicated an entire paragraph to him in the official documents that Spotify filed when it went public on the New York Stock Exchange: "We were able to help Lauv build his brand identity and personal profile," Spotify explained. The form notes that when "The Other" blew up, "approximately 70% of those streams came from our programmed playlists."[6]

By the time of Spotify's IPO in 2018, it seemed that the peak playlist era had produced an aesthetic of its own. That year, one pop songwriter and producer told me that Eilish had become a type of poster child for what was being called a "Spotify sound," a deluge of platform-optimized pop that was muted, mid-tempo, and melancholy. He told me it had become normal for him to go into a session and hear someone say they wanted to write a "Spotify song" to pitch around to artists: "I've definitely been in circumstances where people are saying, 'Let's make one of those sad girl Spotify songs.' You give yourself a target," he said. It was a formula. "It has this soft, emo-y, cutesy thing to it. These days it's often really minimal and based around just a few simple elements in verses. Often a snap in the verses. And then the choruses sometimes employ vocal samples. It's usually kind of emo in lyrical nature."

The chill-hits Spotify sound—or what the pop music critics at the *New York Times* started calling "spotifycore"—was a product of playlist logic requiring that one song flow seamlessly into the next, a formula that guarantees a greater number of passive streams. At times, these whispery, smaller sounds even recalled aspects of ASMR, with its performed intimacy and soothing voices. When everyone wants your attention, it makes sense to find reprieve in sounds that require very little of it, or that might massage your brain a bit. Both traits—seamlessness and chillness—are reflected in music that has become reshaped for the platform, whether this resulted from Spotify's own preferences or the emerging tastes of artists who developed in their wake. "I don't think most people are making it *for* Spotify," the pop songwriter told me. "I think at this point it's just young kids who are products of that. That's just music they like. They're not thinking *I'm going to make spotifycore*—things move so fast. These are just kids that are influenced by Billie Eilish or something."

In 2017, the owner of one long-running indie rock label told me that Spotify was turning everything into "emotional wallpaper." Within his roster, the chilled-out, straightforward tracks were prospering while comparably aggressive music went unheard. "It leaves artists behind," he said at the time. "If Spotify is just feeding easy music to everybody, where does the art form go?" This concern resonated with a lot of musicians and listeners, who were then grasping for a way to articulate something ephemeral: how it felt like music was just becoming totally flattened out in the era of platform capitalism.

Five years later, I spoke with two other independent label managers, who together operate an influential imprint for homespun indie rock and folk. But only certain parts of their catalog were viable on streaming. "Anything that could be put on a coffee shop playlist streams better, basically," one said. The opaqueness of playlist pitching and the "brick wall" Spotify established around its curators made label operations difficult. "Our streaming revenue heavily depends on editorial playlist placements," one of the label managers told me in a 2022 interview. "We used to be in someone's good graces there, but we pretty much just went through a two-year dry spell of barely getting any placements at all, and our revenue now has been cut in half."

According to their distributor, who interacted with Spotify on the label's behalf, there was a moment after 2020 where the "indie" editor was replaced by someone who "didn't like guitar music," and had instead filled the so-called indie playlists with "chill inoffensive Spotify music," as the label co-manager put it. "This watered down pop sound has taken over, and it all sounds more and more similar. . . . I think there are certain labels and certain people who would just say, *Okay, well, I guess we have to pivot to this pop sound*." Part of this sound was the whispery vocal inflection of spotify-core, which carried over into the indie-songwriter spheres too, delivering something I eventually just started calling "playlist voice." The University of Texas professor and author Eric Drott has written that Spotify's use of music to track users' moods and activities incentivizes promoting "tracks that remain in a single emotional register throughout"—which is not only a signature trait of "playlist voice" but clarifies how these sounds create value for streamers.[7]

The two label managers described watching indie-folk artists in their scene leaning into a "vibe-y" softness in order to appeal to mood playlists: "They're getting on playlists like 'Driving at Night,' 'Chilling with Your Friends,' 'Coffee and Tea,' 'Surf Rock Sunshine,' all of these mood playlists," one of them said. "And those definitely have the highest follower counts. It's just the most inoffensive music you've ever heard. It's really easily digestible. It's music that doesn't ask much of the listener."

Over the years, they've both watched artists bend to the whims of platform-friendly aesthetics, falling susceptible to the allure of optimization: "I don't know a single artist who is like, *Yeah, I listen to the 'Hanging Out and Relaxing' playlist*," one of the label managers said. "But they are all looking at the Spotify for Artists dashboard, thinking, *Oh, wow, this is the song that got playlisted, this is the song that performed pretty well, maybe I should lean into that.* I find it to be absolutely horrifying, but I think it could happen to any artist. It's almost just human to think, *Well, this thing is kind of successful, maybe I'll try it.* I have a deep fear of all music starting to sound the same."

As the years went on, Spotify wasn't content to just have artists studying the data and optimizing their music for streaming, or sitting around at their own studio sessions figuring out how to get onto Spotify playlists. In 2019, the company started to host its own songwriting camps, where hit writers would lock down under the same roof together to work on streamable material. Camps are common in the world of mass-commodity pop production, but they are usually coordinated by labels or publishing companies. Sometimes they act as assembly lines for a specific pop star.

Spotify camps, instead, were specifically convened around what streaming services wanted to push as the real pop commodity: flagship playlists. In 2019, it hosted a camp around its R&B-adjacent playlist "Butter" at Alicia Keys's Jungle City Studios in New York. In early 2020, it hosted a session around a playlist for new Irish music called "A Breath of Fresh Eire," in Dublin. In late 2022, there was a camp themed around its UK

R&B playlist "Riff and Runs," described as "beautifully chilled vocals from around the world." According to one songwriter who has participated in these camps, Spotify reaches out to artists who have already performed well on the playlists—another example of the self-replicating data logic that decides winners and losers in this environment.[8]

Ollie Green, a London-based pop songwriter who has worked with the likes of Rita Ora and David Guetta, joined a Spotify camp in 2019 in London geared around a playlist called "The Most Beautiful Songs in the World." According to Green, the writers weren't taking explicit direction from Spotify reps, but the expectation to write playlist-friendly material was implied. "It was certainly not like they said, *you must write this kind of thing*," he told me. "But everyone knew why they were there. . . . Very little had to be said. As a writer you have a bit of intuition. It's partly down to me to know what I should be doing, and why I'm there, and what I'm there to do. I could have just written a bunch of rock songs and then never gotten invited back. It was more like, *okay, we're on the beautiful songs camp, so let's write a beautiful song.*"

"It was all very much geared towards a certain sound," he continued. "Stripped acoustic piano ballads, nice strings, beautiful voices, stuff that would fit the playlist." In other words, music much like what the label owners described: soft-around-the-edges, playlistable fare.

Green was aware of "The Most Beautiful Songs in the World" playlist already, because he had heavily streamed songs included on it in the past. At the camp, he was assigned a room with an artist named Aaron Smith—to whom their songs would be credited—as well as an additional cowriter and a producer. Together, they made a song called "Brother," a melancholy piano ballad with subtle strings and handclaps. When "Brother" was released on April 10, 2020, it immediately appeared in the official Spotify playlists "Fresh & Chill" and "New Music Friday." Over the next few days it was added to "Sad Songs," "Easy," and "No Stress." It was, of course, also added to "The Most Beautiful Songs in the World," where it remained for 340 days.[9]

Throughout our interview, Green repeatedly emphasized what a great time he had at his Spotify camp, and that he didn't have "a bad thing" to say about the company. This made sense: the system, it seemed, was working for him. In 2022, though, David Israelite, the president of the National Music Publishers' Association, called Spotify's efforts to butter up songwriters "cheap gimmicks" to distract from poor payments: "They are in court trying to slash what they pay all songwriters by one-third," he wrote on social media. The relationship between songwriters and streaming services had long been rocky, for many reasons, including that in 2019, when the Copyright Royalty Board ruled it would raise mechanical royalties, Spotify, Amazon, Google, and Pandora responded with a lawsuit, working together to appeal the ruling. These tech companies did not want to raise songwriter fees. "When you compare that to things like songwriter camps," Israelite wrote, "it becomes so hollow."[10]

In 2020, TikTok's pandemic-era success seismically altered the music industry's order of operations. This was the season when the "top of the music discovery funnel" shifted from editorial playlists over to the short-form video app's addictive ultra-personalized feeds, as one former Spotify employee described it in our interview. Musicians now were subject to dueling platform pressures, as the "weird order of having a successful song" was in flux, one songwriter told me. "Up until recently, if Spotify showed love on your song, and if they put it on all the playlists, radio would look at that and go, *Oh, Spotify is getting behind it, we can playlist it on our station*," he explained. "Now, to get Spotify love, you have to get TikTok [hits] on your snippet," he continued, meaning the small clips of songs that users post to test the waters.

With the new pressures of TikTok, artists didn't only need to make songs that would avoid skips and "do numbers on" lean-back playlists. They also had to answer to the harsh demands of short-form video and TikTok's fast-moving feeds. The line between the musician and the meme-maker blurred. Everyone had to commodify their personalities now by becoming a comedian, or making some other sort of clickbait emotional appeal. Artists needed to be dancers and models and lifestyle influencers; they needed to open up about their innermost struggles. An extreme sense of literalism in lyrics triumphed, with songwriters angling to position themselves as easily legible TikTok personalities, as relatable underdogs hustling for streams. It was all so tightly controlled, and somehow often also could feel so random and meaningless. One moment sea shanties were a thing, the next moment there was an unexpected revival of the nineties slowcore band Duster.

The rise of short-form video as a vessel for music discovery brought the logic of streambait to a new extreme. It was no longer about grabbing the listener in the first thirty seconds, but the first three-to-five seconds. The chorus or some ultra-hooky bit needed to hit the app-swiper immediately. Shortly after first joining the app, a video barged its way onto my "For You Page," wherein a self-appointed TikTok-for-musicians expert explained that in order to go viral on the platform, a song needed not only an immediate hook, but "re-engagement triggers" every few seconds.

Songwriting started to revolve around snippets. I will never forget the first time a young songwriter explained to me the songwriting process that was emerging in the TikTok era: artists were releasing short bits of works-in-progress, essentially A/B testing their own hooks in order to see what was *reacting* and figure out what songs to finish writing. In 2022, *Billboard* reported on how labels and artists were abandoning snippets that failed to generate mass enthusiasm, leaving professional songwriters with "dead copyrights" they could no longer place.[11]

In contrast to the tranquilizing effect that the early playlist boom had on songs, TikTok sped things up. In 2022, music fans on short-form video platforms had become obsessed with making "slow" and "sped up" versions of popular songs. The sped up songs were particularly huge, taking cues from what the online "nightcore" scene had been up to for years. But now that these edits were taking off on TikTok, the majors saw dollar signs. UMG set up its own Spotify pages, "Speed Radio" and "slowed radio," the former amassing millions of followers. Some artists simply embraced the trend, like SZA, who released an EP of slowed and sped up versions alongside her 2024 "Saturn" single. Others were less enthusiastic, so some labels started setting up secondary Spotify pages for their artists, mimicking a style of fan-made page to publish alt mixes. Sped up remixes were kind of like retention editing for audio, to borrow a phrase that became popular on YouTube for a fast-moving style of editing engineered to retain user attention. Or perhaps it was like the audio equivalent of uploading a video to CapCut, a ByteDance-owned video editing platform that quickly makes videos more optimized for TikTok. This next phase of the musical attention economy begged some existential questions, such as, what is attention even for? What even is music? One major label executive, in a *Billboard* article about the state of "modified audio," as these remixes were called, said "it's not about recording anymore. It's about what you're offering the user base to say, 'Hey, you're an intelligent consumer. Here are the stems for our songs. Do what you want to it." In the same article, another exec asked: "Is anything in its final form now? Or are we just putting out clay for fans to mold?"[12]

But even before the rise of Speed Radio and the sound-snippet whiplash stoking these reckonings with musical purpose, some artists were feeling burnt out. Oddly, by 2022, TikTok burnout—artists posting about how they were so sick of the game—became its own viral trend, with major label artists positioning themselves as disrupters calling out their label's ceaseless hunger for artist content. Sky Ferreira summarized the weirdness of this pose in a tweet: "Pretending your label has 'asked you to make TikToks' to go viral for outrage clicks is pretty meta." Ferreira was onto something. The mainstream music industry is built on artifice, but TikTok reached new extremes, as major labels searched for ways to game the system.

Take for example the story of a song by a seventeen-year-old Atlantic Records signee named GAYLE. One week before dropping her debut single, she posted a video opening up to fans, soliciting suggestions for song topics. "Can you write a breakup song using the alphabet," one supposed fan commented. GAYLE accepted, sharing a fifty-second acoustic take on a song called "ABCDEFU" with the caption "hope you don't hate it :)." By the end of the year, it was framed as a viral hit, but diligent TikTokers were suspicious; one eventually made a video revealing that the "fan" commenter was actually GAYLE's label's marketing director. It wasn't such an organic viral rise, after all; in fact, the first week it hit streaming, the song was supported by adds on "Pop Rock," "Fierce Femmes," "New Music Friday," plus dozens of lists made by Topsify, the playlist company owned by GAYLE's label. A whole cottage industry emerged around manufacturing the illusion of organic virality. And record industry payola helped prop up the entire culture of TikTok influencing. Labels were engaged in the elaborate campaigns for "seeding" songs into the algorithm through strategic influencer placements, or just through having their own interns create numerous accounts for the sole purpose of promoting certain sound clips.[13]

In the end, TikTok was a platform for promoting music, not monetizing it—the platform pays artists virtually nothing, even worse than streaming. As music became even more lean-back, the devaluation continued. TikTok strategy still involved figuring out ways to send users to Spotify or Apple

Music; oftentimes, whole campaigns would be built around "teasing" a bit of an upcoming single in order to support a "pre-save" campaign, where fans could schedule to have a song automatically added to their collection on release day.

In time, what it meant to "do well on Spotify" and "do well on TikTok" started to fold in on each other. Whether on Spotify or TikTok, discovery inside of a corporate digital enclosure was never actually about discovery; it was about risk management, and reducing the risk of losing a consumer's attention. Ultimately, both environments were driven by different mutations of similar questions: *How long did you dwell on this? How long did this hold your attention before you flicked onward?* The signals of satisfaction or dissatisfaction were lean-back on another level, as behavioral metrics became ever more passive.

The rise of TikTok, in many ways, not only changed the sound of music, and the ways in which it was popularized, but also changed Spotify; it was during this period of TikTok dominance when Spotify reportedly began to deprioritize editorial curation for more personalization; and not just more personalization, but more personalization based on behavioral data. By 2023, Spotify had launched its personalized TikTok-like discovery feed for mobile, as TikTok started launching its own streaming service, TikTok Music, in a few markets. At a certain point, it seemed like the two platforms were on a collision course of sorts, headed to a future where they would be serving the same functions; TikTok has since shut down its streaming service.

The more things change, the more they stay the same, though. "The numbers, I do keep quite an eye on them," one of the pop songwriters told me. "It is quite addictive. But if it wasn't Spotify and streaming numbers, I'd be looking at the radio charts. If it wasn't the radio charts, I'd be looking at iTunes sales data. If it wasn't the sales data, I'd be looking at other metrics. You want to get some kind of feedback of where it's connecting with people." He has a point: platform pressures, in the end, are just business-minded approaches to songwriting, amplified by data optimization.

Music distribution technologies have long influenced the sound of music itself. The entire history of recorded music can be traced through this frame: from the ways in which the limitations of the earliest phonographs shortened the length of songs, to how vinyl inspired classical musicians to embrace vibrato more widely to create more pronounced dynamics, to how the shifting norms of commercial radio in the eighties impacted cadence and volume. In *Capturing Sound: How Technology Has Changed Music*, the musicologist Mark Katz calls these "phonograph effects." Streambait pop was just one modern-day manifestation of how technology has always influenced the sound of recorded pop music. Jeremy Wade Morris has built on Katz's notion of "phonograph effects" by calling these "platform effects"—how the pressures of various digital music platforms shape the sound of music released on said platforms.[14]

These academic terms are especially helpful in breaking down the overly simplistic narrative of what gets called technological determinism—that these powerful technological systems are controlling us like puppet masters, deciding our actions. At the same time, it would be untrue to claim that our lives are *not* shaped by technology and media. In the middle is an idea called "affordances," a concept introduced by the psychologist J. J. Gibson to theorize that the way objects are designed and built informs the ways that people use them, and their functions in users' lives. Veronika Muchitsch, a music and technology scholar and researcher at Stockholm's Södertörn University, explained to me that "affordances can be helpful for thinking about the ways that media technologies inform user behavior, or invite certain behaviors and practices more than others."[15]

Streaming services aren't pulling strings tied to artists' backs *forcing* them to write songs in certain ways. But they afford users space for certain ways of being. When platforms repeatedly prioritize one type of thing over another, the scope of what's possible in a given media environment starts to narrow.

I often think back to something an independent musician told me years ago: he felt that in the streaming era, the only thing that had been democratized was the ability for everyone to think of themselves like a Warner A&R—short for artists and repertoire, the label employees responsible for finding and developing new talent. This idea haunted me for years but truly came to a head when I started researching how Warner A&Rs actually operate. In 2021, a couple of executives from the in-house Warner Music Group data science team explained, in a video, that the company was then processing information about its roughly 4.5 billion streams per day, all of which powered insights to "help inform where we're going to invest in new artist and content types . . . whether it's forecasting, building a propensity model, or some kind of behavioral segmentation or scoring." In other words, the major label was collecting an obscene amount of data every day, and then using it to presumably power algorithms that would tell it what artists to sign in the future. It had even acquired a company called Sodatone, which employed an AI tool using streaming and social media data to "identify unsigned talent by tracking early predictors of success, such as the loyalty and engagement of a growing fan-base, and the potential virality of a track or demo." In the major label system, following the data wasn't a question; it was just part of the mandate of growth.[16]

Commercial music is always in search of what's going to scale. It's why streaming services are always going to be wired for *music that streams well*. This is part of what independent artists are up against today: the supposedly neutral streaming platform that encourages artists to create value on its own terms, one that cares more about playlist streams than creating a sustainable situation for artists. The problem is not the chill-pop streambait musicians, or even the TikTok plants, but these self-replicating systems that continuously reward the same styles—whatever users will stream endlessly, whether they're paying attention or not.

In 2023, I was having lunch at a restaurant in Williamsburg, Brooklyn. The in-house music was familiar: that forgettable whispery washed-over indie pop that seemed to never go anywhere. It sounded made for streaming, but it also made me wonder if maybe streaming has just made everything sound more like the overheard soundtrack to an overpriced lunch spot on Bedford Avenue. "Sorry, can you Shazam this?" I asked my friend, referring to an app that can identify songs playing in public spaces. "What? Oh, sure," he said. "I didn't even notice it playing."

8

Listen to Yourself

When Spotify made its big investment into producing in-house playlists—what some researchers have called its 2013 "curatorial turn"—it was fundamentally becoming a different type of service. Spotify's early years were about making music available, quickly and seamlessly. But as music became available everywhere, Spotify's supposed opportunity became its ability to change the way people listened. It was no longer just about providing all of the music in the world, but about purporting to know what you wanted to listen to, when you wanted to listen to it; to provide the perfect playlist at the perfect moment.[1]

The same year that Spotify brought on Tunigo's curators to build in-house editorial playlists, it also introduced its first "Discover" page, where it housed algorithmic recommendations. The service already offered Pandora-like automated radio stations, but the "Discover" page was, at first, more like a Tumblr feed, a patchwork of recommended artists, albums, playlists, upcoming concerts, and even album reviews and news articles. In 2014, it was relaunched with a more streamlined Netflix-type feel, with shelves grouped by themes, and limited to albums and new releases. The underpinning was a long-used algorithmic tactic called collaborative filtering, which, in basic terms, finds users with similar taste to your own, and then recommends stuff from their library that you've never heard.

Algorithmic music discovery has its roots in the broader history of recommender systems, and predates streaming. In his book *Computing*

Taste: Algorithms and the Makers of Music Recommendation, anthropologist Nick Seaver traces the history of music recommender systems back to July 1994, when a group of computer scientists at MIT's Media Lab launched Ringo, an email-based system that used "social information filtering" to "automate word of mouth." That meant users would email information about their music taste and receive recommendations back. Collaborative filtering was created around the same time. In music scholarship, there's a whole field of study called "music information retrieval" (MIR) that goes back several decades and, since 2000, even has its own long-running annual conference hosted by the International Society for Music Information Retrieval, the "world's leading research forum on processing, analyzing, searching, organizing, and accessing music related data."[2]

This was not Spotify's world, but as the years unfolded, the company started to realize that, with its enormous user base, it could be doing more with all of the data it was capturing. In 2014, the company acquired the Echo Nest, a Massachusetts-based music data firm, for 49.7 million euro. The company emerged from the theses of two MIT PhD candidates: one whose studies involved content analysis, using automated "machine listening" to tag songs with data related to the way they sounded, and another whose dissertation centered on context analysis, gathering data about the way music is understood culturally, by processing the way people talked about it online. The heart of the company was a database of characteristics defining 30 million songs. At the time of the acquisition, the "big data for music" company had been in operation for nine years, providing data to clients across the corporate media—Clear Channel's iHeartRadio, MTV, Vevo, Nokia, Sirius XM, Univision Radio, Intel, all of the majors—who used it to make apps, playlists, and feeds. It was powering nearly all of Spotify's competitors; a source told me the Echo Nest people were particularly excited about what they'd been doing with the streaming service Rdio.[3]

As a result of its hundreds and hundreds of clients, the Echo Nest claimed to have not just a lot of music data, but a lot of data about how app developers were using data. On stage at the 2012 Rethink Music conference in Boston, the Echo Nest's CEO Jim Lucchese explained how they had observed a shift wherein companies were not exactly trying to understand music, but instead were trying to understand users: "How do I understand these fans individually?"[4]

Before Tunigo and Echo Nest, user-generated playlists defined Spotify's curation ecosystem. With no official, employed curators yet hired, the platform's users created their own playlists—over a billion of them by 2013. As users made those playlists, something else was happening: Spotify was collecting a lot of data. Not just your every click on the platform, which it was, of course, tracking, but also data from the playlists users were making: songs for studying, soundtracks to new crushes, tunes for getting ready to go out to. Every playlist that a user made on Spotify—every track, every playlist title, every description—was adding to its pools of training data.

"Training data" is the basis of machine learning, algorithms, and AI. It's a set of data that a machine learning model will use to find patterns and predict outcomes. Machine learning algorithms—which power many of Spotify's recommendations—put forth this basic premise: if you collect enough data, patterns in that data will help generate statistically likely outputs. If you want to train a machine to produce Drake lyrics, train it on Drake lyrics. But if you want a machine that will tell you what to make for dinner tonight, provide a long list of what you ate for dinner every night last year. And if you want a machine to recommend the perfect driving songs, you might want to feed it thousands of driving playlists that users have made on Spotify.

"Spotify had more listening data than anyone," one former machine learning engineer told me. "They made an early decision to collect a lot more information about streaming and store all of it, and keep it for as long as possible. They just had more and better data. The other thing was that they thought about the recommendation problem in a different way than Pandora [and other services] did. Pandora was saying, 'What is the best representation of a genre or related artists?' That was not really what Spotify was trying to do. Their thing was to recommend specific to your taste. And they just cracked the code on how to present it to someone."

Still, Echo Nest brought a lot of music metadata, which they called either "cultural" or "acoustic." The cultural metadata referred to descriptive textual information, like the wealth of aforementioned playlist titles, but also data that was scraped from a process of crawling the web for blogs and press, gathering information about musical connections. It's a process that the company might not be able to get away with today, in a culture where AI firms training models on the work of journalists is more contested.

On the acoustic front, for every track uploaded, an automated audio analysis would log its key, tempo, time signature, acousticness, danceability, instrumentalness, loudness, mode, valence, and energy. Those last two— valence and energy—are the closest that Spotify machine listening gets to the concept of "mood," both measured on a scale from 0.0 to 1.0. The web page for the company's public-facing application program interface (API) describes valence as "the musical positiveness conveyed by a track," noting that "tracks with high valence sound more positive (e.g. happy, cheerful, euphoric), while tracks with low valence sound more negative (e.g. sad, depressed, angry)." Energy, meanwhile, is thought to represent "a perceptual measure of intensity and activity," including: "dynamic range, perceived loudness, timbre, onset rate, and general entropy," the API page reads. "Typically, energetic tracks feel fast, loud, and noisy. For example, death metal has high energy, while a Bach prelude scores low on the scale."[5]

Valence and energy (which is sometimes called "arousal") together are commonly used by those attempting to extract mood data in a combination known as a valence-arousal matrix, or what's sometimes referred to as "Russell's Circumplex Model of Affect." As Seaver, the author of *Computing Taste*, explained it to me in an interview, the idea that a machine listening model can determine valence is "an absolutely goofy idea" but also "totally ubiquitous in a subfield called Music Emotion Recognition." According to Seaver, there is a general understanding in the field that emotional responses are unique, but there's also a belief that "there is something out there that is happy-sounding music, and that you might understand that a happy-sounding song might make you sad, but that does not negate the fact that it is happy-sounding."

The result is a system perhaps better understood as emotional cliché retrieval. Searching various tracks and rummaging through the API meta-data, I could only ever identify a small handful of different acoustically-generated mood tags: happy, sad, chill, amped. But there are other sources of mood-related information, too, like user-generated playlist titles. One source explained to me that when a lot of people put something on a play-list called "upbeat," Spotify's engineers consider that upbeat; that signal is taken as the source of truth.

A paper published by Spotify's in-house research department expands on how those song-mood associations are calculated: it starts with the platform's 4 billion playlists and then filters "down to those playlists that have words corresponding to the mood lexicon in their titles/descriptions." From there, the "co-occurrence between each mood and song" is computed, and finally, the association is calculated using an equation called "pointwise mutual information," which is part of natural language processing, a subfield of AI that tries to understand human language. The same in-house researchers wrote that their "palette of moods" included 287 terms like "chill," "sad," "happy," "love," and "exciting," spanning adjectives (like "somber"), nouns (like "motivation"), and verbs (like "reminisce").

"Different data goes into different components of the algorithms," a former machine learning engineer told me. "There is not a single funnel in which all data sources are being used. Recommendation is not some monolithic thing." He described song-, artist-, and album-specific data descriptions as "item-based" properties. Then there was also "user-based" behavioral data; information about not the thing being recommended, but the person being recommended to, coming from their app interactions and listening behavior. "The more mature system that you often think about when you're using Spotify is the combination of item-based and user-based," he explained. That combination informs user "taste profiles," the term Spotify uses for its datafied take on a user's listening habits, or as the company says, its "interpretation of your taste based on what you listen to and how you listen to it."[6]

For a while, it wasn't clear whether all of this investment in algorithmic discovery would stick, or whether purchasing the Echo Nest would pay off at all. One ex-Spotify engineer recounted some internal frictions that arose among the pre-acquisition machine learning staff, who had mostly been working on the early Radio feature, and the newcomers. In general, the perspectives on Echo Nest I heard in interviews were varied. One former Spotify employee told me they considered it to be the smartest acquisition in the recent history of the music business, while another told me that Spotify couldn't figure out how to integrate the most interesting aspects of Echo Nest's operation and that ultimately the acquisition might have been more of a talent hire or PR move than anything.

But in 2015, Spotify's growing personalization team had its first big hit with "Discover Weekly," a data-driven new music playlist that came out of an internal "hack day." According to a 2015 conference slideshow from DataEngConf in New York, Spotify's engineers had started to notice, through user data, that listeners were spending significantly more time on the "Browse" page, looking through internally-curated editorial playlists, than they were on "Discover," which housed the feed of data-driven recommendations. What if they combined "the personalized experience of Discover with the lean-back ease of Browse"? They tested out the concept with a year-end 2014 playlist called "Play It Forward," and then launched for real in 2015, reimagining aspects of the Discover engine as a single thirty-track playlist rather than rows of tiles, and emphasizing tracks the user had never heard. Surrounding the July 2015 release, product manager Matthew Ogle told *Music Ally* that the vision was to "make something that felt like your best friend making you a mixtape, labeled 'music you should check out,' every single week." It was a big success: by the end of the year, "Discover Weekly" playlists had generated over 1.7 billion streams.[7]

Several former employees commented on how drastically the release of "Discover Weekly" changed the direction of the company. "After 'Discover Weekly,' they turned their focus on, how do we make this a more general concept on Spotify?" one former engineer said. "How do we make everything into a 'Discover Weekly,' so everyone gets their own version of a mood playlist, or a theme playlist, or whatever?"

The year after the success of "Discover Weekly," the personalization products started rolling out at a more serious clip. In 2016 alone, Spotify added "Daily Mix," a series of auto-generated mixes tied to different data clusters on your taste profile; "Release Radar," a mix of new tracks from artists the user follows and related artists; and the year-end "Wrapped," rebranded from what was previously called "Year in Music." Those were followed by algotorial, which the company started working on in 2017, and the introduction of a revamped, ultra-personalized "Home" page in 2018. In 2023, they added "Smart Shuffle," a listening mode that added algorithmic suggestions when a user hit play, as well as "daylist," a personalized playlist that changed throughout the day, and "AI DJ," auto-recs spliced with intros made by a generative AI DJ voice.

A former employee said this proliferation of new features caused friction between the very concepts of the playlist versus the personalization algorithms. "There was this level of competitiveness," the employee recalled, between whether algorithmic curation would triumph or the company would continue to "focus on big editorial playlisting, and turn these playlists into brands and franchises," he added, referring to titles such as "RapCaviar" (the most influential playlist, by far), "Today's Top Hits" (its equivalent to turning on pop radio), or "mint" (its big EDM hub). "There was a lot of money and effort put into these big playlists. But on the whole, I think personalization did win." Another former employee concurred: "Oh, personalization *definitely* won," she said.

The 2017 introduction of "personalized editorial playlists," more often called "algotorial," was particularly impactful, changing the shape of what it looked like to be a playlist editor at Spotify. Rather than curating and sequencing playlists, the work of being an editor started to more heavily involve curating "candidate pools" of tracks associated with certain moods and themes, so that the sequencing algorithm could create the playlist most likely to hook a given user. As time passed, more and more playlists became algotorial.

There was a lot going on to make the experience of being a Spotify user more automated, putting more control in the hands of the platform. In 2018, Spotify made an effort to streamline things further. "One of the major initiatives around that time was shifting consumption," a former employee said. "That was the name of the initiative, 'Consumption Shifting.' And the goal was to move people out of other places of the app, and into the home page. So that essentially there was a single place where you would listen on the app, unless you knew exactly what you were looking for, which would go via search."

"The ultimate goal was to have the majority of consumption happening through a fully programmed surface," the former employee went on. "So it was less of a focus on the library, less of a focus on search, more of a focus on getting it right when someone opens the app, so they start listening from there."

Subtle shifts in the interface could have big implications. I had often wondered if streaming services considered the impact it had on people's listening experience to make "Autoplay" the default after reaching the end of an album, meaning algorithmic recommendations would automatically start up. Was that a big deal internally? I asked one of the ex-engineers. Truthfully, he wasn't so sure. But he was adamant to point out that oftentimes, shifts like that were just people doing their jobs: "I think it is mostly just corporate imperative telling people to move a metric. And they are finding the way to move that metric, and they're turning it on. That can be applied to a lot of instances where there's sometimes these bizarre decisions being made, that can seem sort of malicious. Moving everyone to the home page, the main feed. That feels strange and forced. Well, the reason is because it was forced. Someone made the decision that in order to capture the attention of more leaned-back listeners, we needed to move things over there. And these sort of sweeping changes take hold, and then they become the new normal. A lot of these corporate decisions lead to some of the more brain-turned-off listening."

As Spotify leaned more heavily into machine learning and personalization, its concept of *the perfect playlist* was becoming clearer: it was not just about nailing the most universally beloved song for a given mood or moment, not just about running generalized A/B testing to find the next big global hit, it was about purportedly running personalized A/B tests on you. It was about running millions and millions of A/B tests, different ones for each user, constantly running studies on your listening habits. It was about data-tuning what you were most likely to stream at a given moment. Personalization, driven by machine learning and algorithms, would aim to put the "perfect" in "perfect playlist"; each song data-optimized for max user engagement.

It was subtle, but also huge: the product was becoming blatantly less about connecting users to the world of music, and more about treating your own taste as a world of its own to be studied and sorted, packaged and sold. It wasn't necessarily selling you music recommendations, it was oftentimes selling your own music taste back to you in lots of different types of boxes. Of course, this was all done in the name of "discovery," but over time it became clear that "discovery" was code for keeping users streaming, and keeping users within their comfort zones (or as Spotify thought of it, customer retention zones). In fact, by 2020, the language of "discovery" on the app was sidelined for the broader project of supplying playlists "made for you." It was about behavior modification to serve a corporate bottom line; more time spent on the app meant a user was more likely to retain their account, and it also meant more data. How you responded to the occasional item seeded for "discovery" would then help the app expand its "taste profile" on you.

There were whole teams dedicated to studying the ways users responded to recommendations: Did they listen all the way through or did they skip? Did they add the song to a playlist of their own? Did they click onto the artist or album page and how long did they "dwell" there? But perhaps most consequentially for the shape of Spotify recommendations to come: Did the recommendation contribute to extending the user's total listening session time? How long did the listener stay streaming?

When Spotify went public on the New York Stock Exchange in 2018, it claimed that Spotify-owned playlists, both editorial and algorithmic, then accounted for over 31 percent of users' listening. The company has not released new information publicly in years about the popularity of its editorial playlists. But today, the editorial playlists are largely understood to be far less influential than they once were, as the entire programming strategy has become much more driven by personalization. "Whenever they are not releasing data that they used to release it's because the numbers are probably not looking good," a former employee said. At the end of 2023, Spotify's internal organization chart—called the Band Manager—listed under 200 employees working in the "Editorial" department globally, spread across all markets; there were around thirty editorial employees in the US.

By contrast, there were in 2023 over seven hundred Spotify employees working on its personalization teams. What was the point of it all? The answer would differ, of course, depending on who you asked, and depending on the algorithmic system. The company loved to talk about "delighting" the user with the perfect content recommendation, but there was more to it. "I think they eventually realized that the way to keep people on the platform, which boosts revenue, was to supply people with what they want," a former employee said. "That's basically the Web 2.0 model. Netflix is exactly the same, where they never want you to stop watching. Spotify is basically doing the same thing with how they're trying to drive your engagement."

Platform businesses embrace personalization, usually, to drive engagement, to grow their data pool, and thus their revenue. Across interviews with former Spotify engineers, depending on the recommendation product they worked on, success was determined differently, but several mentioned working on things like extending listening session length, growing engagement, and new user retention. This all echoed what Seaver wrote about in *Computing Taste* when he described something that recommendation system engineers conversationally referred to as "the hang around factor"— how a core value metric upon which recommendation systems tended to be based was general user retention. "The ultimate measure of functionality," Seaver wrote, was "what keeps listeners listening."

For some Spotify engineers, though, there was a breaking point. "One of the reasons I ended up leaving was because I became pretty disillusioned with this myopic focus on just the amount of minutes listened," one former machine learning engineer told me. "It doesn't feel like the way that I want to engage with music. . . . There's value to all approaches to recommendation, but this singular focus on just amount of time listened was something I wasn't happy about."

"What do you want when you listen to music?" he continued. "I don't think there's a single answer. Some of the records that I would consider really life-changing, really profound, are records that in terms of listening time, they wouldn't even show up in my top 100. Partially because they're really challenging records. They're records that opened me up to certain things. But they require a lot of investment. I'm not going to sit down and eat dinner to it. I need to be in a space where I can really devote myself. There is a lot of music that listeners find important but it's not what you want to listen to all day."

Ultimately, he determined that there was really only so much that could be gleaned from a bunch of information about someone's listening history—from reducing a person's music taste to a pool of data. "It's like taking a three-dimensional picture and flattening it to two dimensions," he told me. "It still has some relation to the actual object you're trying to study, but it leaves out a fair amount. To say your tastes are really represented by a list of the things that you've listened to—almost anyone would say that's not exclusively true. They're correlated, certainly. But it's decontextualized. Looking at a stream of all the tracks I've played, it tells you something." But there is, of course, much that the data does not say.

When algorithmic discovery was becoming increasingly influential in the post–"Discover Weekly" years, after 2015, cultural discourse was stuck on some existential questions: Could AI really understand music taste? Was "algorithmic culture" going to supplant music journalism? Were the algorithms making music discovery less human and more boring? These questions may have been imprecise, but could the critics be blamed? Algorithmic discovery was being used to bolster the corporate enclosure of music. It made sense to push back.

At its core, though, a more useful debate might have been one not about human-ness versus machine-ness; both humans and machines can gather data, process it, and make decisions that fail listeners and artists in search of profits. Some more pointed questions for automated decision-making processes, then and now, might be: What types of patterns are the systems looking for? How are those patterns already influenced by how the platform shapes behavior? In a sense, asking what the streaming algorithms of the 2020s are optimizing for isn't too different from age-old music and media questions like: To what extent is commercialism influencing editorial? But there were bigger stakes, too: What systems were being strengthened through all of this optimization?

When the core metrics of "user satisfaction" are directly tied to "things that make us more money," optimization will only ever lead in one direction. On a streaming service that seeks to turn profits, the "perfect playlist" (or whatever other "programmed surface" they're pushing) is always going to be the one that extends user sessions and generates more data.

For all of the data Spotify collects, users actually get to see very little of it. That usually happens only once per year, when the annual year-end advertising campaign "Wrapped" offers a glimpse. It's typically the company's biggest day of the year: it sends listeners and artists alike an annual review of their streaming stats, plus sharable, made-for-you branded content cards detailing their top tracks and artists—a "masterful coup of free advertising," as it was once called in the press.

Each year's campaign is a little bit different. In 2021, users were given their "Audio Aura" to visualize their top two music moods of the year. The service explained that it had enlisted an aura reader named Mystic Michaela to identify each user's "personal energy signature." Some users received a pale pastel square, captioned, "Your top music moods are wistful and kindness," while others were pinpointed as "yearning," "intense," "chill," or "rebellious." The project was a grand gesture in line with Spotify's efforts to make music a more insular and self-oriented experience. "When listeners go into their

Audio Auras, I really feel like they are going to be able to see more of themselves and have an inward conversation," said the Mystic, in a press release.[8]

The very concept of "Audio Auras" bizarrely inverts a different type of understanding of "aura." In his influential 1935 essay "The Work of Art in the Age of Mechanical Reproduction," the German philosopher Walter Benjamin wrote broadly about the hollowing of artistic integrity that comes with the capitalist limitations of mass-produced culture. He wrote about how mechanical mass production causes art to lose its "aura," or its uniqueness. But in the modern music industry, what's valued is not the "aura" or uniqueness of the music itself—it's the "aura" or uniqueness of *you*. In Spotify's vision of mass personalization culture, music exists to express the self; surveillance is required to do so, but it's rebranded as a cool and fun gamified promo program.[9]

Hyper-personalization has championed a new orientation of listening—make the music revolve around *me*—that now pervades different layers of the Spotify product in different ways. This way of approaching algorithmic recommendation has ushered in a deeply alienated way of learning about music. You know what the machine thinks you like, but you don't always know *why* the machine came to that conclusion; you also don't know what the machine thinks *other people* like, or the ways in which what you are recommended relates to what other people are recommended. It is music recommendations as a means of creating silos, not connections.

On streaming services, we hear simulacrums. We are made to believe we are listening to ourselves, but what's streaming is a warped reflection, where our desires are just some of the data that is refracted and served back in order to keep us streaming. We are listening to our slightly off data double. But at a certain point, a streaming listener may very well come to believe that what the machine suggests is indeed what they like, not because it's true, but because they can see or feel no other option.

"Your Music, Your World" was the name of a 2023 Spotify Nigeria commercial, where a woman pops on her headphones, opens up Spotify's home page, and clicks "Your Daily Mix," before heading out for a walk around town. What comes next is strange. She stops to marvel at a wall of TV screens, where she sees several clones of herself posing as newscasters. "Hello and welcome to my daily mix," one of them—her—says. She laughs and keeps walking, before buying a juice from, yes, another copy of herself. She pops into a hair salon, where everyone looks just like her.

Next, she's in a van, bopping along to the music, surrounded by a crowd of people, but they're all *her*. "Playlists made just for you," the narrator concludes. It illustrates in stark relief the deep individualism championed by this system.[10]

On the surface, it seems that in making the music revolve around *us*, the perfect-playlist paradigm has firstly advanced the meme known as "main character energy," perhaps best evidenced by an algotorial playlist like "my life is a movie" (tagline: "every main character needs a soundtrack"). Related patterns emerged in the playlist titles—especially the vibed-out ones approximating authenticity through lowercase titles, catering to Spotify's ongoing company-wide bet to win over Gen Z subscribers. (Using all lowercase to approximate an off-the-cuff, low-key aesthetic is also a trend that major label pop stars have adopted in recent years.) Across the board, in the 2020s, some algotorial playlists seemed to become less about recommending a type of music, and more about recommending a type of listener, or a type of aspirational listener that a Spotify user wished to become. Take for example some subtitles that particularly seemed to be typecasting listeners and offering consumable aesthetics more so than contextualizing music: there was one called "Farmers Market" ("pov: fresh produce is in your reusable tote, the flowers are in bloom, and you're sipping on an iced coffee") and one simply called "aesthetic" ("for those who prefer a curated vibe"). Even the sad girl playlists could potentially extend this pattern, like "sad girl sh*t" ("ummmm i thought i was healed???") or "sad girl starter pack" ("sapphic songs that defined your music taste as 'yearning'").[11]

On the purely algorithmic front, new types of automated "Niche Mixes" overtook more screen space, but the music contained within them never seemed all that different; "Sad Crying Mix," "Sad Late Night Mix," and "Lonely Sad Mix" were all different options, when I clicked around recently, but the offerings were mostly music from my listening history, with just a few new recommendations. The boxes within which Spotify segmented its recommendations were growing more niche and plentiful, but more than anything, it felt like an interface trick, a way to make the user feel a sense of abundance about the rewrapping of songs they already liked, taking algorithmically premeditated low-risk content and making the options seem new—it was, as ever, an illusion of choice.

Clicking through these differently labeled boxes that all seemed to contain the same music, I was reminded of something that the musician and artist Kim Gordon had told me in 2023. She pointed out the ultimate timelessness of this type of marketing tactic, one that French novelist Emile Zola described in the late 1800s. "He kind of describes the beginning of capitalism," she told me. "This guy makes a giant store, and has the idea that if he buys enough quantities of things, he can cut the cost. He calls it the machine. Gradually the other stores all go out of business because he is always changing things around to make them seem new. And he says he has the pleasure of the ladies. He's controlling their desire. Spotify creating these different names of music genres is like this . . . this is fresh, this is the new trend. But it's just a repackaging."

If I hold my breath and squint a little bit, I can start to get a sense of why someone who loves music might be drawn to the field of recommender systems. The personalization efforts were often described in terms of matching users and songs. The thinking was: there are so many listeners looking for new music, and artists looking for new listeners, how do we best match them up? It almost casts music discovery as a sort of dating app, harnessing the world's listening habits in order to help people and tracks find their perfect pairs. Through a lens of optimism, it could seem fascinating. But Spotify is not a purely musical and technological endeavor. It's a business. And if there has been any lesson of the past fifteen years, it is that multibillion-dollar multinational technology corporations cannot be viewed outside of that context. There are a lot of assumptions about the neutrality of technology baked into the idea that the patterns and data gleaned from such a system would provide an honest look at the world of music listening. In the streaming environment, personalization algorithms were employed to retain customers more than anything else. And when the mode of listening (or hearing) is so deeply shaped by economic incentives, what can you actually get from the data? In the end, it's not data about listening to music, it's data about listening to Spotify.

9

Self-Driving Music

"Next up, it's time for a vibe, and that vibe is bliss!" the artificial voice of Spotify's chipper-but-smooth AI DJ quipped one day as I tried out the latest made-for-you offering bestowed upon us by Big Streaming. Some nondescript indie rock tracks streamed, and then the bot came back, announcing that the next block of tunes would include a selection from the algorithmic "Release Radar" playlist. Trained on the voice of a Spotify employee, the system splices song blocks with these brief interludes, a repackaging of pre-existing recommendation models, brought together into a ceaseless, personalized, one-click stream. As ever, the heavy focus is on supplying tracks from the user's listening history. Where a radio DJ might announce the record label, year, or instrumentalists on a track, Spotify's AI DJ contextualizes around the user: Where does this fit into your "taste profile"? It's not about how a song or artist relates to history or culture, but about how the song or the artist relates to *you*. "Next up, some songs that took over your life in 2022," the generated voice announces. "Yeah, you're going to recognize yourself in these."

Introduced in the winter of 2023, the new DJ function immediately seemed like nothing more than an eager attempt at capitalizing on the then-ongoing generative AI hype cycle. But it was also something the company had been working on for many years, an elusive vision they'd long been after: one where the Spotify user could simply open the app, press "play," and instantaneously get the perfect soundtrack for any given moment or context, without having to search, click, or think. It was a fantasy of instant gratification, where the user needn't endure the labor of making choices about the soundtrack to their day. Back in 2013, in some of the earliest press about his approach to playlist strategy, Tunigo's Nick Holmstén would allude to this future. "The whole mission of our music application is to just have a play button," Holmstén said in a 2013 interview. Five years later, during Spotify's pre-IPO Investor Day, co-president Gustav Söderström described the company's long-term view of "self-driving music," where ongoing data collection would inform a music recommendation feed that updated in real time, without any user interaction.[1]

Not too long after introducing the AI DJ, Spotify debuted "daylist" in the fall of 2023, a playlist that changed throughout the day and claimed to know a user's preferred listening mode from moment to moment; this type of time-specific recommendation drew from "day parting," a term from the world of broadcast radio programming that caters to certain demographics according to certain times of day. Rather than targeting different market-tested audiences, though, the recommendation system was targeting different market-tested versions of you. And "daylist" was distinctly not radio—it was a personalized playlist, drawing from niche genres and moods to create extra-long titles like "indietronica 2020s late night" or "optimistic cinematic sunday afternoon," with titles in all-lower-case letters presented over hazy color gradients recalling the "Audio Auras" of "Wrapped" seasons of yore.

AI DJ and "daylist" were two sides of the same coin; two different approaches to "self-driving music," meant to speak the languages of different generations. As Spotify strategized its continued move away from human curation and toward more machine learning, it was debating the correct interface metaphor. "We had to decide, should we have the radio channel as the analogy, or should we have the personalized playlist as the analogy?" explained Söderström in a 2023 podcast interview, foreshadowing the new playlists that were then on the way. "They kind of do the same job. A personalized playlist within a genre like 'chill' is very similar to 'Chill Radio.' You will get the same songs, actually. . . . As you can imagine, older people, they like radio paradigms, and younger people, maybe not so much." The company decided to throw both ideas against the wall to see what would stick. But many of the underlying data sources and machine learning models that propped up these various recommendation systems were the same—listening patterns, of course, but also the data about how music sounded, was bucketed, and big picture ideas like Spotify's systems for understanding and describing music genres.[2]

On a different day, while listening to the AI DJ, the app described an upcoming block as a dive into the world of "metropopolis," which immediately stuck out to me as a Spotify-created genre name. For years, Spotify had been coming up with these bizarre microgenres, a popular subject of conversation on social media especially each year during "Wrapped." Spotify had increasingly come to use the year-end campaign for showing users not only their top artists, songs, and musical moods, but also their top genres, which would often include strangely specific names that most users had never heard of before. And in turn, each December, music fans would take to Twitter to express their confusion that Spotify had called them a top fan of "solipsynthm," "braindance," "traprun," "otacore," or "escape room." Apparently Spotify had been beating the "metropopolis" drum for a while; back in 2014, *Slate* ran a piece under the headline "Stop Trying to Make Metropopolis Happen." I guess no one at the company got the memo.

These genres were not fully "self-driving"—there were Spotify employees involved in their creation—but they were initially made, in part, for the purposes of a related goal, where a user could push one button and get the perfect feed. The microgenre taxonomy was largely the work of a former Spotify principal engineer named Glenn McDonald, who once described his job at Spotify as helping musical knowledge "self-organize," a phrase that evoked a sense of natural order or inevitability to organizing music according to Spotify data.

McDonald came to Spotify through the Echo Nest, and his work was based on a flagship project called "Every Noise at Once," a gigantic data map where he claimed to be visualizing Spotify's artist and listening data, using a scatter-plot to track and analyze thousands of "genre-shaped distinctions" and "teach computers to understand genre." McDonald and his microgenre map were the subject of their own mini-tour of the music press over the years. As he explained in one interview, the project came about back at Echo Nest, when one of their customers wanted a genre-based radio feature: "They were like, *I just want a few buttons, so I can hit 'rock radio' and I don't have to pick artists and tracks.*" So they set out to create a system for understanding genre. McDonald tasked interns with creating lists of "seed artists" for go-to genre names, and then combined with their related artists, they could start approaching the "neighborhood" of a genre. "Every genre gets on the map by some person [adding it]," he said in the same interview.[3]

Take, for example, the "escape room" genre. In 2016, McDonald explained how he started the process of creating it by looking at listening patterns: "I made up the name myself, because I couldn't figure out any existing one to apply," he said, adding that "the vibe" was "an underground-trap/PC-music/indietronic/activist-hip-hop kind of thing." In one of Spotify's blog posts, McDonald noted that sometimes he saw data clusters that didn't quite qualify for a label on the map: "Maybe they're not exactly genres yet. . . . But I can name them, and then I can watch them and see if they turn into a thing."

There were certainly some interesting aspects of the "Every Noise" project—its website included a bunch of helpful ways to find out about new releases from specific countries, for example—but attempting to narrativize genre this way was an overreach. Using streaming metrics to shape culture is a heavily biased practice. Because it relied on studying Spotify listening patterns around certain groups of artists to see if they "became a thing," the biases that motivated users to stream songs in the first place could shape which listening patterns were even considered worthy of labeling. These genre designations existed in service of Spotify's broader goal to keep users streaming.[4]

And while the made-up genre names were often made into jokes on social media—a meme trend that Spotify seemed to be encouraging through "daylist"—it also contributed to a broader breakdown of meaning in music, or as Kieran Press-Reynolds wrote in a 2022 piece for the independent music outlet *No Bells*, "taxonomic misinformation." At what point does a recommendation system stop recommending songs and start recommending a whole idea of culture? And what happens when the quest for engagement starts to shape the fates of real scenes? Or if the genre that Spotify believes it has made up based on data is actually one with a rich pre-existing history that the platform is now obfuscating or rewriting?[5]

Enter: hyperpop, the formerly niche internet micro-scene turned full-blown pop phenomenon, most commonly associated with the British label PC Music, as well as with the maximalist duo 100 gecs and their post-dubstep post-mash-up post-everything computer music. But in the

early 2010s, hyperpop was a sprawling scene with sonically and geograph-
ically varied sub-scenes, all connected by various forums on the web. In a
2021 YouTube series called Hyperpop Origins, music journalist and artist
manager Noah Simon interviewed dozens of artists from small-scale labels,
collectives, and radio shows around the world, including the Australian pop
artist Holliday Howe, who started tagging her music hyperpop as early as
2015. The four-part documentary chronicles how hyperpop people hung
out online in specific chat rooms, and at a digital venue called SPF420.
It was less of a genre and more of a creative impulse, a tendency within
electronic music, and at times a friend group on Twitter or SoundCloud.
Hyperpop was a shorthand for a post-SOPHIE, post–PC Music internet
aesthetic, a more queer and trans alternative to mainstream experimental
electronic music culture, often with pitch-shifted vocals, drawing influence from vaporwave, nightcore, chiptune, J-pop, y2k pop, hip-hop, and
all sorts of dance music. Especially crucial was the sonic variety of it all.[6]

Then, something curious happened. In August 2019, as a direct response
to the viral rise of 100 gecs across TikTok, Spotify rebranded its "Neon Party"
playlist, which featured PC Music artists, into a new playlist, "hyperpop."
The next year, the *New York Times* published an article claiming that hyperpop emerged from the very process described earlier surrounding "escape
room"—that the name was chosen by Spotify staffers studying data clusters.
The piece ran under the headline "How Hyperpop, a Small Spotify Playlist,
Grew into a Big Deal"; Spotify playlist editor Lizzy Szabo was quoted as
saying that "the fact that so many people were talking about [100 gecs]
inspired [Spotify] to look deeper and see if there were any other artists
making music like this" that they didn't know about. Spotify says the name
"hyperpop" was chosen because the word appeared in metadata collected
by McDonald, who told the *Times* he had seen the word used before, but
it did not qualify as a microgenre in his system until 2018: "For our categorization purposes, it was mostly a matter of waiting to see if enough artists
would coalesce around a similar ebullient electro-maximalism." (The fact
that Szabo and McDonald were both involved in the press appearance was
telling of how the "hyperpop" playlist involved both the editorial curation
and the personalization teams working together.)[7]

Hyperpop was a web scene—it's not like there was no digital or data
footprint for these artists—but for Spotify, it wasn't considered *real* enough
until the data was on Spotify. It's an equation that brings to mind what

the author and academic researcher Maria Eriksson wrote in a 2016 paper on the Echo Nest, building on the work of Geoffrey C. Bowker: "We seem to be entering a point in time in which you do not exist unless you are data." In Spotify's understanding, the hyperpop scene did not "exist" on the platform until enough data had been accrued to make it legible.[8]

The official Spotify playlist did to hyperpop what streaming giants do to culture at large: it worked as a flattening, making a scene that was previously sprawling and complicated into something commodified and palatable, cutting out many of its original voices along the way. In return, hyperpop artists varyingly embraced or rejected the Spotify playlist, and many started to reject the label outright. "That was a dissonant thing for me: seeing artists that were a part of this scene, detaching themselves from it because of how this name kind of took off," Noah Simon, the creator of Hyperpop Origins, told me. "If you're an underground artist, you don't want to be attached to a conglomerate like that. It's frustrating, because hyperpop wasn't a term coined by Spotify. They just co-opted it for their own purposes."

On YouTube, Simon's documentary is introduced with this direct debunking: "Hyperpop was not invented by Spotify in 2019." On the screen, interviewees spoke about how the playlist turned hyperpop into a "game to win," while others mentioned feelings of hostility and exclusion. "Why does it feel like we were all erased?" asked the artist and producer Omniboi, in the documentary. The founder of Hyperpop Records, which launched in 2016, recalled how the label's demo submissions became clogged with producers trying to reach the Spotify curators. At another point, Omniboi commented that "the term itself used to be way more conceptual. . . . You couldn't have a YouTube video about how to make a hyperpop song in five minutes. We were in this Twitter family, we were all going to the same shows, but we didn't really sound the same." In fact, a YouTube search for "how to make a hyperpop song" for 2019 (the year before the Spotify playlist) turned up no relevant results, while a search for "how to make a hyperpop song" for the year 2020 (the year after the Spotify playlist) turned up several. Hyperpop had, in some ways, become like a warped sped-up edit of the 90s commodification of grunge—another attempt to take a scene, cartoonishly flatten it out into a single aesthetic, then blast it out through corporate media. But like the music itself, it was all happening faster—even the major label gold rush.[9]

"At the time, there was a direct pipeline off SoundCloud, into the 'hyperpop' playlist, and onto major labels," said Simon. But he pointed out that the artists that were getting singled out for major label contracts seemed to be—for the most part—straight, male, and cis. As the artist quinn told Press-Reynolds for the 2022 *No Bells* piece, "The creation of the Spotify hyperpop playlist and the invitation of labels led directly to the erasure of trans influence. . . . What it's about for us, is us trans and POC people not having yet another thing ruined or taken away from us by the guys in suits. . . . It's deeper than any numbers can go."[10]

The New York City-based producer umru, who has worked with artists across the vast landscapes of PC Music and hyperpop for nearly a decade, also pointed out a critical mass of artists who were grouped into the hyperpop playlist who didn't identify with it all, especially a strain of producers who were more influenced by the SoundCloud rap scene, but were somewhat arbitrarily thrown in. "A lot of people's disdain for it also kind of brought them together," he told me, with a laugh.

umru saw the effects of the hyperpop playlist as related to the effects of the playlist ecosystem more broadly. "It made it so easy to be a fan of a sound without being really interested in the community or the specific artists," he explained. "It made that the path of least resistance." Some Spotify users were becoming fans of the playlist, not the artists—though the scene had advantages over others that had been subject to the same process. "The stuff on there was still very unique," umru said. "Even the fact that the music has lyrics makes it harder to just turn it into a pure vibe, like how lofi hip-hop is a whole genre where people just put it on as a vibe and they're not interested in who's making it."

In some ways, the embrace of hyperpop's kinetic maximalism felt like a direct response to the drowsy nature of the chill music that had consumed certain corners of internet music for years. umru recalled a 2016 tweet that made a big impact on him, from a PC Music–adjacent producer named Igloohost: "NO TIME FOR 'CHILL VIBES.' . . . IT IS 2K16 LIKE CMON SPEED IT UP MY GUY !!!!" It made such an impact on umru that he printed it off and hung it above his desk.[11]

As with lofi hip-hop, the introduction of an influential Spotify playlist brought monetization to the scene in new ways. It was complicated: some artists were able to pay their rents from music for the first time ever thanks to a single playlist placement. But it also illuminated Spotify's immense platform power: when the playlist was refreshed, artists could see their rent checks disappear.

For a lot of the artists involved, hyperpop hadn't started as a commercial pursuit. The "Hyperpop Origins" documentary is filled with stories of artists connecting around a noncommercial creative impulse, hanging out and making friends and going to each other's virtual shows, starting small-scale labels to release music no one else was paying attention to, lifting up those whose voices were obfuscated by the mainstream. Those are types of connections a cluster-map driven by engagement metrics and audio analysis cannot possibly perceive. Recommender systems working in service of corporate media exist to sell a product and uplift artists driving engagement for their financial benefit. In distilling music scenes down to metadata tags, Spotify fundamentally misunderstands much about genres and scenes and sounds that operate in opposition to a streaming-friendly ethos, which is to say: it misses a lot of what makes participating in music worthwhile.

Meanwhile, Spotify's microgenre as a general concept—or branding opportunity—seems to have more influence over how music is found on the platform than ever, as "Daily Mixes" become hyper-specified into a limitless scroll of "Niche Mixes" and "daylist" produces new targeted word clouds of microgenres every few hours. McDonald pointed out in a blog post that the "Every Noise" map was only one "ingredient" in "daylist," which he did not create, and that "daylist" reflected "the endemic tech-company fondness for unsupervised machine learning over explicit human curation." As Spotify leans even more intensely toward machine learning, it seems its systems will only become even less accountable.[12]

During the same years that Spotify employed a genre whisperer to map, pinpoint, and label over six thousand microgenres, the company championed another narrative about genre: that it's going away. The company launched its genre-less campaign in 2018 with a playlist called "POLLEN," with the tagline "Genre-less. Quality first always." The idea that streaming has ushered in a post-genre landscape has been widely discussed in music criticism, but also raises questions: Is genre-less curation even possible on a technical level under a system that requires so much metadata to function?

In any case, the post-genre curation effort is yet another branding exercise, more rebel capitalist posturing, Spotify's way of positing itself as more adventurous than the old-school music business. But the very notion that Spotify could banish genre is at odds with the reality that the platform has dizzyingly created more and more of it.

For all the talk of genre-lessness, "POLLEN" seemed like a pretty steady stream of alt-pop and chill R&B imagined through a corporate faux-indie lens, like an Urban Outfitters CD for the Spotify generation. As the designer who was hired to "brand" the playlist explains on the design studio's website: "Moving away from traditional playlists that target one specific genre or mood, POLLEN instead assembles an overall 'vibe' more akin to a lifestyle: a collection of moments rather than a singular category." The website lists a masthead of sorts, detailing twenty different individuals and entities who were involved in the development of the playlist, including visual artists and floral designers. Spotify also developed corresponding "studio" programs, where artists created tracks, videos, and features associated with the playlist for YouTube and social media.[13]

In an interview, one Spotify playlist curator told *Complex* that playlists like "POLLEN" are the platform's attempt to "contextualize around user communities, like what types of music are younger audiences ready for based on their other habits? What types of apps are they using, how are they engaging with our platform?" It seemed similar to microgenre trend-spotting—following the data to pinpoint supposed user communities—but at the same time, much of the language around "POLLEN" also seemed to parallel that of its advertiser-facing materials around "streaming intelligence," where Spotify pitches its various audience segments for potential brand partnerships. If the very idea for the playlist was built around targeting a specific segment of its audience, then Spotify could all the more easily advertise to this base. It didn't need to draw listeners in and then try to define them for advertisers. It had already defined the audience and built the product around them.

"POLLEN" positioned itself as a sort of authoritative playlist for people who did not want authoritative playlists to tell them what to listen to. One curator mentioned on a conference panel that "POLLEN"—and other playlists that are part of the genre-less project, like "Lorem," "Oyster," and "Alter"—were "where we question the status quo in terms of programming." A curator for "Lorem," which is like "POLLEN" but specifically targeted at

Gen Z, said that if she checks Instagram and an artist's vibe seems to be in line with Lorem, "we'll go through it and put it in without any data." Brave![14]

Speaking with Taja Cheek of the New York band L'Rain, who has been featured on the "POLLEN" playlist, served as a reminder of how insufficient phrases like "genre-defying" and "genre-bending" can be. "There's something about it that just feels like it actually isn't taking into account the specificities of the music it's talking about, and feels lazy in a way," Cheek told me. "And it's more a way to appeal to people's sense of individuality and uniqueness than it is actually defying any sort of real boundary."

She was evoking a dynamic that has played out more broadly across the streaming landscape: the appeal to the type of listener a user wants to be, or to lifestyle, rather than to music. "The music industry has long treated audiences like they're kind of dumb," Cheek continued. "And undermined their interest and knowledge of the music that they're consuming. People listen to lots of different kinds of music. That's not new. But the music industry has presented things by genre for so long, that it seems groundbreaking to do something else, even though it's just reflecting how people are already listening to music."

In 2020, one of the music business trade press outlets hosted a panel discussion that featured various Spotify employees alongside artists whose careers had blossomed with streaming playlists. A young musician on the panel, one who started out playing ukulele songs before becoming a poster child for Spotify-aligned bedroom pop, spoke to how helpful playlists had been in her career. "It's been really pivotal for me growing up in this era of playlisting as an artist, because it's helped me to find my sound," she said. "Which is odd, because it's supposed to be genre-less! As an artist, it shows me who my peers are as I'm looking at the landscape of artists and music." This quote stuck with me: the idea that a young artist would be using data-driven playlists, the ones essentially created from a process of defining advertiser-friendly audience segments, in order to identify her peers. It pointed to another risk of this environment: allowing not only the language of musical context, but the very connections being made, to be dictated by data biased by the influence of engagement and advertising imperatives.

"If we're willingly letting corporations create culture, or determine culture, for their own financial gain, that's unequivocally bad," Cheek told me. "And what makes it so much worse is that it's couched in all of this language of individualism that people buy into and believe. It's an era where we can't agree on basic facts of history in general, and then we're giving corporations the power to create their own versions of culture, and therefore their own versions of history. And then they make a lot of money off of it, while the people who are actually creating the work and the art that make it possible for them to even do this whole scam are not getting paid anything."

"Data is described as this pure source that is untainted by culture or opinion or location or anything like that," she continued. "It's just not true. Algorithms are made by people and people have biases. There is nothing pure about data at all. It's just a way of describing something from a particular viewpoint."

As I've spoken to artists and independent labels over the years, many have agreed that there is something profoundly *off* about the way that Spotify maps, charts, and packages music, and in turn, creates meaning in music. Perusing Spotify's playlists over the past decade, it has at times felt like a bizarre parallel music world has taken root, beyond just the ghost artists and streambait.

When the recommendation systems are optimizing for extended listening sessions, when they are filled with made-up genres, when *music that sounds like other music* is what's most data-blessed, the reality of what we're hearing on the playlists and AI DJ streams isn't music culture, it's Spotify culture. It's a weird data-refracted version of music culture. It's a top-down version of culture branding itself as a bottom-up version of culture. When I look at a Spotify bedroom pop playlist, it doesn't feel like I'm learning about bedroom pop, it feels like I'm learning about the SEO-optimized version of bedroom pop that exists on the Spotify servers. The same goes for just about any micro-scene or musical tradition that Spotify has attempted to map. The creation of finer- and finer-grain data points to label artists and users with exists, in part, to make it easier to market to users by dividing them into advertising segments. It often has nothing to do with the artists or songs themselves, or the intentions of the artists or the scenes that they came from; instead, it's music culture writ large recast as fodder to fuel streaming-friendly one-click buttons for different moods and lifestyles, a whole environment that meets music in the context of only data; captured, commodified, and managed.

10

Fandom as Data

One night in the spring of 2023, I found myself stuck shoulder-to-shoulder in the packed-out lobby of the Williamsburg club Baby's All Right, during the changeover between two industry showcases. The later gig, with doors at ten, was an installment of something called "Spotify Stages," part of the company's then-ongoing attempt at entering the live music market. As I waited for the doors to open, I was wedged at the bar beside a guy shouting to his friends about playlists, specifically his theories on why so many musicians failed to successfully pitch playlist editors. It was, he said, because they couldn't summarize their vibes succinctly enough. Artists were too verbose; they just needed a few words.

The 280-cap Baby's All Right space is recognizable on social media for its full wall of gemstone-shaped stage lights that look like a giant Lite Brite. That night, the venue's signature lighting had been turned Spotify green. The walls were green, the floor was green, the ceiling was green. The entire venue was consumed by neon green. *Is this really what it's come to?* I thought to myself. For so many years, live music was held up as the ultimate Band-Aid for the exploitations of the ultra-consolidated recorded music economy. Streaming wasn't paying, sure, but artists would make their livings out on the road—or so we were told. Were the streaming companies coming for this now, too?

The show was fine. The headliner was an artist who had gone viral on Instagram six years prior; at the time of the show, he had 2.5 million monthly active listeners, and appeared on some mid-tier rap and pop playlists, including one called "goosebumps" (tagline: "you up?") found on mood- and romance-themed "shelves." (That's the term for the themed rows of playlist tiles a user might see on their personalized home page.) This was his first live show ever, someone in the crowd told me.

Outside the venue, I polled showgoers: What brought them out? One told me that she had been to a bunch of Spotify-presented shows. Another said that she learned about this artist six years ago, when she was fifteen, through the "editing community." "Editing what?" I asked. "Videos," she explained. "On Instagram." I even happened to catch a former Spotify employee, who spoke exuberantly about the company's attempt at taking on Live Nation and Ticketmaster. "Spotify has so much data on who is rising but not there yet," he told me. "Music is a very archaic industry. It's a boys' club based on who you know. Hopefully [Spotify Stages] will make it a little more democratic." And he was a big fan of this artist. "He was on my 'Wrapped' last year. I have like thirty-five-ish songs saved from him. He has a very niche following."

A couple of weeks later, I stood on the sidewalk outside Market Hotel—a long-running all-ages music venue above Mr. Kiwi's grocery at Bushwick's Myrtle-Broadway intersection—talking to a pair of teenagers who had traveled from Pennsylvania to see another "Spotify Stages" gig. They told me about a genre called "aesthetic rap," which described the artists they had crossed state lines to see tonight. "It's, like, rap that has a pleasing beat over it," one of them explained.

Another person waiting outside had found out about the show from a Spotify email, another said he found the headlining artist on his friend's gym playlist, but the vast majority of the kids I spoke with told me they were there because of TikTok. "It was one of those videos where someone was walking down the street asking people what kind of music they were listening to," a twenty-year-old showgoer told me. Another said they found him "on Spotify, I think it's called aesthetic rap. I don't know how to explain it. It's like a subgenre." Aesthetic rap: What was it? My interviews did not offer much clarity, but in the moment, I wondered if it might be one of those microgenres from the "Every Noise" map. And while there is an "Every Noise" page for this descriptor, some further digging around the internet reveals a more complicated origin story involving a group of kids who converged on Discord during the pandemic. One Reddit user calls it "cringe"; a YouTuber calls it his favorite genre of all time. The kids

I spoke to outside Market seemed genuinely enthused. But as I headed home, I was struck by how palpably it seemed that most of those conversations were more concerned with a niche vibe fandom—which no one could even really explain—than the artists themselves.

Over my years of reporting on Spotify, conversations about music culture's burgeoning obsession with microgenres—or maybe they were really microvibes—kept popping up, not only with the terms coined by Spotify, but more generally across music fandom online. Another perspective on the phenomenon came when I called up two of the moderators of the wildly popular Facebook group "oddly specific playlists"—one with nearly four hundred thousand members, averaging over eight hundred posts per month—to ask how its users thought about curation and context. There are groups and forums dedicated to Spotify playlists all around the internet, but this one is the most popular; and whereas other groups allow playlister self-promotion and "follow-for-follow" type hustling, "oddly specific playlists" is different.

To some extent, "oddly specific playlists" is charmingly pointless, a wacky corner of social media where basic playlist themes are strictly prohibited; no chill vibes, no running playlists, no study mixes, no thank you. Instead, users write posts requesting song suggestions for their most out-there playlist ideas. On a recent scroll through the group, members were asking for suggestions like: "songs about rotting/decomposing/returning to the earth," "songs a jellyfish would listen to," "jazz music for a drunken stumbling tragicomic clown." Occasionally they are musical—looking for songs with epic vocal harmonies, songs prominently featuring a certain instrument. Interestingly, many of the requests have to do with lyrical content, something recommendation algorithms never seem particularly good at. But for the most part, it is all about niche aesthetics and matching mood boards; users will often post a meme or some sort of image pulled from Instagram, and say, "this, but a playlist."[1]

On Zoom, the Facebook group's moderators Philip and Shelby told me about some of the other ways the playlist group has taken on a life of its own in recent years. "A lot of people treat it like a game, like a brain teaser or a puzzle," Shelby said. "It makes you think about music in terms of more than just whether it makes your ears happy. It makes people think, what are these lyrics actually saying? Or how is this composed? They're hearing those little instruments in the background that they wouldn't have thought to listen to."

The moderators, who approve every post individually, get a close-up view of the ways these hundreds of thousands of members are approaching playlists. They've noticed that members tend to treat the requests like confession booths, or spaces to vent, kind of like therapy. "People do find community in it," Shelby said. "Like if someone's grandma died, or they broke up with their boyfriend, or they're moving to college away from their family for the first time. They'll go to the group and say, *Hey I'm starting this playlist, this is the subject matter, or tone that I'm looking for, this is my situation.*"

The moderators have also observed that people tend to recommend the same songs pretty frequently. As a lighthearted in-joke, they made their own playlist called "We Don't Know What Your Playlist Is About but These Songs Are For Sure in It" (description: "you need therapy but you asked for a playlist") with songs like "I Know the End" by Phoebe Bridgers and "Nobody" by Mitski. Still, the moderators reflected on how they felt that the group provided an alternative to the algorithms. "I feel like most people have, at best, an ambivalent relationship towards algorithms," Philip told me. "They can be useful tools for finding music, but you start to feel uncomfortable when it starts to predict your tastes too well. I feel like this group is sort of a way to disrupt that feeling of just being in the feed or the echo chamber of the algorithm."

As I perused the group over a series of months, I searched for that feeling. To me, the group felt a bit more like a meme community than a music one; it was more playful than just receiving automated recommendations, but it also had a utilitarian feel. The comments on most posts were usually floods of Spotify links. And I couldn't help being hyperconscious of the fact that so often, what was being asked for or discussed did not have to do with music per se, but the pursuit of some sort of vibe or aesthetic described in painstaking detail. Words are a form of data, too. Maybe, in the end, it was some new third thing: not an algorithmic experience, but not fully an alternative either.

Philip said that over time in the group he started to observe the broader tendency toward describing music through microgenres like cottagecore (a pastoral, countryside aesthetic that flourished on TikTok during the pandemic) and dark academia (mood board: poetry books, dusty libraries, black coffee, classical music). He also started seeing "a lot of requests for liminal space type vibes," referring to an internet aesthetic fixation on photos of abandoned, eerie old back rooms and basements. "That's not really a genre of music but a lot of people keep asking for it," he told me. "Usually it ends up being, like, vaporwave. I was intrigued when that meme came out but now I find it kind of repetitive. The funny thing about it is, every liminal spaces playlist I found had a different vibe completely."

After our interview, to further illuminate the point, Philip messaged me a link to a video essay investigating something called Aesthetics Wiki, a website documenting hundreds of aesthetic microtrends. There was talk of goblincore, kidcore, witchcore. It seemed like any random word or phrase could be cast as a descriptive signifier with -core added to the ending. "Everything has become an aesthetic or a vibe," Philip said. "You lose the depth when you box things into a category. But we live in a capitalist world where everything is a cliché. It's just part of consumerism."

"Now I'm seeing 'coastal grandma' a lot," he told me. "You can see those microgenres being created in real time when you are admin-ing this group." At the time of our interview in 2023, I had no idea what he was talking about with this "coastal grandma" meme. But soon after, I noticed an official Spotify editorial playlist while perusing the "Pop" hub on "Browse," titled "Grandma's Home," with the description: "It's giving coastal grandmother, it's giving Diane Keaton, it's giving apple pies." Was someone from Spotify spying on the Facebook group? No, they were just all looking at TikTok. The year before, an influencer had posted a viral video outlining a whole aesthetic universe of white flowy outfits, airy open kitchens, and Ina Garten recipes. "I even made this playlist on Spotify so you could have the coastal gran ambience with you everywhere you go," she says in a voice-over paired with the mood board.

Cottagecore, dark academia, liminal spaces—not only were these terms floating around the "oddly specific playlists group" and Aesthetics Wiki and TikTok, they each had their own official Spotify editorial playlists, too. As culture became fixated on niche aesthetics, the company absorbed these ideas into its broader understanding of mood, vibe, and genre. These are all different ways of understanding music, but on Spotify, these types of distinctions blurred into each other. Ultimately, mood, vibe, and genre had all just become different ways of tagging music with descriptive data, different ways of sorting music into buckets that served the necessary functions of streaming curation, which is to say, the function that genre has always played: marketing. They were all just ways to narrow audience segments and influence the pipelines of programming, in hopes something might make someone click "play."

Take one telling example: "cottagecore." There is no "Every Noise at Once" page for "cottagecore," which suggests that Spotify doesn't necessarily think of it as a genre. But there is an official "cottagecore" Spotify playlist that a user might find while clicking around the "Wellness" page, and then clicking around the "Nature & Noise" subpage. It comes with a lengthy description: "you're gathering flowers in the forest, listening to birdsong, humming a sweet melody." It's pure vibe, pure aspirational aesthetic, and it's also pure PFC—filled with stock content dutifully tagged up by the Strategic Programming metadata team. And while the playlist can be found through "Browse," it seems that "cottagecore" more likely exists to catch users who might be searching the term, to point them in the direction of cheaper content for Spotify.

Online fandoms built around naming microgenres and aesthetics feel directly connected to this rise of metadata as an organizing standard of algorithmic culture. In the early 2020s post-peak playlist era, Spotify staff responsible for playlists were curating tracks as much as they were tagging them; their work involved labeling tracks in order to insert them into the appropriate "strongly seeded candidate pools," as employees discussed on Slack, and thus making them more legible to algorithmic systems. Spotify has an entire team dedicated to "defining and harmonizing the relationship between humans, algorithms, and sets," and there are strategists that oversee things like "content attributes," "setchecking," and "setwatching," components of algorithmic systems that suggest what users might want to hear next. As online music cultures were organizing music by granular descriptors, they were fulfilling a similar role, sorting music so it could be better perceived by algorithmic methods like natural language processing.

The pop music philosopher and scholar Robin James, in theorizing why music culture has become entwined with the language of "vibes," has argued that in embracing vibes, we've adopted the language that algorithms use to perceive and to organize us. She has explained vibes as a way to typecast users not based on identity but on their actions and data breadcrumbs, in terms of the "trajectory" that someone might be on as a user. "We've learned how to interact with algorithms so that they perceive us in ways that we want to be perceived," she said in a 2023 podcast interview. "You're pre-packaging yourself as a data subject."[2]

It took a long time for me to understand why so much start-up culture of the late 2010s was invested in metadata. Diving into the world of Aesthetics Wiki, reflecting on Spotify editors becoming taggers, I was reminded of a music business conference presentation I had attended in 2022, where the CEO of an AI mood data start-up walked attendees through her company's "tagging product," where a client could simply upload a track, and based on a sonic fingerprint, the AI would tag-up the track with niche descriptors from the AI's proprietary "taxonomy" of genres, moods, and emotions. Clients often uploaded more than one track though; they were uploading tens of thousands. The product was being used by streaming services to generate playlists, and by private equity companies who needed to understand the curatorial possibilities of their new portfolios, during the catalog royalty gold rush of the early 2020s, in which investors were paying hundreds of millions of dollars to buy out artists' and publishers' royalty rights. "We're an artificial intelligence company for the music industry," the CEO said. "But that's just a fancy way of saying we're a data processing company." This was only one of a few different companies offering a similar product: mood data taxonomy as a service. Tagging was a big business opportunity, and big businesses will always look for free and cheap labor to exploit—including the labor of tagging and sorting. Why process the data if you can get fans to process the data for you? Aesthetics Wiki itself was eventually absorbed as a data source for a number of generative AI companies.

The new paradigms of being a fan online—the niche vibes, the meme playlists, the infinite descriptors—started feeling more attuned to this broader project of data processing and corporate exploitation than, say, musical understanding and appreciation. It was the datafication of not just music, but fandom. If microvibes are a form of metadata, and metadata works to make artificial intelligence systems operate more efficiently, it's worth following that logic a bit further and remembering the broader ramifications of AI systems. In his introduction to Jacques Attali's *Noise:*

The Political Economy of Music, the philosopher Fredric Jameson describes the concept of "autosurveillance," under which "capital and the state no longer have to do anything to you, because you have learned to do it to yourself." This was fan culture reshaped by algorithmic ubiquitousness, which is to say, by tools of surveillance.[3]

11

Sounds for Self-Optimization

I n 2023, Spotify temporarily prohibited a generative AI start-up called Boomy from releasing new music to the platform. The app has been around since 2018 and claims to have released over 14.5 million songs, which it says account for nearly 14 percent of "the world's recorded music." Boomy's CEO has asserted that his company is not just software but a "platform, label, and publisher representing a new creative class of technology-enabled musicians"—that it's an indie label just like any other. [1]

Boomy's output could hardly be called music, though. The app feels more like a novelty generator that mixes vibe-specific fragments. A user is prompted to select from a list of prefab styles (like "Lo-Fi," "electronic dance," "relaxing meditation"); selecting "Lo-Fi," for example, then leads to choices between three sub-styles, "Morning Sun," "Afternoon Nap," and "Nights"; from there, a track is generated, which can be posted to streaming services or edited further. The track can be ready to monetize within minutes, with Boomy keeping 20 percent of streaming revenue. The app also owns the track outright, and licenses it back to the "musician" to earn royalties. "Musician" is in heavy scare quotes there; there is no music-making involved. It is a systematic streaming-enabled grift to generate exploitable copyrights.

Spotify didn't ban Boomy because of its artificially generated tracks, though. It was banned because its tracks were revealed to have been streamed by artificial listeners—meaning that someone had likely bought bot streams from one of many available third-party "stream farms" offering play count boosts as a service. Fake mood music streamed by fake listeners: Is that where the arc of recorded music industry "innovation" eventually leads? "We shouldn't let any industry's lack of creativity hold the artists back," the Boomy CEO would say on stage at the 2023 "Music Ally Next" summit. Indeed, music-tech innovation relies on a never-ending cycle of self-styled outsider businesspeople finding new ways to extract capital and position it as rebellious. Boomy's brand revolved around hyping the fact that it did not train models on copyrighted material without permission—differentiating itself from AI music companies like Suno and Udio, who were sued by the majors in 2024 for "mass infringement" of copyrights—but this does not necessarily mean it was operating ethically. It also hyped up its potential to enable people to become content creators "even if they lack expensive tools or a formal music-making education," it wrote in a press release, the latter of which, to be clear, has never been necessary to make art.[2]

As a result of the artificial stream detection, Spotify took down roughly 7 percent of Boomy's tracks, which the *Financial Times* reported to be tens of thousands of songs. Spotify, at the time, said that it was working to stamp out "stream manipulation" to "protect royalty payouts for honest, hardworking artists." But the company made one thing clear: Boomy was not being penalized for releasing generative AI content. It had already been doing so for years: in fact, in its first year, tracks generated with Boomy software had seen so much success on Spotify, the company said they were even getting surfaced on algorithmic "Discover Weekly" playlists. By the end of 2023, Boomy had struck up a partnership with Warner Music Group, ensuring its place in the streaming universe anyway.[3]

The race for cheap content was clearly charging onward, with the digital services, major labels, and VC investors alike all looking for the next frontier of that sweet, sweet commodified attention. Streaming turned to TikTok; crypto turned to AI. The vibes shifted ever on. As the fight for market share between the majors continued, a new factor arrived. How would artists—and the whole system for that matter—be impacted when streaming services were inevitably (always inevitably!) flooded with thousands and thousands of AI-generated tracks? Would "streambait" be supplanted by the generative AI content? Would all of those "fake artists" just be auto-generated one day? Daniel Ek, for one, was into it. On a 2023 conference call, he noted that the boom in AI-generated content could be "great culturally" and allow Spotify to "grow engagement and revenue."

His company was also figuring out new ways to use the emerging generative AI narratives to ship new playlist products. Similarly to Boomy, Spotify used the language of creative empowerment to describe the beta version of "AI Playlist" in 2024, a chatbot-inspired tool with users supplying prompts to generate new algorithmic mixes; the press release claimed it would allow users to "effortlessly turn [their] most creative ideas into playlists"—by typing prompts—"whether you're a beginner or an expert playlist creator." It was a new way to extract data from users, pitched as a democratizing means of expression, rather than what it really seemed to be: the next step in replacing human editors with fully machine-driven processes riddled with musical misinformation. [4]

While the cultural impact of the flagship editorial playlist may have waned, certain elements of Spotify's lean-back environment were only growing more pervasive as personalization took a stronger hold on the product: music-as-utility, music-as-mood-stabilizer. Click here for happy, click here for sad, click here for chill-out study beats. The long-term effects of how Spotify evangelized lean-back functional music were not just felt on Spotify. Whether through editorial or algorithms, the perfect-playlist paradigm—the idea that a user, through a light-touch interface, could get the perfect soundtrack at any moment—had helped shape new incentives across the music and culture industries. The ripple effects were everywhere. It was in the way that pop artists were rearranging their catalogs into mood playlists, like when Taylor Swift released her 2024 album as five playlists reflecting "five stages of heartbreak." It was in how labels, artists, and managers alike were thinking up new ways to remix and recast their song assets into streaming-friendly content. And the ripple effects were also felt in the AI start-ups going after the worlds of made-for-you mood music, a whole cottage industry catering to the playlist-trained, functional music listener.

"Functional music" is now thrown around so much, it can be confusing to even know what it means anymore, or what it is meant to do. Rebranding mood music as "functional" seemed like no more than an attempt to make it all seem more scientific than it was—and there was clearly a historical precedence for that marketing tactic in the narrative of Muzak.

When critics started questioning the impacts of all this lean-back filler content on culture, the execs spun a new narrative. One of the very first times the phrase "functional music" occurred in the archives of the music-biz trade publication *Music Ally* was in 2018 when a music publishing CEO called critics of the background music boom "elitists." On stage at a conference, he reportedly remarked with a heavy dose of sarcasm: "It is scary, the democracy, isn't it? That any plebes and idiots can go and vote. I think this is horrible! I prefer Universal deciding for me what I should listen to." Again, there was that pervasive myth: that whatever succeeded on streaming was simply the will of the people. That would be a useful line as various industry players made their next moves to capitalize on growing their streamshare via AI functional tracks.

Companies like Boomy, Suno, and Udio weren't alone in supplying a glut of miserably dull auto-generated audio and passing it off as the future of collective creative expression. In the summer of 2023, I found myself at a beachside start-up expo in Santa Monica, California that called itself a "music tech carnival." At tables set up surrounding an indoor merry-go-round on the Santa Monica boardwalk, enterprising individuals hawked their visions for the future of music. And investors, including reps from major labels, perused the tables, looking for their next big bet—their next Spotify, perhaps. (Major labels essentially function as venture capitalists in their signings, but Sony and Universal both also fulfill that role in departments dedicated to incubating and investing in tech start-ups.)

One corner of the music tech start-up carnival was dubbed "A.I. Alley," a row of tables for founders claiming to be optimizing artist success by harnessing the power of big data. I dutifully stopped from table to table to speak with those working at the cutting edge of automated mood music, metadata tagging, and more. As one of the many brochures proclaimed, they were "turning up the volume on innovation." My first stop was the table of a company claiming to revolutionize background music by auto-generating royalty-free bleeps and bloops called "infinite albums." As with Boomy, a user would start by clicking a "Create Vibe" button, select a general style or emotion from a premade list, and then "click anywhere inside the emotion wheel" to tune the emotional range using eight emoji-type faces: angry, happy, calm, sleepy, etcetera.

There were "A.I. music co-pilots" that would provide song seed ideas; "A.I. band practice," a piece of hardware that would use animated bandmates to help guide a user through instrument lessons; one app where a user could paste the link to any song and pull up royalty-free versions of songs with the same sound. At one table, I met the CEO of a beta voice model marketplace, which would "allow" artists the "opportunity" to sell their voice tones for a small fee, after which part they're considered "royalty-free" for subscribers. I asked if the fee would increase if, say, someone making a song for a Super Bowl commercial came along. The answer was no. I heard more men than I could count utter some version of this at various tables: "Sounds cool, man. I'm working on something similar. What are you training on?" If there was any running theme from table to table, it seemed to just be rich people looking for new ways to get more rich, with little regard for the impact they might have on working musicians.

The AI hype cycle could be disorienting to keep up with. As it unfolded, the very term "AI" felt increasingly useless, especially in music, where so many different concepts fall under its umbrella, and so many pre-existing products were being rebranded as AI for metallic tech-forward sheen. Every day, a press release for some new AI start-up landed in my inbox, selling some new song-starter tool or metadata management service or predictive A&R thing. There were AI apps for voice enhancing, cloning, and simulating. Some were commercial consumer-facing products; others were industry-facing partnerships and deals. Some of the AI was for relatively uncontroversial purposes, basic audio functions like volume and signal correction. But some of it had more serious implications, including the various apps for generative AI music. It was challenging to make sense of it all; to separate the smoke and mirrors from the legitimate threats, the real from the fake, the creative potential from the get-rich-quick schemes. Most of all, it seemed like the meaning of the word "intelligence" had really been put up for debate.

AI skeptics worried about a future that was seeming increasingly imminent: How would musicians know if their work had been used as training data to create a generative AI system? What intellectual property rights would apply? Who could control unauthorized sonic deepfakes? On the other hand, more optimistic artists and technologists urged that AI could open all sorts of new creative possibilities, that artists had already been using forms of it for decades, that consent and transparency and opt-in protocols could lead to collaborative tools harnessing musical collectivity on an unprecedented scale. There would be new types of randomness and chaos shaking artists out of the patterns they'd grown too comfortable with.

"The issue isn't the technology itself," said Philip Golub of Music Workers Alliance, one of several artist advocacy groups organized during the pandemic. We spoke a couple of days after I'd joined MWA on a picket line with the Writers Guild of America, in the summer of 2023, where the musicians showed up in solidarity with writers fighting, in part, to not have their work replaced by AI. "The issue isn't that these tools are fundamentally bad, or nefarious, or immoral," he explained. "It's that we don't have consent over how the things that we make are used, and that is a fundamental right that we all have, but that we need to remind ourselves that we have, because we live in a world where that right is often trampled on and taken away. We forget that we have that right."

Consent was at the heart of a heated debate about "AI ethics," which spawned so many different corporate manifestos and white papers in 2023 that the music industry research group Water & Music published its own "Music AI Ethics Tracker," writing that they sensed these codes had more to do with "safeguarding revenue and market share than with actually setting a comprehensive ethical agenda for AI." The tracker listed what these ethics guidelines most commonly called for: labeling AI-generated content, training data transparency, centering human artistry. The organization found that besides its own list of recommendations, none of these AI ethics guidelines specifically addressed "employment or job displacement—even though those issues are top concerns for many working artists today."[5]

As these conversations played out, an open-minded musician could, in theory, see interesting points from all directions. In practice, though, what was emerging was a lot of trash audio content made from generic stems, as major labels and overeager start-up investors ran full speed ahead. It just seemed like AI was being used to create the cheapest possible content from which corporations could most efficiently profit.

The most controversial stories tended to dominate the news. In 2022, Capitol Music Group faced backlash for its attempt to "sign" a partially AI-powered virtual rapper named FN Meka, whose music included racial slurs and whose social media included illustrations of the avatar experiencing police brutality. After a Black activist group, Industry Blackout, called the project "an amalgamation of gross stereotypes" and "disrespectful to real people who face real consequences in real life," the label abandoned the project and issued a public apology. At that point, the Brown University assistant professor and musician Enongo Lumumba-Kasongo, who records and performs under the moniker Sammus, had already written critically on the rise of Uberduck, an AI-based text-to-speech synthesis engine where a user could choose a rapper's voice, enter text, and generate a track. Lumumba-Kasongo wrote that "the ease with which creators and developers have co-opted and presented the voices of notable Black hip-hop artists like Kanye West and JAY-Z actually represents the latest development in a broader history," pointing to musicologist Matthew D. Morrison's work around "Blacksound," or the "sonic and embodied legacy of blackface performance as the origin of all popular music, entertainment, and culture in the United States." The music industry seemed set on using generative AI to author a new chapter in its long history of exploiting marginalized voices.[6]

Another AI music controversy consumed the music press in 2023, when a viral AI-generated Drake song took the internet by storm, generating countless headlines and several million streams, including six hundred thousand on Spotify, before UMG ordered its removal. The song was released under the artist name "ghostwriter" along with a bizarre TikTok video where the supposed artist wore a ghost costume and big black sunglasses, claiming to be heralding the AI revolution in music. Questions abounded. One was the extent to which the song was actually made with AI; the lyrics, it turned out, were written by "ghostwriter" himself, and it was only the voice filter that had been generated through a long-available technique called timbre transferring. And then there was also the question of whether, in the end, it was all just a stunt for clicks; one diligent YouTuber (@yokai) excavated enough digital ephemera to convincingly trace the track back to an AWAL Records-signed pop singer named JVKE, whose viral rise via TikTok pranks had been well documented in a *Vox* documentary years prior covering the "TikTok-to-Spotify pipeline." And his manager was a longtime architect of short-form video marketing campaigns going back to the days of pre-TikTok app Musical.ly. Interestingly, by the year's end, many music industry power players were coming to describe "ghostwriter" in interviews not as a fraudulent scammer who needed to be stopped, but as a conversation-starting radical who was pushing culture forward. The major label execs didn't have to be scared: AWAL was owned by Sony, and JVKE was one of their own. As it turned out, stream-fraud schemers were only considered as such when they didn't personally benefit the big players in some way.[7]

In the hands of major labels and streambait consultants, AI was looking likely to become just another tool of what the writer Cory Doctorow called platform decay, or "enshittification," and it was all going to be monetized by streaming.

Spotify supported AI-generated music for the same reason that other industry power players were clamoring to harness its potential: it opened up a possible new pool of cheap content.[8]

When people were paying attention, the debate about generative AI was fierce. But what if it could be deployed in the corners of music where people weren't paying attention? Indeed, this seemed to be the area where the imminent AI infiltration of music was most feasible: the replacement of lean-back mood music. Spotify certainly showed no signs of stopping its PFC partners from making use of AI software; it wasn't hard to imagine the "Spotify Originals" sliver on the PFC charts growing larger with music made in "collaboration" with such tools. And the majors were starting to look for new ways to increase their market share through passive AI mood music, too. That's where another component of the AI content gold rush came in, a whole suite of start-ups offering one-click self-generating make-your-own-lifestyle-content streams.

Another one was Endel, a German generative music start-up launched in 2018, claiming to personalize not just music discovery, but the music itself, with soundscapes tailored to *you*. Their sales pitch was "personalized functional soundscapes" making use of time of day, weather, and biometric data to better optimize your daily flow state, wind down, and sleep routine. And while this was happening outside of the streaming platforms, the mood music norms set by Spotify had clearly helped set the stage for this type of company. And Spotify generally seemed on board: Endel tracks would soon be found on flagship editorial playlists like "Brain Food" and "Deep Focus." Playlist culture had encouraged musicians to treat their output like mood playlist filler, and flattened the complexity of moods into a small selection of standardized presets. The industry had spent years treating music as data and nudging artists toward more machine-legible output. Of course it all led here.[9]

Endel wasn't the only company angling to get in on this market. The co-inventor of Siri also had one of these start-ups, LifeScore, offering AI remixes tuned to activity and genre prompts. There was another app called Vibes, promising "personalized background music" to "help you focus, relax, sleep, and stay in the moment," made in real time from thousands of stems. WiredVibe was yet another, claiming its personalization would "elevate your mental health with music." These were the streaming era's answer to time-tested gimmicks; the press materials around the Endel and Vibes apps felt like techie takes on the hyperbolic sales copy for the 1970s Environments series, some of the first commercially available nature sounds, captured and sold by a man named Irv Teibel, whom *Pitchfork* once called an original "New Age hustler." Teibel famously created not actual field recordings but edits using a mix of field recordings and studio flourishes; like the Edison corporation, he distributed forms for mood change feedback and printed overblown testimonials on the backs of the LPs. (The *Environments* albums were reissued by Numero Group in 2018 as both a box set and a $2.99 iPhone app, pitched as long-form field records for work, meditation, and sleeping.)[10]

Endel's VC-chasing founder had a track record for building apps in order to sell them to bigger companies. He could often sound like Mark Zuckerberg in interviews: "We're trying to create a technology that will help us evolve as a species," he once said. Endel's company "manifesto" included laughably lofty statements about how they were going to "reshape our collective future."[11]

In the beginning, Endel attempted to distance itself from the music business, calling itself a "soothing sounds app" and strategically avoiding the word "music" in its own branding materials. Within a year of its founding, though, the company had struck up a partnership with Warner Music Group, who went to the trade publications with a story claiming they'd been the "first major label to sign a record deal with an algorithm." Mood music was making up an increasing percentage of overall streamshare, and the majors wanted in on it. Endel had found its new niche: helping major labels improve streamshare on DSPs by generating tracks—based on major label catalogs—that could better fit the different mood categories offered by streaming services. Soon, it would also strike deals with Universal Music Group and Amazon Music, and receive several rounds of venture capital funding.[12]

Endel sold itself on the premise that it wasn't trying to pit human artists against stock music libraries, but rather that it would work with record labels to help them re-contextualize their back catalogs into more streaming-friendly mood content. Like the very term "functional music" itself, the premise offered them an opportunity to do so while also wrapping the content in the appearance of science-y innovation. In claiming to not pit "real artists" against stock libraries, Endel merely helped those artists sound more like stock libraries themselves. It claimed that its early collaborations with James Blake and Grimes, for example, represented a "whole new category . . . of deeply human music created in collaboration with an AI." It wasn't about using AI to impersonate James Blake, but using stems from his songs to make some James Blake-themed sleepytime beats. "Tens of millions of dollars and years and years of work were spent to create this framework and technology," Endel's CEO wrote in a *Variety* op-ed, which is kind of a shame, because it sounds like something the labels could have hired a kid off SoundCloud to make in an afternoon. (Or better yet, created some full-time jobs for music producers.) In the same op-ed, the CEO wrote about his vision that one day his engineers could get on stage to accept a Grammy, "standing shoulder to shoulder with the fellow artists they've created their award-winning music with," contradicting the company's earlier claims that it existed outside of the music business.[13]

For all of the AI branding, one Universal Music Group employee told me that the Endel collaboration was essentially "moods-based remix content," where Endel would take items from the label's back catalog and assist in making versions that "fit the buckets that already existed" to help the label increase streamshare and stay competitive in the "functional" landscape. "They probably will end up making a lot of money," the UMG employee said of Endel. "But I don't know if they're part of the solution or just another part of the problem." Soon enough, Endel started rolling this stuff out: there was a suite of chill-out remixes of Roberta Flack's "Killing Me Softly With His Song," sleep-themed versions of Sia's Christmas album, to name a couple. To be sure, these AI-generated remixes existed only because there was a financial incentive for endless streams of lean-back content. The major labels loved the ability to partner with AI start-ups because of their shared interests in finding new ways to harvest streams and funnel capital to corporations. In other words, their goals were often aligned.

Much of the marketing around Endel also centered on its narrative of being "backed by science," cementing its position in the long lineage of mood music merchants before it. As the Edison Company had done ninety-seven years prior, Endel funded research on its own catalog's ability to change moods; it was carried out by a company called Arctop, which claims to create "real-time brain decoding technology" for commercial purposes. Participants wore "a light headband only for the brain decoding," which "picked up on the brain's impulses and tracked its responses to the audio in relation to the task being carried out," a scientific approach that is not only unproven but also highly invasive to normalize. On social media, Endel celebrated when the Arctop study had been peer reviewed by a journal called *Frontiers*. But *Frontiers* has been riddled with controversy. In 2024, the *British Medical Journal* (BMJ) questioned its reputation after it made "wide scale retractions," and in 2015, *Nature* reported that *Frontiers* had been added to "a list of questionable publishers," leading to "backlash" that split the research community. While the Arctop study looked at Endel's "Focus" soundscapes, the company partnered with a different organization to supposedly validate its "Sleep" offering: SleepScore Labs, a joint venture between the television host Dr. Oz, known for spreading misinformation, the medical devices giant ResMed, and the private equity firm Pegasus Capital Advisors.[14]

Still, this didn't stop the music industry. In September 2023, Universal Music Group hosted reps from Endel and other self-styled innovators at the questionable intersection of corporate music and health for something called the "MUSIC + HEALTH" summit. At the event UMG CEO Lucian Grainge talked about how throughout his life he'd seen "countless examples of how music can change people's mood, comfort them in times of emotional crisis, or even help them physically," and how AI-accelerated wellness products would become a "key component" of the company's strategy.[15]

"The fact that functional music as a market is rapidly growing is just a testament to the power of sound and the power of music," said Endel's CEO in a 2023 interview with a fitness blog. "A lot of people have recognized that, and they are turning to sound to help them feel better or feel different. They're self-medicating with sound." Whether the research is legitimate or not, wellness and self-medicating should not be in the hands of Endel, Universal Music Group, Spotify, or any other corporate entity, but that's a hard sell in a country where health and well-being are by design left to private sector profiteers.

Spotify's mood music system had evidently inspired Endel, but by 2022, the streaming giant was taking a page out of the German start-up's playbook. According to a review of internal messages, throughout the year, Spotify's Strategic Programming team—the editors who oversaw the implementation of PFC strategy—had dedicated part of its team to developing a new product called "Soundscape," where users could press one button and a personalized PFC-only ambient stream would commence, themed around a loose concept like "Floating in Space" or "Breathe." The idea was that, similar to its AI DJ product, no track list would surface: just an endless stream of ambient mood-enhancing sounds. After months of work, the product was eventually put on indefinite hiatus. But the very fact that it was being considered provided a fascinating glimpse into a streaming company's scramble to compete with marketplace shifts that it had played a significant role in creating. It was a look into the future that Spotify wanted, the logical conclusion of its quest for ultra-passive, one-push, AI-driven mood music.

12

Streaming as Surveillance

"It's an outrageous amount of data," says a former Spotify machine learning engineer, about thirty minutes into our phone call. "Even having worked with it, it's almost unfathomable. It's fair to assume that every click that you've made in the app has been logged somewhere, whether or not it's actively being used to make the recommendations. You should be under the assumption that any interaction you have within the Spotify app is going to be recorded."

As a twenty-first-century social media user, familiar with the basic concepts of surveillance capitalism—what the author Shoshana Zuboff calls "a new economic order that claims human experience as free raw material for hidden commercial practices of extraction, prediction, and sales"—I conceptually know that this is true, that every click is a tracked transaction creating value for the platform. And yet it still feels jarring to confront the sheer magnitude of my Spotify account data when it lands in my inbox, or at least the parts of my data profile that the company is willing to share. As of this writing, Spotify users can request a download of their account data by navigating to "Account," then "Privacy Settings," then "Download your data." Within the folder provided, there are several files, like "Playlists," which includes the titles, descriptions, and tracklists for every playlist I have created on Spotify, and "Search Queries," a list of everything I have typed into the search bar, the date and time it was searched, and the type of device used to search it. A document titled "Streaming History" bundles track information for everything I've played over the past year, though there is also an option to request an "Extended Listening History," which would include the number of milliseconds for which the track was played, details of whether it began from a playlist or was manually chosen, whether I hit the skip button, and more.

The "Inferences" doc is the most interesting: a glimpse into the list of market segments that Spotify associates with your account, based on both streaming history and data obtained by third-party sources, like advertisers and data brokers. My account is apparently included in audience segments like "Enthusiastic_Mood_Listeners," "Confidence_Productivity_Motivation_Listeners," "Happy_and_Uplifting_Playlist_Streamers," "Heartbreak_Playlist_Listeners," "Made_For_You_Power_Playlist_Streamers," "Mindfulness_Seekers," and "Soothing_Sounds." There are odd inclusions like "Verizon_Users_All" (I'm not a Verizon user), "Disney_Marvel_Playlist_Streamers" (pretty sure I've never clicked those), and "Parenting" (nope). The segments based on intel from outside data brokers can lead users to also be included in groups specifically for ad-targeting, like "Buyers of Clean Beauty Products_US," "Campbell's Soup Buyers_US," and "Captain Morgan Drinkers_US," to name a few, according to various social media posters, plus attempts to target based on credit card types, income levels, investment portfolios, and more. Spotify users discussing their data profiles online varyingly joked about how the information was both invasive and also so often bizarrely incorrect.

Spotify claims to collect billions of data points daily to power its recommendations and targeted advertisements. The company is less forthcoming about its other business: selling this data to data brokers. The implications of all this data collection are complicated. Within the broader picture of mass surveillance today, it can feel low stakes that Spotify is always spying on its users. It's just music, right? Each year, during the "Wrapped" campaign, streaming-as-surveillance becomes its own meme, with some users decrying the normalization of mass data collection, and others responding with jokey resignation about how Spotify has made surveillance seem cute and fun. It all reveals just how comfortable many users have become with this compromise—but it is a compromise, on principle and in practice.

Spotify loves proclaiming its ability to *know users better than they know themselves*; since as early as 2015, the company has sold advertisers on its ability to target listeners using playlist data to approximate their moods. "What we'd ultimately like to do is be able to predict people's behavior through music," Les Hollander, the former global head of audio and podcast monetization, said in 2017. "We know that if you're listening to your chill playlist in the morning, you may be doing yoga, you may be meditating . . . so we'd serve you a contextually relevant ad with information and tonality and pace to that particular moment."[1]

The company also has a tendency to oversell advertisers on its unique glimpse into users' inner emotional lives, which it says is possible because music is so intimate. And despite how, to some users, even a cursory look at their Spotify Account Data calls this into question (how intimate, exactly, is it for an advertiser to consider me a "Mindfulness_Seeking Heartbreak_Playlist_Listener"?), Spotify only continues to double down on these claims. "The more they stream, the more we learn," read the tagline for another piece of advertising for its advertising business, asserting that Spotify data could reveal its audience's moods and mindsets. "User engagement fuels our streaming intelligence—insights that reflect the real people behind the devices," explains yet another Spotify ad promo. "We've found that how people stream actually tells us a lot about who they are. . . . The most exciting part? This new research is starting to reveal the streaming generation's offline behaviors through their streaming habits." These marketing messages might only constitute the company's aspirations, but they're telling all the same.[2]

Advertising brings in a considerably small but not inconsequential percentage of Spotify's total revenues: around 13 percent. The company is always trying to grow that number, of course, with a stated goal to eventually make advertising 20 percent of the business. On the Spotify Advertising website, it finds new ways to sell advertisers on the platform, with "studies" and "insights reports" promoting its first-party data pools. In one such 2022 "study" on Gen Z users, Spotify Advertising reported that younger listeners used audio to "explore the most niche sides of themselves and discover identities they never even knew they had." Spotify claimed that 80 percent of its Gen Z users "are tuning into audio that spans their emotional spectrum, from 'melancholy' to 'passionate' to 'dramatic'" and said "brands that integrate more edgy, out-there, or experimental concepts into their products or campaigns will resonate with Gen Z audiences seeking access to these different sides of themselves." Perhaps the most amusing claim was that "Gen Z's aspiration to be seen as unique is reflected in their affinity for 'weirdcore,' a music genre they streamed 3X more on Spotify than millennials in Q1 of 2022," just one example of how its attempts to label music and users with increasingly granular genres and metadata become part of its advertising strategy. The deck ended with a sales pitch, encouraging advertisers to embrace playlist-related campaigns to help Zoomers "reveal something new about themselves," specifically suggesting that advertisers can capture this young, pro-fluidity market segment by sponsoring the "genre-less" "POLLEN" or "Lorem" playlists.[3]

Spotify has since taken its surveillance-driven marketing to new conceptual extremes, partnering with the marketing agency Neuro-Insight on "neuroscience research" to bolster the claims of its targeted ad business. The partnership entered Spotify into the dubious realm of what's called "neuro-marketing," a scientifically shoddy practice claiming to study consumer brain patterns in order to more effectively deliver ads. Neuromarketing is not exactly new, and some researchers have questioned its scientific grounding for decades. By 2013, *Slate* reported that nearly one hundred companies worldwide were selling some sort of neuromarketing service. "The clients who employ these researchers are rarely interested in the subtleties of what the results might mean," wrote neuroscience researcher Matt Wall in *Slate*. "They care about loose concepts like 'engagement' or 'emotion' related to their products or TV commercials, and this is what the neuromarketers claim to deliver: science-y-looking graphs with wiggly lines that show (putatively) when people are pleased by a commercial and when they're bored."[4]

Reviewing the materials that Spotify and Neuro-Insight created together, it seems that the two companies were after something similar. In 2021, Spotify claimed that the studies revealed that people were happier on its platform than on others, and that its targeted ads worked better as a result. "The more listeners pay attention to the content, they pay attention to the ad," says the voice in one of these marketing videos. "The research proves it! Spotify outperforms all other forms of media in engagement." In a different video, Spotify and Neuro-Insight claim to look at "the brain on music," as participants sit around a table wearing brain-scanning headbands, presumably listening to their favorite "Heartbreak_Playlists" or "Confidence_Productivity_Mindfulness Mixes." "Our goal is to use signals like this to make sure we're serving music and podcasts to the user that they want before they know they want it," an exec told *Axios* at the time. It was yet another contemporary marketing campaign recalling the Edison Mood Change surveys, but instead of asking participants to record responses, it used hundreds of participants wearing brain-scanning headbands to reveal that "music allows people to be in touch with their emotions, elevate mood, and connect with others." (No way.) Not exactly a groundbreaking revelation, and surely one that could be gathered through less invasive research methods. Similar to other Spotify advertising campaigns, the insights seemed at times incredibly obvious and unscientific, and at other times, incredibly overblown.[5]

These marketing schemes are dubious, but to understand the deeper issues of streaming surveillance requires further context. It requires focusing less on individual bad actors and instead trying to understand the broader systemic power imbalances. "If we want to be really effective in the struggle for privacy and protecting our information, if we're really serious about it, we have to consider this as a system and not as individual actors," Stefano Rossetti, a data protection lawyer with the Austria-based privacy rights organization NOYB (short for "None Of Your Business"), told me. "If you look at Spotify, individually, the answer will always be *yeah, it's just music.* [They] can see that maybe I'm in a breakup, or I'm obsessed with some sort of anti-Christian song, or whatever. You can get some stuff from the bits and bytes that I leave on Spotify."

But more often than not, he explained, on Spotify and across the web, the data does not just stay with the platform—it goes to a whole network of data brokers and ad-tech platforms, to be incorporated with other third-party data to create, repackage, and sell more nuanced profiles on individuals. "Maybe it turns out Spotify shares the information with a data broker, which is, in turn, absolutely happy to share this information with another actor to make a very detailed profile about me," Rossetti continued. "It's Spotify, it's dating apps, it's what I read online." This practice is called "ID syncing," in which companies compile data from various sources, from cookies and mobile identifiers, fingerprinting on browsers. Taken altogether, these companies attempt to map detailed user profiles that could be used for job selection, background checks, political micro-targeting, and more.

Spotify has taken part in such collaborations through its direct partner-ships. In his book *Streaming Music, Streaming Capital*, the professor and researcher Eric Drott notes that Spotify has partnered with Facebook, Uber, Tesla, Tinder, and Virgin Airlines, as well as Ancestry.com and 23andMe, offering the last two companies "not only a new customer base but a new source of behavioral data, one that might profitably complement the genetic data they already possess." And to more broadly illustrate why else marketers and ad-tech firms as well as "credit agencies, banks, health-care providers, insurers, governmental agencies, and finance companies" might want music-related data—beyond just Spotify and streaming data—Drott points to examples that already exist: a start-up called Creditvidya, which has used music streaming data as part of its algorithm for approving loans, and the microcredit start-up Lenddo, which media scholar Robert Prey has noted uses concert ticket data as part of approving students for loans to buy textbooks.[6]

These examples illuminate why it matters that Spotify is a partner of Acxiom, one of the world's largest data brokers, which as of 2021 claimed to have detailed data profiles for 2.5 billion people across sixty-two different countries. And as of 2023, there are sixty-seven different companies on Spotify's "cookies vendor list" that "use cookies and similar technologies on the Spotify Service in order to provide services to Spotify and our advertising partners." In 2016, Spotify began selling its first-party mood data to WPP, one of the world's largest global marketing firms; in 2023, the companies reaffirmed their "ongoing synergies" with a new partner-ship, promising that WPP would make first-party Spotify data available to its clients. As part of the partnership, WPP would also revamp Spotify's Neuro-Insight research into "client-specific" repackaging, working with a global media services company called Mindshare.[7]

When I spoke with Rossetti, I told him about something that had been stumping me for years. I find issues of privacy and surveillance to be deeply important, but I also suspect that Spotify seriously inflates its own capabilities. Was criticizing their invasive, surveillance-driven advertising practices actually contributing to the hype? It seemed like a lose-lose situation. If the company is capable of all of the hyper-invasive practices it boasts about, that is obviously harmful. But if it sells adver-tisers on targeting it is not capable of, that also seems harmful, because it contributes to the normalization of surveillance and deception. How do you simultaneously say its recommendations are bad and the surveillance is too invasive?

Actually, the question itself gets to the core of the issue. The very fact that we don't know proves that these companies have violated our privacy. "There is a problem of asymmetry," Rossetti told me. "Because they know a lot, and you don't know what they know, and you don't know what they're doing with what they know." As he explained, the whole data protection framework in the EU, the General Data Protection Regulation (GDPR), exists in part because of this, in his words, "asymmetry of control, asymmetry of power." GDPR was put into law in 2018; there is no federal equivalent law in the U.S., but some states have passed versions locally. In the EU, GDPR maintains that because of this asymmetry, individuals are entitled to have rights aimed at reducing this gap. It mandates the right of access: an individual can ask a data controller, like Spotify, Apple, or Amazon, to deliver them a copy of the data they have stored on the individual. Other rights include the right to erasure, also known as the right to be forgotten, and the right to rectification, where users can require the service to rectify incorrect information on them. (In theory, maybe an entire EU-based micro music scene could even coordinate to exercise its right to be forgotten by the "Every Noise" map.)

If the user feels that the data provided is incomplete, they have the right to go to a Data Protection Authority or to a court and start a case against the company, and to have the matter investigated. When Rossetti's organization made its first Spotify data requests post-GDPR, it received back only sparse information related to listening history. "They gave us what playlists we had, how many times we listened to a song," he told me. "But [not] the profiles they had created on us and that they would in turn sell or share with data brokers for advertising purposes." NOYB suspected this might be a violation of the law, so they filed a complaint with the Swedish Authority for Privacy Protection (previously known as the Swedish Data Protection Authority). Around this time, NOYB also began requesting data from other tech giants—Google, Meta, Apple, Amazon, and more—to make sure companies were operating in compliance. Most of them weren't. With the Spotify case, the Swedish privacy authorities remained "absolutely silent" for nearly four years, Rossetti told me, after which point a Swedish court ordered them to make a decision. Within a few months, in June of 2023, they fined Spotify 5 million euro and ordered them to bring their data processing operations into compliance, and expand their standards for making user data accessible. (US users can also now request versions of a data profile, as described.) "It's not perfect, but way better," he continued. "We won this case."

Spotify calls its mass data collection practices "streaming intelligence," a term that, like the popular use of the phrase "artificial intelligence" by corporations today, is merely a way of reframing surveillance. As Meredith Whittaker, the President of the Signal Foundation, which runs the encrypted messaging platform Signal, noted in a 2023 conference talk, the artificial intelligence industry is but "an exacerbation of what we've seen since the late nineties and the development of surveillance advertising." That is certainly the case with Spotify, which under the guise of AI-powered recommendations has developed a surveillance apparatus driven by emotion profiling and pseudoscience.[8]

In 2018, Spotify applied for a patent for emotion detection technology, or more specifically, for a tool that would harvest a user's voice (in the context of, for example, an Alexa-like prompt) and decipher "intonation, stress, rhythm, and the likes of units of speech" so the "emotional state of the speaker" could be "detected and categorized." The patent, granted in 2021, also claimed it would create environments where "extractions of a user's changing emotion during a sequence of interactions" would be possible. Another 2018 patent saw Spotify signaling plans for "methods and systems for personalizing user experience based on [user] personality traits," drawing on mood, music tastes, and demographic to "correspond to different personality traits of a user." The patent explains how the company would create a "personality model" based on traits such as "openness, conscientiousness, extraversion, agreeableness, and neuroticism." These aren't Spotify's only creepy patents related to moods and emotions—it also aspires to create personalization tools based on user "nostalgia metrics," combining a user's age with their preferences for music from decades past, to estimate generational affinities—but these ones illustrate how connected Spotify has become to the bigger space of emotion detection AI and its surrounding controversy.[9]

"Emotion AI" is an area within artificial intelligence that deals in the collection and analysis of emotion and mood data, and attempts to simulate and respond to human emotions; since the nineties, it has sometimes been called "affective computing." These supposed "emotion detection technologies" often deal with the face, and sometimes are discussed as an offshoot of facial recognition tech, though certain companies specifically focus on voice and audio. In its 2019 annual report, the AI Now Institute, an accountability organization, put a microscope to the unfounded science upon which emotion recognition companies claim to be based; it called the rise of affect recognition a top concern "not only because it can encode biases, but because we lack a scientific consensus as to whether it can ensure accurate or even valid results," and made a strong recommendation for a regulatory ban on this tech "in important decisions that impact people's lives and access to opportunities." Despite issues of privacy, profiling, and bias, some commercial applications of emotion AI have reached the market in recent years, in advertising, customer service, health, and other industries. According to one estimate, the global "emotion detection and recognition market" was valued at $20.26 billion in 2021—and is projected to be triple that number by 2030.[10]

It might seem like *just music*, but streaming services are susceptible to what's called "surveillance creep," or "function creep." A surveillance system might start out with one purpose, but over time, its purpose might shift and expand beyond its original use case. We might know that a streaming app is watching our every move, but it's just to recommend us music, we think—and so, we are conditioned to consider it low stakes. So much so that when, for example, a music app starts also monitoring and mapping our voices, or tracking down our search engine activity off-app, maybe we don't even notice. Or, when it takes the most basic facts of our listening behavior and sells them to data brokers as "mood data," which they then use to assemble more complex profiles on us, maybe we don't even care. But these are fundamental violations of our privacy, and whether that right is encoded into law or not, it matters. The UK privacy advocacy group Privacy International puts it this way: "Privacy is how we seek to protect ourselves and society against arbitrary and unjustified use of power, by controlling what can be known about us and done to us, while protecting us from those who aim to exert control over our data, and ultimately all aspects of our lives." As the tech and music industries alike aspire to ever more invasive ways to extract data and profits from us, it's crucial to remember the bigger picture.[11]

What's more, privacy is just a basic human right, one that we should seek to protect wherever possible—not only for ourselves, but for others. Issues of privacy and surveillance do not fall on individuals equally; these are technologies of enforcement and discipline that tend to disproportionately target already marginalized and over-policed communities, especially communities of color. It is on all of us to fight for the human right to privacy, and to remember the distinct ways in which music communities have long been surveilled by the state: from the era of McCarthyism, when radical protest singers were stalked and jailed, to COINTELPRO infiltration of jazz, to the NYPD's fixation on hip-hop scenes, and beyond. Making music isn't a crime, but it's often been treated as such, and mass surveillance that comes with corporate platforms and AI systems needs to be fought in this context.

Another consideration is how streaming surveillance integrates AI practices into everyday life, rendering them commonplace, so that by the time more egregious applications of AI arrive, users are desensitized. Take this example: in January 2019, Spotify announced it would open up the algorithmic "Discover Weekly" playlist for brand sponsorships, with in-playlist ads. The first advertiser to jump on board was Microsoft, which used the opportunity to push its "Empowering Us All" campaign, advertising how its AI technology could make advancements in education, healthcare, and philanthropy. In a statement at the time, a Microsoft media rep said that its partnership with Spotify allowed it to spread its message about how the technology would "unlock human ingenuity . . . within a personalized entertainment experience powered by AI." Microsoft was specifically invested in associating its AI business with musicians at the time: the campaign also included a TV commercial where the musician Common walked around a city street performing a spoken-word poem about the opportunities of AI. This was all mere months after Microsoft had announced it would be selling its AI technologies to U.S. military and intelligence agencies.[12]

Microsoft is hardly alone in its military contracts. It matters that Daniel Ek has used his fortunes from Spotify, in part, to invest in AI militarism, through a 100 million euro investment in the German military-AI company Helsing, putting that company's valuation at 400 million euro. Helsing alleges to use its software to "assist battlefield operations" by using live data to "identify and assess multiple collected forms of data via sensors in order to assemble a picturesque viewpoint which military agents could then use at their discretion." Ek sits on the board of Helsing, and has publicly advocated for the expansion of investment in its technology. In 2022, he coauthored an op-ed for *Politico* arguing in favor of what he dubbed "New Defense," urging for a new wave of AI military companies. The piece was riddled with tech-culture buzzwords, calling out the need for defense contractors to be "digital natives" with "agile and iterative development practices." It should go without saying that many musicians would prefer the profits made from circulating their work did not fuel the war machine, as was evidenced most recently by the United Musicians and Allied Workers' 2024 "War Profiteers Out of Music" campaign.[13]

Years into its normalization of everyday streaming surveillance, and despite how much information Spotify already has on its users, its appetite has not been satiated. In late 2023, Spotify's head of innovation smirked on stage at a summit hosted by BlackBerry, nearly laughing as he talked about how users were so "spooked" and "scared" about giving up their personal data. "We had insane rebellion when we just asked for location permissions," he said, seeming to feign disbelief. "Even those little things scare people, let alone trying to introduce things that . . ." He trailed off, before launching into an explanation of how Spotify can detect and target users based on moods and sentiments. "That kind of stuff tends to spook people, so I think it's . . . how do you make it digestible and slow roll it?"[14]

13

The First .0035 Is the Hardest

What is a stream worth? For years, a rough figure has circulated in conversations about just how poorly artists are faring in the streaming economy: $0.0035 per stream. This infuriates players across the record industry—because, technically, the very idea of this number is meaningless. Spotify does not pay artists per stream, but rather through a complex pro rata revenue share system. And in fact, Spotify does not directly pay artists: it pays "rights-holders," entities like record labels, distribution companies, and aggregators, which maintain deals with Spotify on behalf of artists—deals that vary depending on the negotiating power each company holds with the streaming service. Still, on a conceptual or perhaps even spiritual level, the $0.0035 figure has played an important role: it has helped publicly communicate the reality of what most musicians earn from streaming services, which is basically nothing. As the long-running punk label Don Giovanni Records has quipped, referencing the even lower average rates paid by YouTube, these days, "the first 0.0014 is the hardest."[1]

The penny-fractions discourse also tells us something else: over fifteen years into the era of music streaming, most artists and listeners cannot explain how the value of a stream is calculated. The U.S. Congresswoman Rashida Tlaib estimated in 2023 that it would take over eight hundred thousand streams per month to make the equivalent of a $15/hour job. But as a representative of the United Musicians and Allied Workers (UMAW) told me in an interview, an outsized percentage of working musicians cannot accurately delineate what percentage of their income comes from streaming, simply due to the absurdly complicated nature of the system. This problem of explainability is part of the record industry's long tradition of keeping artists in the dark; when industry execs say that *it is all just too hard to explain*, that's also how artists are disempowered by the so-called expert class.

Despite all the complexity, one former employee insisted the impact was clear: "A child could understand what they're doing and how it's hurting artists."

Spotify makes its pro rata payments on a monthly basis, paying labels and distros based on not their catalog's number of streams, but the percentage that number comprises of the total streams that occurred on Spotify within the month. If a major label's catalog accounts for 20 percent of all streams on Spotify that month, then that label is owed 20 percent of the royalty pool. It might seem simple enough, but the number of factors shaping every step of that equation is dizzying. "We have per-stream and per-user royalty calculations," wrote an employee on an internal Slack channel. "Each product-market-licensor combo has a unique royalty calculation." Other complications are the systemic payola-like practices that exist through various "promotional rates" that labels or distribution companies might accept on an artist's behalf, meaning that companies have agreed to accept a lower royalty rate in exchange for promotion on the app.[2]

On a very fundamental level, though, pro rata is a system that benefits music that generates massive numbers of plays, whether that be through big marketing budgets, viral hits, or background-friendly streambait. In its 2021 report on music streaming, the UN's World Intellectual Property Organization argued that the "big pool" pro rata system means "major-label superstars tend to derive the bulk of the revenue from streaming platforms." This is a definitive flaw at the heart of streaming remuneration: not all music is meant to be streamed endlessly on loop, but that doesn't mean it should be rendered value-less.[3]

According to Hunter Giles, the cofounder of the royalty accounting company Infinite Catalog, whose clients include indie labels such as Merge, Polyvinyl, Topshelf, and others, the pro rata system creates a "layer of abstraction" that creates mass confusion among artists. "You lose so many people. It's not made clear by anybody," he told me. Giles is instead a proponent of streaming services shifting to "user-centric" models, wherein a user's monthly subscription fee would go directly to the artists they listen to: if I only listen to L'Rain and Kim Gordon, then after Spotify's cut, the remainder of my monthly fee would go to L'Rain and Kim Gordon (or, more precisely, their respective rights-holders). Musicians' unions and advocacy groups, like the UMAW and the UK-based Musicians' Union, have long called for streaming services to embrace user-centric models.

"Instead of one royalty pool, it's hundreds of millions of royalty pools," Giles continued. "It's a much harder task. But that's what computers are for. You can definitely do this. Pro rata was built because that was the easiest way to get from A to B, and it was an acceptable system for the original majors and Merlin. But we've seen in the fifteen years that it's been around that it can be abused. Pro rata is too esoteric. It's just one too many calculations. And that has served as a very effective sort of smoke screen."

The precise calculation that Spotify uses to allocate royalties is sometimes explained as "Net Revenue x Share x Pro Rata." Net revenue is the total money brought in from subscribers, minus certain taxes and fees. The net revenue must then be divided three ways, with (1) one share going to Spotify, and a share each for the two types of royalties that streaming services pay: (2) to the recording rights-holders, and (3) to the publishing rights-holders. Recording rights-holders own a particular recording of a song, while publishing rights-holders own the composition of the song itself. (When a person writes a song—puts, for example, a combination of notes, lyrics, or a melody on paper and then publishes that work—then regardless of who later records the song, that original songwriter is entitled to some degree of compensation.) The calculation of publishing royalties is complicated; for streaming, these are often mandated by law—in the U.S., for subscription services, it's a percentage of what the recording rights-holders get—and the streaming companies have long lobbied in DC against these rates increasing. And as it happens, the vast majority of the publishing market is controlled by the same companies that control the recording market: Universal, Sony, and Warner.[4]

Another complicating factor is that the share of net revenue that comprises the Spotify recording royalty pool, from which pro rata payouts are then calculated, is determined by individual deal negotiations: for example, one contract might determine the pool to be 50 percent of net revenue, where another contract might determine the pool to be 60 percent of net revenue. This is but one of the aspects of the streaming royalty equation that remain mystifying due to the top-secret, black box contracts major rights-holders have with streaming companies. Several studies and music industry sources confirm, though, that the average split tends to land with around 52 percent going to the labels. From there, that 52 percent is split on the pro rata basis according to usage data, with reports also supplied to the rights holders listing how many streams went to each artist.[5]

The way in which each stream is weighted in the pro rata equation is affected by all sorts of factors: What country did a stream come from? What plan tier—free, standard, student, duo, family—did a stream come from? When an artist is paid from a premium stream, payment is calculated as a percentage of subscription money; when an artist is paid from a free stream, payment is calculated as a percentage from ad revenues. The plan tier also impacts payments in part because, despite the fact that a lesser amount of revenue might go into the royalty pool from users on discounted plans, major labels have negotiated themselves mandatory minimum payouts per user that other rights-holders are unable to command.

Once the rights-holder receives its payout from Spotify, it in turn pays artists according to their own deals, which also varyingly contribute to the ultimate size and fairness of the payments that artists receive. Typically when an artist signs with a label, they'll get a royalty advance—essentially a loan paid back through future royalties, which they use to fund the making of the record—after which the label will also get a percentage of future royalties for the course of an agreement, in exchange for marketing, promotion, and other services. Major labels tend to offer big advances in exchange for big cuts. Independent record labels tend to offer smaller advances, but there is a deep tradition of indies adhering to a fifty-fifty split after expenses for the duration of a contract. Streaming has blurred many of these lines though: some bigger indie labels will take larger cuts these days, while some major labels over the years have been pressured to offer less exploitative terms.

There is so much more about the nature of streaming royalties that remains unknown to the public. But some additional details have come to light over the years. The UK Music Managers Forum, in the 2020 edition of its book on the modern royalty system, *Dissecting the Digital*

Dollar—drawing on a survey of fifty artist managers, working with artists across all three majors and over one hundred independent labels—confirmed that the majors are often "guaranteed certain income based on consumption oblivious to the streaming service's revenues," in addition to "other kickbacks." But even to such insiders, streaming royalties can be opaque. Due to NDAs, nearly all recording artists are prohibited from reviewing the contracts their labels and distributors have struck with streaming services, and are often operating in the dark. "Because of the total lack of transparency, you often don't know the question you need to ask—and that's the big problem," one anonymous music manager says in *Dissecting the Digital Dollar*. "If you don't know what's going on you can't properly assess how the label arrived at x, y or z." Another study, aptly titled "Streaming in the Dark" and published in 2023 by the DC think tank Public Knowledge, came to a similar conclusion: that the "NDA curtain" was preventing meaningful reforms to streaming royalties.[6]

This is all to say: the digit on an artist's royalty statement is much more complicated than a per-stream rate. And artists are almost always systematically shut out of any sort of transparency around the calculations creating their livelihoods.

For almost as long as Spotify has existed, artists have been showing their receipts detailing the penny fractions they're paid and calling for something to change. In the fall of 2011, just a couple of months after Spotify launched in the U.S., the *LA Weekly* ran a blog post about indie labels that had decided there was "no upside" to being on Spotify. The following year, the musician and writer Damon Krukowski penned "Making Cents" for *Pitchfork*, a widely read status check on how artists were faring in the brave new "better-than-piracy" era. Krukowski explained in detail how his former band Galaxie 500, an influential dreampop trio who released classic albums on Rough Trade Records in the late eighties and early nineties, was paid for 5,960 quarterly streams of its single "Tugboat": on the publishing side, they'd made $1.05, and on the recording side, an estimated $9.18. Split among three members, that was approximately $3.17 each.[7]

At the time, Spotify told Krukowski that he should check with his record label to see where the money went, he recalled to me in an interview. "I am the record label," he told them. The band had been in control of its own catalog for years, and for years, they'd watched royalties from record sales decline; not just since the dawn of Spotify, but from the launch of Apple's iTunes Store. "It looked terrible from the start," he said of the general Spotify payment model. It was a serious moment of reckoning over how he might sustain life as a musician going forward, with his current band, Damon & Naomi. "There are moments when you feel like you can see a way forward. But in 2012, it was *What the hell are we going to do? Where do we go from here?* Those first Spotify checks came in, and we were just like, *Oh, this is not going to work.*"

When Krukowski published "Making Cents," he was navigating unfamiliar terrain: he had recently taken his first-ever full-time office job, writing wall text and catalog copy for a museum. For Krukowski, declining album sales and the dawn of streaming meant getting a second job. He wasn't alone. In the streaming era, it's practically a given that working, independent musicians have additional, non-music-related income. In a 2019 piece for *Vulture*, the music journalist Larry Fitzmaurice interviewed over a dozen considerably well-known independent musicians about what they were actually doing to make ends meet: teaching, making coffee, email marketing, truck driving, the list went on. "Any other job makes more money than being in a band," New Zealand dreampop songwriter Tamaryn told Fitzmaurice. "Even if you're working full-time at McDonald's, you're gonna make more money than a lot of my peers. The industry structure is built against the artist. It's not a lucrative dream. I still consider it a total privilege and luxury to be an artist. It's not something that makes me money." In the same article, Ryan Mahan, of the Matador-signed post-punk group Algiers, whose day job is in refugee advocacy, put it this way: "Until people in the creative arts are recognized as cultural laborers deserving of a living wage that supports their work, we'll be forced to have multiple jobs."[8]

There has been no shortage of anecdotes like this in the streaming era, documenting the struggles musicians face in attempting to piece together a living. In 2023, the first-ever UK Musicians' Census pointed toward some hard numbers. Conducted by the UK Musicians' Union and the nonprofit organization Help Musicians, it surveyed six thousand musicians and found that the average annual income from music work was 20,700 pounds, but that nearly half of musicians earned under 14,000 pounds annually. Over half of the musicians surveyed sustained their career with a form of income outside the music industry. And 44 percent reported "a lack of sustainable income [as] a barrier to their music career."[9]

This tracked with earlier smaller-scale studies. A 2018 study conducted by the Princeton University Survey Research Center, in partnership with MusiCares, surveyed 1,227 musicians in the U.S. and found that the median musician earned between $20,000 and $25,000 per year from a mix of music and non-music jobs. The most common sources of music-related income were live events and teaching lessons; and while over a quarter of the respondents earned some income from streaming, it amounted to less than 5 percent of their music-related income. Sixty-one percent said "their music-related income was not sufficient to meet their living expenses."[10]

"When I started making records, the model of economic exchange was exceedingly simple: make something, price it for more than it costs to manufacture, and sell it if you can," Krukowski wrote in his 2012 *Pitchfork* piece. "The model now seems closer to financial speculation." It was a prescient assessment. As the financial picture has grown increasingly bleak for musicians, the streaming era has led many to opt to put their royalties up for sale to the highest bidder, creating something like a stock market for streaming royalties.

Through the late 2010s and early 2020s, a whole industry developed around the buying, selling, and exploiting of streaming royalties as an asset class. There are consumer-facing marketplaces like Royalty Exchange, where artists can auction off their rights, and SongVest, which describes itself as a marketplace for purchasing "fractional shares of music royalties" from songs and artists: "Buy SongShares® of your favorite hit songs and earn royalties as they accrue." SongVest is also part of a royalty advance loan shark market that offers musicians up-front cash for their future royalty streams. Yet another player in that business is Utopia Music, through its "Accelerate" product, which claims to "empower creators with the financial autonomy they need to succeed in their careers by providing a risk-free solution to deliver accelerated royalty payments." On a much larger scale, private equity companies have snatched up pop star song catalogs, leading to the development of companies like the Hipgnosis Songs Fund, which were buying up rights for hundreds of millions of dollars during the pandemic, ushering in what some called a whole new era of music industry financialization encouraged by streaming. Some have pointed to this dynamic as a sign that recorded music's value has returned, but the reality is more grim: a lot of artists are really just desperate.

As independent artists have come to terms with the state of streaming, some have pondered this question: Is $0.0035 really better than nothing? It's one thing to make nothing from the free circulation of your work, but it's another to make nothing while Daniel Ek and Martin Lorentzon become billionaires, and the majors earn higher and higher revenues. Another reckoning came in late 2023 when Spotify announced a substantial update to its royalty system. In a supposed attempt at fighting fraud, it would be demonetizing various types of white noise and "non-music content." In addition, the new model also would demonetize any track garnering fewer than one thousand streams annually—an estimated 86% of the tracks on the platform, to which Spotify now seemed to say, *Actually, we do think this is worth nothing.*[11]

Fighting against the AI-muzak profiteers was understandable enough, but the music business seemed fine to throw all types of independent and DIY artists under the bus along the way. That's because the new royalty system wasn't as much about fighting fraud as it was about protecting major label market share. As it turned out, the new royalty scheme was part of a campaign waged by Universal Music Group to revamp streaming in its favor. Starting in 2022, major label revenue growth had slowed, and major label streamshare was reportedly declining. While major label revenues had been increasing by 20–40 percent annually for several years, in 2022, that number only grew by 5 percent, to $13.2 billion, and major label stream-share was down from 85 to 75 percent, according to MIDiA Research. UMG—which owns 40 percent of the recorded music market—wasn't about to concede that type of market share to anyone.

As UMG CEO Lucian Grainge wrote in his annual address to employees in January 2023, the company wanted to divert revenue away from the "ocean of noise" on streaming and toward "professional" musicians. The major labels called "amateurs, bots and white noise" producers "bad actors." But this fight was incredibly broad: the new policies did not sufficiently define "amateurs," and instead effectively grouped DIY artists and what they called "hobbyists" in with all sorts of scammers and bot-makers. Still, the industry embraced a new plan devised by UMG to divert royalties away from low-streaming tracks, starting with the French streaming service Deezer in the summer of 2023. They deemed it "artist-centric" streaming—a misleading title, for many reasons—and the business press called it the first major update to the royalty system since Spotify's debut in 2008. After the "artist-centric" system was announced, JP Morgan forecasted that UMG's revenue from streaming would lift by 9 percent. According to the *Financial Times*, in 2023, when UMG and Spotify renegotiated their deal, "UMG made Spotify's participation in the 'artist-centric' process a stipulation of that agreement."[12]

In the fall of 2023, Spotify announced that it, too, would adopt UMG's new model. In the press release, Spotify said the new royalty system would help take on those who were "gaming the system with noise" and specifically called out "functional" genres as part of the problem—declaring that in the streaming era "white noise, nature sounds, machine noises, sound effects, non-spoken ASMR, and silence recordings" had become popular content to play on loop for hours, and how this was being "exploited by bad actors" who cut their tracks into thirty-second clips to maximize profits. That statement wasn't *wrong* per se, but it certainly didn't cover the full scope of how functional music permeated the platform, or the full scope of how it was affecting artists. Come 2024, Spotify committed to requiring functional noise recordings to be streamed for two minutes to generate a royalty, and said it would start to "work with licensors to value noise streams at a fraction of the value of music streams." It all sure did sound familiar—kind of like the PFC program, even. Ultimately fraud tracks would then make a fraction of what they were making before, "freeing up that extra money to go back into the royalty pool for honest hard-working artists," Spotify wrote in a press release. "It also creates a more fair playing field for artists in these functional genres, by eliminating the perverse incentive to cut tracks artificially short with no artistic merit, at the expense of listener experience." What wouldn't be eliminated, though, were the secret, privileged partnerships with select functional music companies.

The news of the new royalty structure spread as quickly as its critiques. It became clear that this move wouldn't just be impacting AI bots—it seemed like the majors were waging an attack on not only all sorts of DIY and "amateur" musicians, but also artists working with noise, field recordings, and nature sounds. A whole range of musical traditions and practices was set to be affected. Meanwhile, UMG CEO Grainge called critics of the "artist-centric" plan "merchants of garbage" releasing "content that no one really actually wants to listen to." CEOs are by nature often disconnected from reality, but this really put it on display.[13]

One label that was particularly concerned about this new royalty system was Smithsonian Folkways Recordings, the nonprofit record label founded as Folkways in 1948 and absorbed into the Smithsonian Institution Center for Folklife and Cultural Heritage in 1987. "What we have here at Folkways is a collection of sounds, and expressions of culture, from all over the world," its curator and director, Maureen Loughran, told me. According to Loughran, over 50 percent of the Folkways catalog will be demonetized by the royalty model update. Some of these tracks didn't meet the thousand-stream threshold, but some were part of Folkways' robust collection of field and nature recordings, which Spotify and other streaming services were now deeming "non-music noise content."

Loughran pointed to a classic Folkways record that had recently been reissued on vinyl as part of the label's seventy-fifth anniversary celebrations: *Sounds of North American Frogs*. "That is an underground hit for us," she said. "People love this record." She also pointed to another Folkways classic, the 1964 record *Sounds of the Office*, which makes a collage of sounds many office workers today might find obscure: the electric typewriter, bookkeeping machines, addressographs. "The sounds of the office are very different today. It creates a whole universe of imagination about how people lived their lives in that moment," she explained. "Obviously that is not going to hit one thousand streams on the DSPs, but that's not its function. Its function is to tell a story about a certain moment in time, and having that accessible to people is important."

The issue was not just about the demonetization—these are, to be sure, not records that Folkways ever planned to get rich from—but a broader delegitimization of the history and integrity of the catalog that comes from the songs being deemed "spam," and how that positions them within the broader music landscape. According to Loughran, the label's responsibility is not just turning a profit, but acting as responsible stewards of an archive. That means ensuring accountability for the royalties—which go to the families of the artists in the archive—but also that the recordings are properly contextualized: "This affects a whole heritage of music and families that we have a responsibility to as the stewards of this collection."

Like many other independent record labels, Smithsonian Folkways maintains an educational mission that can often be at odds with the values of the entertainment industry. On our call, I read off the names of some playlists that Folkways-affiliated greats appeared on, like the legendary blues guitarist Lightnin' Hopkins being featured on the official Spotify playlist "pov: you sold your soul to the devil" (description: "down at the crossroads you made a pact in the name of rock and roll"). "I can hear every musicologist just throwing all their books out the window now," Loughran said with a laugh, before clarifying: "You don't want to indict a whole generation's ability to discover music. That might be the door that they open to get here and then they create other ways of engaging. But I do think it detaches the context. Was the artist's intention to produce that vibe? Most likely not. And you could misinterpret what an artist is trying to present just because you think it fits some emotional point you are trying to put together."

"If somebody is engaging in the catalog because it gives them a *vibe*, but then they don't understand that the track has a cultural function within a community and a society, that is disrespectful, to engage with it as though it's just sound, it's just vibes," she continued. "Maybe it's ceremonial, maybe it's something of an important community tradition, and we're just removing all of that context from it because we just like the way it sounds." As an antidote, Folkways had recently launched its own subscription option, where albums stream from its website alongside elaborate liner notes and artwork.

The music industry's focus on stamping out individual scammers can often seem like merely an attempt to distract from the systemic grift of it all—of streaming, of platform capitalism, but also the oligopoly of the recorded music business, period, and how it constantly finds new ways to extract more and more from musicians and listeners. The dawn of streaming may have been, at times, a contentious collaboration between the old bosses (majors) and the new bosses (technology corporations). But it was still a collaboration. The goal was corporate profits, not establishing a fair system for artists. In the years to come, this core discrepancy would reveal itself over and over. At a music conference in 2019, Spotify executive Jim Anderson appeared on a panel, after which a concerned musician stood up during the Q&A to ask about the financial model, and whether it was fair to artists. A disgruntled Anderson replied: "The problem was to distribute music. Not to give you money, okay?"[14]

Spotify's public representatives have been inconsistent in their messaging about fair pay, sometimes claiming, like Anderson, that artists should just be grateful for whatever exposure and crumbs they receive, while other times claiming fair compensation to be one of the company's core missions. Anderson's comments came just a year after Daniel Ek stood on a stage in Stockholm giving his usual spiel for the company's pre-IPO Investor Day. It was March 2018, one month before Spotify would go public on the New York Stock Exchange, and the company was holding a live-streamed video event to sway potential shareholders. Standing before a neon-green screen, Ek, then thirty-five, ran through his standard talking points: about the promise of streaming, about fairness for musicians, and his favorite, "leveling the playing field."

"For us, the most important day isn't our listing day," he said into a cordless headset, before debuting the company's new mission statement. "It's the day after and the day after that. This is when we'll continue the hard work of helping *one million artists to be able to live off of their art.*" Spotify's mission had never been coherent, but on that day in 2018, it allegedly became this. But how far off was it? And more importantly: What constituted the ability to "live off of" music to Spotify?[15]

"First of all, that mission is incredibly vague," one former Spotify employee told me, in an interview. "What does that mean? Does that mean living wage? Also what is their work? Is their work *music* or other things? I found that to be a very vague ambition."

Internally, Spotify actually does have a system for attempting to quantify this: "artist tiers." On the company's backend for assessing playlists and general artist data, every artist is assigned a number: Tier 0, Tier 1, Tier 2, Tier 3, and so on. The tiers are based on how much money an artist *generates* in royalties each year—the phrasing is specifically attuned to the fact that Spotify actually does not know how much artists ultimately get paid, since it pays their rights-holders, not the artists directly. Tier 0 artists are superstars, generating over $5 million per year in royalties. Tier 1 artists span a massive range, between $500,000 and $4.9 million. Tier 2 is similarly wide-ranging: artists generating between $50,000 and $500,000 per year. "The threshold for where artists are starting to be able to make a living sits in Tier 3," a staffer wrote in a company Slack chat. And while the Tier 3 range spans between $5,000 and $49,000, the "typical" Tier 3 artist generates an average of $13,500 per year. "This is where the future professional artists reside in 2023," the chat message continued.

In 2022, Spotify publicly estimated that approximately two hundred thousand "professional or professionally aspiring" artists existed on its platform and that more than a quarter of them made over $10,000 that year; they suggested that because Spotify accounts for one-third of the streaming market, and 20 percent of the recorded music market, these artists must have made $40,000 total from recordings—also suggesting that their own equation for whether an artist is "able to live off of" streaming factors in what they assume the artist must be making from other sources.[16]

Even on the higher end of Spotify's floor for being "able to live off of their art," in its various estimations, these are sums that would be meaningful, in most cases, for individual solo artists, self-releasing their music. Indeed, the tier system, in general, does not seem to account for musicians working with teams—whether that be songwriting collaborators, bandmates, producers, or record labels of any scope, all of which would dramatically impact the profits reaching the actual musicians behind a given artist moniker. This is a crucial distinction: when streaming services issue scraps of payments, this does more than ensure the precarity of artists' livelihoods. These financial realities also shape the image of the streaming era's model musician, systematically pushing artists toward staunch individualism.

14

An App for a Boss

"My job is to make them feel like they can grow," I am told by a member of Spotify's "Creator" team—the department within the company that exists to interface directly with artists, podcasters, and other "creators." The specific choice of words is striking: how the employee describes the job not as *helping* artists grow, but *making them feel like* they can grow. "It sounds corny, but we are always thinking about how to make a tool that will increase creator sentiment. We care about making them feel like they can have a good experience on Spotify. That they can make money, and that it's worth the effort." This is part of what the record industry has long sold to young hopefuls: the excitement of feeling like in the future they, too, could make it big. Spotify's emphasis on selling the *feeling* of potential also reflects a broader tendency of 2010s platform capitalism: the prevalence of hope labor, a term that academics have used to frame the aspirational work that users do for free in hopes that it will lead to future work. In a sense, it is not too dissimilar from the classic assumption that artists of all types ought to be grateful to work for exposure while someone higher up the chain profits.

The "Creator" team is the department that houses Spotify for Artists, or S4A as it's called internally, the program through which the company sells artists on the general idea of streaming. In a more direct sense, S4A is also where it pushes artists to save their credit card information and purchase advertisements. A lot can be understood about the Spotify model by understanding how the company sells itself to musicians—whom the company sees as a type of customer more so than as workers creating the valuable material it circulates. Spotify has long referred to itself as a "two-sided marketplace," where on one side it sells a product to listeners, and on the other side it sells a product to musicians and podcasters. This conveniently overlooks its business selling advertisements and user data, which arguably comprises a third "side" to the marketplace, commodifying attention harvested through the other two "sides."

The creators-as-customers dynamic is not exclusive to Spotify, but it has only intensified on the platform over the years: as Spotify has clamored to find new revenue streams, it has doubled down on creating new promotional products to sell to musicians, both through the direct sale of advertisements, like when an artist or label might buy a banner or pop-up to promote a new single, and through "promotional opportunities" offering exposure in exchange for lower royalty rates. As a former employee put it: "The mission was basically, how do we create new revenue streams from this relatively untapped source?" Artists. Fittingly, while its artist-specific pop-up ad product, "Marquee," is often pitched as a "creator tool" within the Spotify for Artists program, internally it is housed within the "Native Ads" department. Internally, the company refers to the mission to make artists into customers as "Marketplace."

Spotify for Artists was first launched as a PR tool. It appeared in 2013 as a stand-alone website, offering an explanation of the royalty system and introducing the launch of "Fan Insights," an analytics dashboard for artists and managers. Its blog launched the following year; the very first post in its archive was penned by Daniel Ek himself. It was November 14, shortly after the Taylor Swift catalog disappeared from the service, and an op-ed by Swift in the *Wall Street Journal* explained her supposed motives: "I'm not willing to contribute my life's work to an experiment that I don't feel fairly compensates the writers, producers, artists, and creators of this music." And so Ek took to the pages of artists.spotify.com to reply. "Taylor Swift is absolutely right: music is art, art has real value, and artists deserve to be paid for it," he wrote. "We started Spotify because we love music and piracy was killing it." Forgetting, it seems, that Spotify had been launched as an ad-tech product in search of a "traffic source," which happened to eventually become music. "So all the talk swirling around lately about how Spotify is making money on the backs of artists upsets me big time," he continued.[1]

S4A was relaunched as a stand-alone app in 2016, and in the pre-IPO years, the program grew, eventually becoming more of a content resource, with video interviews and blog posts commissioned from music journalists. The S4A blog was produced by a content agency called Third Bridge Creative, which notes on its website that after purchasing their services, "Spotify for Artists measured an 18 point uptick in Artist Sentiment score among artists who engaged with our content." This was the whole point of S4A: making artists feel better about an extractive media product that existed to enrich major labels and tech executives.[2]

The model musician depicted in the pages of the S4A blog was the one most benefiting from the financial system: the solo creative. "It's almost like propaganda," a former employee of the Spotify Creator team told me. "The way they discuss artistry is almost always individuals. . . . It's not communal." To substantiate this ex-employee's claims, I reviewed the S4A website in detail, making a list of every artist featured for its first three years of existence. I found over 70 percent of the artists featured on its blog were solo acts. As I write in 2024, there are six artists featured on the front page of the Spotify for Artists website, and they are all solo individuals.

The S4A app is designed like a little command center, displaying streaming statistics and offering portals for pitching songs to playlists and launching (paid) promotional campaigns. "25 people listening right now," read the top of the home screen when I logged into an artist's account one afternoon. Along the side of the screen were stats from the past seven days: the number of listeners, streams, followers, top songs, and the playlists that drove the most traffic to those songs. Then there was a feed of self-help guides for aspiring musicians: a "fan study" ("What can super listeners do for you?") and a guide to Spotify success ("Find your path to progress . . . you choose your goals."). Another guide promised that artists can "learn how fans discover [their] music with Made To Be Found," linking off to a study on the "three pathways to get discovered on Spotify": playlists made by editors, playlists made by algorithms, playlists made by users.

The app's primary function, though, is breaking down those stats into tabs for "music" and "audience" data. On the music side, there are metrics for each release: streams, listeners, views, saves. On the audience side, there are "segments," "demographics," "location," and "release engagement."

There are metrics for listeners, streams, streams-per-listener, saves, playlist adds, and followers. There are some charts and graphs, like ones displaying the artist's listenership demographics by gender and age. "You have 806,806 listeners on your total audience on Spotify," read the "audiences" tab on the account I reviewed. "This is the total number of unique listeners from the last two years. It is the sum of all listeners in your active, previously active, and programmed audiences." Part of the reason this number is displayed is to sell artists on ways to "re-engage" that total listenership.

It's a lot to parse. In part, providing all of this data is how platform companies sell "creators" on the feeling that they are in control, and not the other way around. It's part of how platforms distract from the grim reality that these tools are governed by programs and policies completely out of the "creator's" purview. And what Spotify doesn't actively emphasize to artists is that in the process of guiding them through their "audience segments," it also logs their own behavior on the Spotify for Artists app, from which it in turn creates its own "segments" of artists, too, tracking patterns so it can figure out how to best sell Spotify ad space to them. In one internal report, S4A staff broke down the different types of artist app users into different archetypes: What features are they using? What stats are they interacting with? What are they spending? For the musicians, it may have felt like they were tracking their listeners, but the company was tracking them, too.

The "creator" is a twenty-first-century invention. According to the internet culture reporter Taylor Lorenz, the term was coined by YouTube in 2011 as an attempt to rebrand the concept of the "YouTube star," the phrase that had taken hold to that point describing its power-users. But the platform companies needed a term that could encompass not just YouTubers who were famous already, but YouTubers who hoped to become famous. The creator is related to, but not exactly the same as, the "influencer," a phrase more synonymous with Instagram, social media users with big followings who turn their whole lives into advertisements, building audiences and then selling them to brand sponsorships. Creators are also not to be confused with "creatives," whose work has more to do with corporate branding, design, and advertising—as I was reminded by one Spotify employee, who repeatedly corrected me during one interview, while I struggled, at first, to understand the difference. Ultimately, the concepts of the "creator" and the "influencer" both contributed to reimagining the position of the musician in the platform era.[3]

Creator is sometimes thought to be short for "content creator," which might be a fitting designation for YouTubers and influencers, but there are stark implications for the blurring of art and content. It's worth remembering what we're talking about when we're talking about the difference between the two. The dictionary definition for "content" is "things contained," or "that which is contained," but its Latin roots are in the word *continere*, which means "to surround, enclose, contain, or limit." I often think back to something that Jesse von Doom, the cofounder of now-defunct open-source platform CASH Music, told me once in an interview: "When you subjugate something and call it content, that means it's contained. I don't want art to be contained. I want it to be free and to run around and be weird and messy." It can seem like a mere semantic difference, but it's true: art-making and content-creating are different undertakings, not just spiritually, but also practically.

When music biz people talk about "the creator economy," they are usually talking about platforms like Patreon and Substack—software platforms that allow fans and followers (often rebranded as "communities") to directly pay or subscribe for content, with the idea that, after platform fees, a bigger percentage of that payment will land in the creator's bank account. This basic idea has spawned a billion-dollar industry, with creator platforms attracting venture capital investments in the 2020s; some business analysts claim the creator economy will be a $480 billion industry by 2027. In this sense, the idea of Spotify as a creator platform is murky: the company's own "creator" tools don't involve fans paying artists, but rather, artists paying the company.[4]

Still, the mythologies of the creator economy—build your brand, grow your audience, be your own boss, hustle—run deep in Spotify's messaging to artists. They are mythologies that intertwine and overlap with what was once called "the gig economy," referring to Uber, Grubhub, and other precarious app-based work. Selling artists on the gig economy is a particularly perverse dynamic: in some ways, musicians were the original gig workers, and in today's economy, the image of the free-agent musician who loves what they do, and trades job security for passion projects, is often deployed to soften the image of so-called gig work and its egregious labor model. "It's especially incumbent upon artists that we deeply analyze and be very critical of the current paradigm," the writer and filmmaker Astra Taylor once told me in an interview, "because the creative ethos is being used to bolster this very exploitative new form of capitalism." It is both bizarre and concerning that the music industry, in turn, sells this model and faux-independence back to artists today through "creator tools" and "artist services." When Spotify calls itself a "two-sided marketplace," it lays bare the similarities between today's musicians and gig workers more broadly: precarious work where your boss is an app.[5]

In 2017, just a year before the IPO, Spotify was at a crossroads. And it wasn't just manifesting in PFC. In an interview, a former employee, who was also working on the Creator team, explained it to me this way: "They were trying to decide whether or not they were going to invest in long tail creators and independent artists, thereby changing the way that value is exchanged in the music industry, or if they were going to invest in the system as it currently was, and uphold the industrial music system that has been evolving for one hundred years. Daniel Ek is an incredibly savvy businessman, and also had unlimited resources. He had this problem: Which way are we going to go? And he decided to fund both solutions simultaneously, and see which one won out. Ultimately, especially after going public, the industrial music system won."

The concept of the "long tail creator" harkens back to an idea first put forth by *Wired*'s Chris Anderson, first in a 2004 article and then in his 2006 book *The Long Tail*, suggesting that the internet would democratize culture by ushering in an era of niche, small-scale artists, demoting the cultural power of the superstar system. It argued that low-demand products could, in aggregate, amount to a larger market share than the blockbuster hits. And that this mass sea of obscure books, movies, and music would not just make culture more interesting—it would also be great for business. In the mid-2000s, this idea was very convincing to many tech entrepreneurs. Daniel Ek was hooked; before his company had launched in the U.S., a 2010 profile in the *Telegraph* reported that Ek was "so inspired" by *The Long Tail* that he gave out copies to the Spotify staff. Indeed, Ek's professed personal mission of "one million artists making a living off of their music" can feel like a randomly chosen target, but it makes more sense in this context—in fact, it seems like a mission statement that could have been written by Chris Anderson himself.[6]

Through 2017 and 2018, Ek and his teams invested heavily in "long tail creator"–facing initiatives, with a focus on so-called DIY and independent artists. Spotify bought Soundtrap, a Swedish music creation start-up. It bought a stake in DistroKid, one of the self-serve distribution companies that artists need to go through to get their work on Spotify and other platforms. And it piloted a program called "Direct," which allowed artists to upload music straight to the service, without the need for a distribution company at all. These were the years when Spotify unveiled a pop development incubator program, "RISE," and an event series for aspiring professional musicians, "Co.Lab."

Several Spotify employees I spoke with said they were shocked when this interest in supporting long tail creators segued into monetizing them. One former employee I spoke to recalled a story from 2018: "We had all flown out to Mexico for an off-site. Because they used to have these very lavish off-sites. And [there was] a presentation on the future of creators at Spotify. And it was all about monetizing their work. And the whole creative team was like, what the fuck. I remember that felt like a turning point, where suddenly people were realizing, there's a shift happening. . . . There was a creeping feeling that the company had lost any kind of moral center."

"If Spotify is guilty of something, they had the opportunity at one point to change the way value was exchanged in the music industry, and they decided not to," the former employee told me. "So it's just upholding the way that things have always been."

It's a fascinating insider's perspective, but it's also worth questioning whether the decision was truly made by Spotify, or forced by the majors. And it's also worth questioning who really would have benefited if the company had continued on its journey to become more like a massive record label. For some musicians, data-driven streaming platforms were already starting to feel like their bosses—their algorithms like disciplinary tools utilized by those seeking to control the marketplace.

In a 2020 media appearance, Daniel Ek asserted that "some artists that used to do well in the past may not do well in this future landscape, where you can't record music once every three to four years and think that's going to be enough. The artists today that are making it realize that it's about creating a continuous engagement with their fans. It is about putting the work in, about storytelling around the album, and about keeping a continuous dialogue with your fans."[7]

Ek was essentially telling artists to pull themselves up by their bootstraps and work harder, produce music faster, and to do it on terms amenable to the streaming industry: a constant drip of shorter, quick-hit releases to engagement-bait and trigger playlist algo-recs, rather than the thoughtful pace of album cycles past. In Ek's world, the model artist seemed to be one who was continuously pumping out new content, pitching playlists, gauging reception on the Spotify for Artists app, checking the stats, and responding to what moved the needle. And not only moved the needle, but moved the needle in an environment built entirely on Spotify's terms. At what point do these motions stop comprising an artistic endeavor and start becoming something entirely different?

Sure, that type of musical pace might work for some, but the suggestion that artists struggling to make a living under the platform era's harsh and anti-art conditions just needed to hustle and get with the program was unsurprisingly not received well.

"You are a Spotify employee at that point," Daniel Lopatin, the prolific producer and artist behind Oneohtrix Point Never, told me. "That's fine. But that's what it is. That's something other than just being in a band. That's being a multimedia marketing enterprise." Reflecting broadly on the different ways platform economics have shaped art-making, Lopatin asked a question that has stuck with me: "If your art practice is so ingrained in the brutal reality that Spotify has outlined for all of us, then what is the music that you're not making? What does the music you're not making sound like?"

Even seemingly small changes to the interface could create new work for artists wanting to keep up. For instance, in 2022 when Spotify's "Music Expression" team decided to revolutionize album art by introducing a type of track-specific looping-clip music video feature, artists suddenly had a new type of visual asset to produce for each new song. When in 2023 the company decided to revamp its app's home page to more closely imitate the experience of a TikTok feed, all of a sudden artists and their labels were expected to produce "clips"—short-form excerpts meant to stoke engagement. As ever, it was not just Spotify: when Apple decided to give "added weighting" to "spatial audio" tracks, suddenly artists needed to invest in new types of mixing and mastering to keep up. And following the rules did not guarantee success.

This is not even to mention other pressures artists were feeling to stay in their lanes. One independent musician told me that she felt like the nature of streaming algorithms made musicians hesitant to change their sounds, because so many factors in Spotify's algorithmic systems were determined at the artist level, and not the track or album level. "I don't think a massive sound shift from an artist is well served by Spotify. Once you're in the algorithm, it's hard to escape where you fit into. . . . The related artists are set," she said. This was yet another way in which artists' output was being shaped by the demands of their new artist-bosses: content is more valuable when it is manageable, when it more legibly fits advertiser-friendly categorization. It discouraged adventurousness.

Within the broader Spotify organization, S4A is just one team that interfaces with artists. For those with privileged access—with major label contracts or well-connected managers, for example—the vast majority of artist relations and marketing efforts will happen within the dedicated artist relations teams; S4A is where those activities get scaled for those without such direct lines of communication. But even for the artists whose distributors get direct access to an artist relations rep, the general feeling is still often mystification.

By 2018, a new tactic was becoming central to Spotify's artist relations strategy: Times Square billboards. If you follow a decent number of musicians—independent and mainstream alike—who regularly release new music, perhaps you've seen a photo like this roll across your Instagram feed. An artist stands in the glowing heart of New York City, surrounded by tourists and cops and Coca-Cola ads, looking up at their own giant face in disbelief. *Thank you so much @Spotify!!!* They were words music fans had become accustomed to reading; over the years, artist managers and labels would encourage artists to publicly thank Spotify and other streaming services whenever a song was added to a playlist, for example, in a feeble attempt at holding on to the attention of their streaming overlords.

The billboards—which also existed in London, L.A., and other cities—reflected something singularly strange though: an illusion of success in an era where whatever that meant was becoming obscure to many artists and fans alike. As the streaming era unfolded, quantifying success from media attention seemed increasingly arbitrary—ask anyone in the music biz what they think of using "monthly active users" or favorable press clippings as a barometer and they'll likely shrug. The billboards seemed to put forth something substantial. But speaking with label staffers whose artists have landed on the billboards is a fascinating little snapshot of the artist as customer in a moment of total spectacle.

If Spotify personalized playlists are, in part, meant to feed the contemporary social media user's unabating enthusiasm for moments of main character energy, then the Times Square billboards are meant to make the artist feel like their life is a movie. When I spoke to three different big indie label managers whose artists had landed on Spotify billboards in the past, they largely agreed that the value was more about having a photo of the band in front of the billboard than the actual billboard itself. "The actual exposure is questionable," one label manager told me. "It's one of those things that artists can show their parents, and be like, *Look at this, oh my god, I'm in Times Square, isn't that crazy?*" Another label manager shook his head and laughed at the idea that these billboards were actually leading to streams.

In a way, the billboards serve a similar function to the "Wrapped" campaign, in that they also almost guarantee an added Spotify social media marketing push from any artist featured: Who is going to get their face on a billboard and not hard post it to their Instagram grid? As one label manager explained it to me: "While we were there taking pictures with the billboard, there were definitely people who were like, *Oh my god, that's you guys!* And saying hello to the artists. But the actual growth is hard to quantify, especially because it goes up around or on the release day of a record. And naturally the release day is usually one of the strongest streaming days." Like other creator-facing efforts—the songwriting camps, the S4A blog posts—the billboards seemed more about selling Spotify to artists than selling artists to listeners, boosting "artist sentiment" via making a select few feel like celebrities for a day.

For one of the label managers I spoke with, landing a Spotify billboard was an arduous process. As one of her bands finished up their latest record, she started looking into the possibility of a Times Square billboard. As a smaller label, she wasn't sure if their pitch would be competitive enough. "All of these companies—Spotify, Amazon Music, YouTube—have billboards in Times Square that they will give to different artists," she explained. "Sometimes certain artists will have a royal flush, like Mitski or the Yeah Yeah Yeahs, where all three will support those records."

To start the process of pursuing a Spotify billboard, she reached out to the digital rep at her distributor, who is the point of contact for streaming relations. "The distributor reaches out to Spotify and says, look, this artist is a priority release, they've done really well on your platform in the past, we feel like they warrant this kind of marketing. Then we did a meeting with the Spotify rep. We made a deck with all of the information about past playlisting, past streaming, upcoming tour dates, past festivals they've played, glowing reviews, anything that paints an awesome picture of the band. And then we played a few songs, told them about the record, the timeline. And then we just kept emailing them, like, all the time."

Then it was just a waiting game. "They don't tell you until the week before," she explained. "So you're just kind of crossing your fingers for it." According to the label manager, even though the impact of the billboard is questionable, they do provide an opportunity that most labels couldn't afford on their own. Her label had once considered trying to rent a billboard themselves and researched the pricing. "It's usually thousands of dollars, but if a company rents it out for a month, then easily hundreds of thousands of dollars. It just depends where the billboard is and how long," she explained. Of course, it raises the question: What is Spotify doing spending hundreds of thousands on vanity billboards when it has barely ever turned a profit? The label manager wondered, too: "Where does this money come from? There are so many questions there."

Quite conspicuously, the Spotify billboards existed to advertise Spotify. "It's marketing for the service," Simon Wheeler, the director of global commercial strategy at the British record company Beggars Group, told me, reiterating that it's not just Spotify but all of the DSPs who are investing in these billboards. "The services have been pretty smart to get the artists to be one of their biggest marketing channels, really." In the end, it was a perfect symbol of the winner-take-all system; a materially meaningless gesture holding up the charade that the system totally worked.

15

Indie Vibes

There's this one Spotify for Artists blog post that has stuck with me for years. It's a 2018 profile of an instrumental guitarist named Lance Allen, whom Spotify describes as a family man from Tennessee, and calls independent "in the truest definition of the term." The post starts with an overview of the concept of DIY, calling it the "philosophical manifestation of punk," and describes artists getting in vans and sleeping on floors with a "back in the day"–type tone. *Now* DIY can look different, the post explains. It can look like Allen, whose life was changed forever when he was added to the official editorial playlist "Acoustic Concentration."[1]

Through the magic of playlists, and self-releasing via the distributor CD Baby, Allen was able to start paying his mortgage from Spotify checks, and eventually, after cracking 3 million monthly streams, even treated himself to a new Subaru Outback. Being added to "Acoustic Concentration" sent him down the rabbit hole: it led him to another official Spotify playlist, "Peaceful Guitar," and he "made it his life's mission to get on there, like a major-label radio promoter trying to crack a pop act on the commercial airwaves." Allen describes how he would look up the artists who were already on "Peaceful Guitar," see which user-generated playlists they were on, and pitch those curators to seed his music in the recommendation system. "I even created my own playlist with the same artists on there, and started marketing that on Instagram, because there's a lot of Spotify users on there," he explained in the blog post. He would pay for the social media ads out of pocket. His daily efforts paid off in June 2017, when he was added to "Peaceful Guitar," after which he began appearing on many other official editorial playlists, amassing millions of streams. When he realized there was playlist potential in recording instrumental pop covers, or alternative versions of songs angled toward different moods, he started recording those, too.

Spotify for Artists didn't only chronicle Allen's playlist hustling, but called his approach "a new set of tricks that every DIY artist should take note of." And Allen was hardly the only solo entrepreneur being used as an example of the model streaming-era independent artist. This was a time period when Spotify was doubling down hard on selling the meritocratic myth that enterprising individual artists could make careers for themselves with enough determination, grit, and playlist pitching. In reality, it was more like playing the slot machines and crossing your fingers: even Allen pointed out, in the article, that he had no idea how he got that first life-changing "Acoustic Concentration" placement, despite his extensive attempts to track down Spotify's editors.

In all of the time I've spent contemplating that blog post, I've never blamed Allen for trying to make the most of a convoluted system. Music is vast, and different approaches work for different artists; his approach could be viable for some, even if what's described can at times feel more like platform gamification than advice for running a sustainable DIY project. Rather than music culture, it was platform culture: norms and practices emerging because of specific platform demands rather than because of shared musical affinities or social connections between artists. Streaming wasn't making more room for independent music culture, per se, but rather shaping a new model of independent musician, reimagined by the platforms, optimized toward streaming success. And in time, even Allen's story would feel a bit like a cautionary tale.

"Independent music," taken literally, refers to music released on independent record labels, which can technically mean any label other than the majors. But historically, the idea of "independent music" that has loomed large in the popular imagination has evoked more. When we talk about independent music, we tend to also be talking about the alternative networks that exist separately from the mainstream record business: labels, yes, but also independent distributors, record shops, zines, blogs, radio stations, and venues, all catering to music that exists outside of, or sometimes in stark opposition to, the status quo of popular music; all equally vital in giving life to music culture.

To be sure, "independent music" isn't a monolith. For some, independence is a refusal—of commercialism, or of corporations, or of capitalism—while for others, it's just a stepping stone. Music scenes have long debated the meaning of words like "independent," "DIY," "community"—and not all who take on those labels live up to their promises. Some might even argue that independent music doesn't exist at all anymore. But at best, independent and DIY communities are places where these debates can occur, where there is some sense of purpose beyond the cold hard demands of the marketplace, where a diversity of practices can flourish. In my estimation, a defining characteristic of the classic independent record labels of the 1980s—like Dischord, an evergreen touchpoint for discussing independent values—had to do with the transparency and directness of the agreements, with the norm being a straightforward fifty-fifty split after expenses. Whether a label upholds that simple arrangement and lets artists retain ownership of their copyrights remains an important question, but not the only one.

Today, independent record labels remain crucial not just because they might offer up-front cash to underground artists to make records, but also because of the ways in which they help connect the dots within music scenes, like a grassroots glue across regional and aesthetically like-minded communities. Many independent label operators tend to think of what they do as more than business, but as curatorial or archival work, driven by a sense of purpose. Independent labels can help provide context at a time when discovery can often feel contextless; they can help root new music in a sense of place at a time when it feels increasingly placeless. Scotty McNiece, the cofounder of International Anthem, a label focused primarily on jazz and improvised music, once explained the task of running his label to me like this: "There's this whole world of people out there who want to hear new things, and are looking for new things. But people need entry points that are appealing."

"Independence" often evokes more than just the major-indie dichotomy, but also particular values: allowing for smaller-scale cultural production, promoting new and challenging ideas. In 2016, Maggie Vail, the former vice president of the legendary independent label Kill Rock Stars and current label manager of Bikini Kill Records, gave a presentation on independent music and the dwindling openness of the internet. "VC funding has led to an obsession with scale," she explained. "But not all business scales. Not all art scales. Scale is a shitty measure of impact. Scale means that everything has to get bigger and bigger and bigger, and if we demand that of the web, we're going to miss out on small changes that actually change lives." It's a point that is relevant to thinking about streaming platforms, and also to thinking about independent music. As it stands, the per-stream valuation of music created by streaming works for artists aspiring toward mass-scale success; for the artist who is trying to reach as many people as possible. But not all music scales, and that's not a measure of its worth. For a lot of people involved in independent culture, the goal is sustainability, not scale.[2]

That is precisely why Ben Parrish, who has worked across several long-running independents with storied histories, including Kill Rock Stars, Joyful Noise, and Sahel Sounds, was hesitant at the dawn of streaming. In an interview, Parrish reminded me that even in the music world that calls itself independent, a lot of decisions are made "with the idea that an artist will hopefully cross over and be a hit." As he explained, this seemed, at the dawn of streaming, to be underpinning many independent labels' embrace of the new model. He recalled being concerned, knowing that the artists he cared about weren't going to scale up to be huge streaming-era stars. "When you are interested in niche genres and music scenes, and stuff that mostly appeals to weirdos and record collectors, even one person switching to streaming from buying a record more than cancels out however many people might algorithmically stream the song," he told me. "The whole idea just seemed extremely short-sighted, and like it was giving the shaft to the majority of artists for the possibility that a few might connect with millions."

Independent music encompasses a wide variety of practices, sounds, and scales, but streaming seemed to flatten out all of the rough edges with a winner-take-all, one-size-fits-all model. In time, it would become more clear that it was also a model where all music became fodder for the profits of shareholders, advertisers, and data farms; grist for the algorithmic re-imagination of culture writ large. For independent musicians and labels especially, streaming turned out to be a brutal system, with artists essentially giving up their work for free to a platform that bulldozes scenes and treats music as an asset class for the wealthy. To engage in its system is a compromise that works not for the many, but the few.

The staunchly independent art-rock band Deerhoof, formed in 1994, lived through this shift. According to its drummer Greg Saunier, the dawn of social media and the corporatization of online life brought mythologies about "leveling the playing field"—the same ones upheld by Daniel Ek and his fellow champions of the "long tail" model. The false promise was that soon, any "Joe Schmo was going to be able to compete with Beyoncé" if their song was good enough, as Saunier put it to me.

"There's a kind of twisted irony at play," Saunier said. "Someone like Daniel Ek hopes he can fool us into seeing this as a golden opportunity to compete with major pop stars, with their million-dollar production values and slickness and marketing. It's presented as some kind of chance to compete. But in fact, you are forced to compete. You actually have no choice," he explained.

Not all artists want to be stars, just like not all workers want to be billionaires. When Deerhoof formed, there was a clear definition of independence, Saunier said, which often simply meant being on an independent record label, rejecting corporate influence, and working to avoid ending up like a number on a spreadsheet to be crunched to improve margins.

"Now the word 'independence' just slots in so perfectly with the neoliberal project," Saunier reflected. "The word has been redefined to mean, you're on your own, we're not helping you. . . . You get no investment, you get no brainstorming meetings, you get no marketing help. It's purely based on if your track happens to go viral, or conversely, if you happen to already be famous, in which case your track is going to go viral anyway. It's the shifting of all responsibility and work to the individual, which is the main tenet of this stage of capitalism that we're in. It is perfectly illustrated by the new definition of the word 'independence.'"

"Leveling the playing field" is a difficult, if not impossible, task in a marketplace where the major labels have such an outsized amount of negotiating power. What really happened was a forced consolidation, where independent musicians are made to compete with major label artists and mass scale–aspiring solo pop artists, the enterprising pop-preneurs, in order to appease a system that was set up to compensate the majors. And that consolidation, it seems, has made major label problems into everyone's problems.

In early 2024, a headline circulated: Spotify had paid out $9 billion to rights-holders in 2023, and half of those royalties went to the independent sector. On its face, that is an astonishing number. But, like any other stat supplied by a media giant to justify its own existence, it's worth unpacking. On one hand, it's of course good for independent streamshare to grow. We shouldn't want a music world that is 70 percent owned by three gigantic global corporations. That's bad for artists, and it's bad for culture, for all of the reasons that corporate consolidation is harmful more broadly. As within media, a highly consolidated music industry means it's harder for challenging ideas and marginalized voices to find audiences.[3]

At the same time, it's worth questioning what Spotify really means by "independent" and what its motivations might be for growing the pool of non–major label streams. As it stands, because of the gigantic size of the majors and the sheer volume of popular copyrights that they control, the Big Three functionally control the recorded music industry. While their literal ownership stake in Spotify has dwindled over the years—at launch, the majors owned a collective 18 percent stake in Spotify, while today that number is closer to 6-7 percent—their influence is enormous. Streaming services cannot exist without the major label catalogs, which puts the majors in positions of power when it comes to negotiating contracts. It's an abuse of power: the major labels should not be able to bully the rest of the record industry simply because they sit on enormous swaths of copyrights. If Spotify can come back and say to the majors, *Well, actually, your catalog only accounts for 50 percent of streamshare*, that claws back their negotiating power just a bit.

But what exactly comprises that 50 percent independent share? Unsurprisingly, it is not just independent record labels. "In today's world when people say indie, it can mean anything that's not three companies," said Simon Wheeler, of Beggars Group, a label group that includes legendary legacy indie labels 4AD, Matador Records, Rough Trade Records, XL Recordings, and Young. "That's kind of mad. You've got all of the long tail creators, you've got AI companies, you name it. And apparently we're all the same. We're all just indie. One of the things from my perspective that we should work on is evolving that sort of lexicon to define what an indie is."

One day in spring 2024, I decided to take stock of Spotify's "Top Songs—Global" chart for a snapshot of how even some of the world's biggest pop songs, with massive marketing budgets and major label connections, might get classified as independent, by way of not being released by Sony, UMG, or Warner. On that day in March, forty-one of the fifty charting tracks were major label releases. The remaining nine could technically be classified as "independent": there were songs from Kanye's YZY brand, the South Korean BTS-affiliated label BIGHIT, and Bad Bunny's label, Rimas. There was one track each released on Domino and Dead Oceans, labels with roots in independent music culture who now represent some of the most popular artists on Spotify—in this case, Arctic Monkeys and Mitski, respectively. There was one self-released song by rising reggae star YG Marley, the grandson of Bob Marley.

And then there were two tracks released through the "streaming label for independent artists" AWAL, or Artists Without a Label. AWAL has prided itself on "Powering Independent Artists," per its company tagline, by letting artists retain ownership of their copyrights; AWAL distributes the music, and might pay for marketing or playlist pitching, in exchange for a cut of the royalties. This has become big business: in 2022, Sony Music Entertainment bought AWAL for $430 million.[4]

The AWAL model epitomizes how streaming has not made room for more independent artists so much as it has created a new archetype for what the independent artist can be: "We're at our strongest when we're empowering creative entrepreneurs and individual artists," one AWAL executive told *Music Business Worldwide*. In other words, the ideal artist that is best served by streaming's financial model: the enterprising solo artist.[5]

AWAL and Spotify's close relationship is well documented: the company's executives routinely appear in Spotify's promotional videos, and AWAL artists can often be found on flagship playlists. In 2017, when AWAL launched its own streaming data app for artists, the press release included a blurb from Spotify's then head of creator services, Troy Carter, claiming its approach would "shape the future of the music industry."

AWAL embarked on a press tour touting the power of Spotify playlist placements, and its unique ability to help artists access them.[6]

AWAL's model speaks to how data-driven A&R has become in the streaming era. The company offers three tiers. Its entry-level service, AWAL Core, is a boutique distributor—similar to self-serve options like TuneCore and DistroKid, but with an exclusive application process. AWAL takes 15 percent of royalties, but the appeal is that if an artist gains traction on streaming, they can be "upstreamed" to the second tier, "AWAL+," where in exchange for 30 percent of royalties, they get some advance money, a dedicated AWAL rep, and playlist pitching. "Playlist pitching is an important part of our services," the company explains. "Something we've cultivated via strong relationships with curators." From there, AWAL crunches more numbers to decide which artists are primed for a global pop audience, signing a select few to "AWAL Recordings"—Artists Without a Label Recordings, meaning those artists do, in fact, have a label. And now, under its major label ownership, the pipeline doesn't stop there: there's always the potential that Sony might swoop in, too (though AWAL is adamant it's not part of their contracts).[7]

Throughout the first decade of streaming, AWAL worked with artists who became synonymous with streaming: Lauv, the chill-pop songwriter who was name-dropped in Spotify's NYSE filing; Finneas, Billie Eilish's brother and closest collaborator; and mxmtoon, whose "bedroom pop empire in the making" was chronicled by the *New York Times* in 2019, in a piece that quoted a Spotify marketing executive commenting on the "high indicators of engagement" around her catalog. AWAL started working with Laufey, a young artist merging viral jazz and TikTok literalism, at the end of 2021.[8]

At the time of the AWAL sale to Sony—which the UK parliament investigated for potential monopoly issues—*Rolling Stone* wrote that the deal was "really about the unstoppable explosion in DIY indie artists." But most of all, it seems clear that those words have become quite meaningless in most contexts. If that explosion of independent streamshare was in part funneling back to Sony, how "independent" was it really? The newsletter *Penny Fractions* astutely referred to AWAL as the "minor league training ground for Sony"—Sony could now use AWAL as an A&R data pipeline, where they can still make money off of artists even without ultimately signing them.[9]

Surely, the viability of companies like AWAL may be part of the pressure major labels have felt to offer slightly less rigid deal terms over the years. It may very well represent a new way of pursuing a pop career that for some artists could be more beneficial than signing a major label deal. But conflating this sector with independent music creates confusion. What version of "independence" is it when an artist lends their music to a platform using data and algorithms to determine which artists have potential to break into pop success? The truth is, though, that this is what most music has become in the streaming era, as major labels use streaming data to track and sort potential signings, following the data to reduce their risk.

Like other digital platforms, Spotify's priorities can partially be gleaned by studying the user interface. For example, to get a sense of how the company thinks about "indie" music, a user can click onto the "Search" page and then click over to the hub called "Indie." As of this writing, the top three playlists being promoted on the "Indie" page are "Front Page Indie," "Lorem," and "POLLEN." When I perused the "Front Page Indie" playlist in the spring of 2024, about a quarter of the playlist was made of major label music, and roughly another quarter was credited to independent labels with major label distribution.

As one might guess, Spotify's primary concern is not the long and rich history of independent music, or with providing a platform exclusively for artists on independent record labels, but is rather more aligned with the long history of the music industry flattening "indie" into a specific sound, genre, or as Spotify calls it, a "vibe." Indeed, its flagship "no genre, just vibes" playlists, "Lorem" and "POLLEN"—which were being touted around on a music press and spon-con tour where Spotify's PR team branded them the "future" of its playlist curation strategy—occupy much of the visual real estate on the "Indie" page. Not just through the playlists, but also through rows of playlist recommendations titled things like "welcome to the world of lorem," "POLLEN picks . . . best new albums," and "Lorem: artists to watch 2024."

"Lorem" is curated by what internally gets called the Indie Global Curation Group, a group of editors from Spotify offices around the world who collaborate on certain playlists. As when Spotify rebranded the "Neon

Party" playlist into "hyperpop," "Lorem" was previously known as "Left of Center"; according to one of the strategists behind "Lorem," "Spotify wanted to create a playlist lifestyle brand for the youth. The idea and name of the brand is that the music is so new it doesn't even have a name yet. Just like dummy text. Lorem ipsum." In a Spotify-produced video advertisement for "Lorem," a voice asks "How does 'Lorem' make you feel?" To which mxmtoon replies, "Like I'm the main character!" Another artist says that "Lorem" has "the best vibes," while a third says, "I don't know what 'Lorem' isn't." "Lorem" is, quite literally, all marketing; less about a particular musical idea, and more about getting inside the head of the ideal Gen Z consumer and figuring out how to sell Spotify to them.[10]

In the depths of Spotify metadata associated with "Lorem," I kept coming across this one especially peculiar Spotify-created microgenre. It was called "pov: indie" and seemed to include a selection of viral singer-songwriters and generic alt-pop. But what was it? As I searched the Spotify interface for "pov: indie" music, the results seemed quite random. When I typed "pov: indie" into the search bar, Spotify suggested I check out "Bubblegrunge Mix," the song "we fell in love in october" by girl in red, or Kanye West. Maybe the auto-generated playlist "The Sound of pov: indie" would be more instructive? That playlist was topped by the artist Cavetown, a Warner-signed YouTuber-turned-musician with billions of streams, who is a sort of face of the mainstreaming of "bedroom pop." There's a lot of geeky mid-2000s synth-pop that sounds like OK Go. According to Spotify's metadata, songs that are "pov: indie" often are also categorized as "indie pop," "pixel," "modern rock," "bedroom pop," "alt z," and of course, "weirdcore."

It seemed to me that "pov: indie" was really just "pop" music hyper-targeted to a specific Gen Z user—and that the tag had less to do with the music itself and more to do with the target listener, how Spotify conceptualizes them, or how it wants them to think about themselves. One poster on RateYourMusic.com described the subgenre as focused on "personal experiences and emotions" and "characterized by its introspective lyrics." The name seemed to suggest that the songs might evoke the sense of relatability rewarded by TikTok, like "POV" memes that aim to serve the user a jolt of main character energy. Do you relate to this? Can you see yourself in this music? Or, if not, then put this music on, and you will become this person.

Spotify loved to talk about how "Lorem" was all about the "community" that had formed around it, using that word as a shorthand for the cohered audience, or consumer base—one united around a shared affinity for certain internet aesthetics and content creators. Like elsewhere in the aspirational vibes economy, it was data-flattened music wrapped up in niche descriptors that would make the listener feel unique by hitting "play" and then letting it drift off into the background. "Indie" was once short for "independent," but at some point it became this. Similar to many a great marketing scheme before it, the goal was to capitalize on a user's aspiration to feel like an individual.[11]

Meanwhile, actual independent labels were mystified by what was happening on the so-called "indie" playlists. As the founder of one indie rock imprint explained to me in 2022, word had started to spread among independent labels and distributors that things were changing at Spotify. "Their indie playlists have turned into pop playlists," the label founder told me in 2022. "Most indie labels are aware of this and have been really upset about it," he continued. "Our distributor is constantly trying to talk to Spotify about it. They've pushed a lot of what we would think of as indie to the rock category, which has a much smaller listenership. So even when we do get playlisted now, it doesn't really translate into very many streams, or much revenue. Lorde and Taylor Swift and all of these pop stars are on the indie playlists constantly now."

The independent label owner said it was becoming impossible for their artists to get onto playlists like "All New Indie." "We've been doing this long enough," they told me. "All of our guitar bands used to be on those playlists. And now it's just this watered down pop sound that has taken over. We no longer know what playlists we're aiming for. They become more and more abstract as time goes on, and they all have a sound that is very similar."

By 2023, a digital strategist for another independent record label told me he had all but given up on the prospect of his artists landing playlist placements; that everything was algorithmic now, streaming income was down across the board, and it seemed like there was little he could do about it. "My optimism comes from hoping for the imminent collapse of these 'attention economy' structures," he said.

While Spotify was busy capitalizing on the hollow idea of "indie vibes," these truly independent artists and labels were struggling in a music business that seemed set on finding new ways to alienate and disempower them.

As the solo-preneur emerged, direct-uploading their songs via third-party digital aggregators, so did a whole cottage industry of middlemen selling services to help these enterprising "indie" artists act more like pop stars without labels. To these businesses, the "aspiring creators" were their target customers. And on sale was the promise of a music career. The streaming services seemed to be dangling a carrot of success, and then monetizing the experience of trying to reach it.

The major labels have long been capitalizing on independent music—through ownership of distributors focused on independent record labels, like Sony's The Orchard and Warner's ADA—but streaming-era consolidation was even more extreme. It wasn't just Sony's purchase of AWAL. Universal Music Group had inked a deal with the digital distributor DistroKid, giving them access to artist data for an "upstreaming program," where they could study the data patterns of DIY artists and pursue leads for potential signings, and had bought a stake in streaming-focused management company mTheory and appointed its cofounders in charge of a so-called independent artist and label services company. Warner, meanwhile, struck a deal with the AI company Boomy, cutting into the AI slice of independent streamshare. And then, in early 2024, Warner revealed that it had "initiated discussions" about potentially acquiring the French company Believe, the owner of TuneCore, one of the largest distribution companies for self-releasing musicians. The bid was thought to be 1.65 billion euro, before it was ultimately dropped.[12]

The majors were hell-bent on growing their market share—of taking home a bigger piece of the pro rata pie—and acquiring portions of the DIY and independent distribution sector seemed to be a high priority of the playbook. It appears now that the already-richest forces within music are set on exploiting DIY artists in new ways, whether through artificially deflating the value of their streams or outright buying the aggregators they rely on; on consolidating solo direct-uploading musicians' catalogs, converting them en masse into a type of asset class for the rich to trade in.

If DIY artists banking on the "opportunities" of the streaming landscape was like playing the slots, then there's another phrase from the casinos that comes to mind: "The house always wins."

When individuals are atomized, they are more easily exploitable. In promoting staunch individualism, the hyper-centralized corporate streaming economy leaves most artists in a state of powerlessness. Indeed, Spotify's image of "independence" is one that makes it harder, rather than easier, for many artists to advocate for themselves. Case in point: a few years after I had initially come across the story of Lance Allen, I decided to check up on his social media accounts and see how he was doing.

While Spotify had once packaged and sold Allen's story for its own promotional materials, in order to sell artists on the mythology that streaming-era success was possible with just enough playlisting, years later he was facing the same issue that so many instrumental musicians reliant on Spotify editorial placements were facing: he had been replaced by stock music. In December 2023, Allen took to Twitter: "30 releases now, all pitched and promoted to @Spotify No editorial support. Sigh...... There was once a time that there wasn't fake, royalty-free, pseudonym artists. . ." He followed it up with a plea to Daniel Ek himself: "@eldsjal I would love for you and Spotify to fall in love with the music I create. It's so hard as an indie to compete with Epidemic Sound and Firefly Entertainment."

16

This Is . . . Payola?

Rarely are we made explicitly aware of the full extent to which commercial interests shape our experiences online. Looking through algorithmic social media feeds today, a user is met with a whiplash-inducing barrage of ads, influencer garbage, and other clickbait content. It can be stressful and overwhelming. Perusing search results, too, it can be hard to tell what's trustworthy or reputable—to comprehend how you even came to be looking at a certain photo, video, or text. On news sites it can be hard to decipher sponsored content from an editorial. The internet has long stopped feeling like a town square—it feels like a shopping mall. And streaming services are part of that shopping mall, even if their sleek interfaces don't currently frame it that way.

Simultaneously, research shows that audio, in general, has an affective quality that lends a type of intimacy and unearned trust. A 2023 Pew Research Survey found that the "vast majority"—87 percent—of American podcast listeners believed the information they heard to be mostly accurate, despite trust in news being at a historic low. This all despite the fact that podcasts "blur the lines further between trained journalists and commentators," noted the news website *Axios*, in an article about the study. Perhaps owing to the parasocial relationships encouraged by the human voice, the lean-back environment allows audio to get away with a lot. And while podcast consumption is clearly different from music listening, this may be useful context for considering how streaming services capitalize on an uncritical audio culture. What streaming services have done well is influence content in ways that are aligned with corporate interests—namely, selling placement in playlists and "programmed streamshare"—while maintaining a sense of feigned neutrality, especially aesthetically through the lack of contextualization in the interface. Businessmen might say this is genius, but for the public, it's a disservice. It's not neutrality; it's deception. For users and artists alike, it creates confusion.[1]

In November 2020, Spotify further contributed to the confusion with an opaque headline on its company blog: "Amplifying Artist Input in Your Personalized Recommendations." The post introduced a new program called Discovery Mode, which would ask artists to accept lower royalty rates in exchange for algorithmic promotion. It was pay-to-play, but Spotify unsurprisingly introduced the perverse scheme using the most neutral language it could come up with: artists would be able to "identify music that's a priority for them," the company wrote, which would become one of "thousands" of data inputs influencing how it delivers "the perfect song for the moment, just for you." Rather than charge an up-front fee, "labels or rights-holders agree to be paid a promotional recording royalty rate for streams in personalized listening sessions where we provided this service."[2]

Spotify initially hesitated revealing too many details about the program. In 2022, I spoke with one independent label owner who was testing out Discovery Mode, and he did not even know what percentage of royalties Spotify was keeping. But more information has since surfaced: artists participating in Discovery Mode take a 30 percent royalty reduction on tracks enrolled in the program, when they are discovered through its channels. Discovery Mode started with Radio and Autoplay, but was later expanded to influence all auto-generated "Spotify Mixes," like "Daily Mix," "Artist Mix," and mixes associated with moods, decades, and genres. Only tracks more than thirty days old are eligible.

Notably, from the start, there were no signs that Spotify planned to label, on its platform, which songs were enrolled in this royalty-siphoning scheme. This lack of disclosure is what has most made Discovery Mode seem like the radio payola of the 1950s, which was eventually outlawed by the Federal Trade Commission. And while Spotify could not get away with directly asking for cash payments up front—it would draw attention to their pay-for-play arrangement, and raise questions about how ad-free the ad-free service really was—the program was almost immediately regarded as a payola-like practice by many music advocacy groups.

Spotify, of course, framed Discovery Mode as democratizing. Speaking to *Music Business Worldwide*, one Spotify employee explained it this way: "We're not asking for any upfront budget or payment, which means there's no barrier to entry. We were looking for a model that would be more accessible, democratic and fair, so we're not going to ask any artists to spend any cash." More artists would now have the freedom to devalue their work, the opportunity to participate in an extractive system, and that was somehow democratic.[3]

Discovery Mode's inner workings are, in part, a product of how playlists have evolved more broadly, especially in the algotorial direction. Recall how these days, many of the recommendation systems on Spotify start with curators identifying a pool of "candidates," or tracks associated with a given playlist. For example, a curator might identify hundreds or thousands of candidates for songs eligible to be included in a certain activity playlist, and then a personalization algorithm will decide which fifty actually end up on a user's playlist. From the pool of candidates, a tracklist will be generated by a sequencing algorithm that chooses songs a listener is most likely to identify with. Similarly, with the eligible auto-mixes, the Discovery Mode algorithm comes in to re-rank the tracks from the relevant pool before they are delivered, meaning a track that is enrolled has a higher chance of being boosted to the tops of those pools and served to users, a source explained.

Internally, Discovery Mode's success was measured in terms of what percentage of total artists (per tier) were onboarded, and how much cash they were saving Spotify. By 2023, Spotify employees celebrated an "exciting Discovery Mode milestone," according to a review of company Slack messages. More than 50 percent of Tier 2–3 artists had now tried Discovery Mode. "Last year we set out with an ambitious goal of getting to 30%," an employee wrote. "Surpassing 50% felt beyond our wildest dreams and yet here we are. Congrats all!"

Spotify has made a lot of money from Discovery Mode. In May of 2023, an employee shared a chart on Slack documenting the previous year in Discovery Mode profits, under the headline, "DM Gross Profits continued exceeding goals due to higher than expected opt-in." Between May 2022 and May 2023, Discovery Mode had brought in a total of 61.4 million euro in gross profit. As a snapshot, in just May of 2023 alone, Discovery

Mode brought in 6.6 million euro in gross profit; that month, the biggest spenders were listed as Believe (1.8 million), "Indies" (1.6 million), and Merlin (1.9 million); the rest came from Warner Music Group (0.6 million), TuneCore (0.1 million), and "Self-Serve" customers (0.6 million). Glaringly missing were Universal and Sony. Indeed, it appeared that there was a direct connection between the musicians who were opting into Discovery Mode—largely independent and DIY artists—and those who already stood to be affected by the "artist-centric" royalty policies demonetizing tracks with under one thousand streams. But in the long term, it also seemed like an economic arrangement that only the most moneyed labels could afford.

"We do feel that Discovery Mode is very insidious in that, with that product, it doesn't matter whether you do it or not, you're affected by it," one indie label employee told me. "You may well be affected if all of your competitors are using Discovery Mode and you're not, because your share is going to go down."

In the early *Music Business Worldwide* coverage of Discovery Mode, a Spotify employee called it a "model that allows the smallest artist [to act] on the same terms as a big label." What, precisely, were those major label terms that smaller artists were now getting access to? As it turned out, Discovery Mode wasn't the only algorithmic promotional tool—or "Algorithmic Promotion Tech" (APT), as these are called internally— influencing Radio and Autoplay at the time. Internal employee Slack exchanges alluded to another program, one specifically for promoting UMG tracks. It was originally called the Catalog Incentive Program, which was replaced with a new program called the Repertoire Discount Program (RDP), running through 2025. As ever, the opaque nature of major label streaming deals remains an issue for all.[5]

Reviewing employee Slack discussions on the inner workings of Discovery Mode was like watching people speak a different language. They chattered away about "inventory efficiency" and "utilization forecasts" and "set expansion" and "lift targets" and "market level tunings." For RDP and Discovery Mode alike, there were goals for both "utilization targets" and "streamshare targets" across promoted Autoplay and promoted Radio, which changed depending on "content pool size."

Three years after the 2020 launch of Discovery Mode's pilot version, an employee nostalgically reflected on Slack about all that the architects of this payola system had accomplished: "Please join me in wishing Discovery

Mode a happy 3-year Spotiversary!! . . . It's amazing to look back on our progress on how we improved the product and scaled to >160 licensors and >20k independent artists. Some of our most exciting updates are still to come in the new year. Let's go team!!"

But Spotify's sights were set higher, as explained in an internal Discovery Mode explainer: "In the long-term (2025+ time scale) we envision between 30-50% of all recommendations on-platform will be influenced by Discovery Mode."

The disingenuous promotional copy around Discovery Mode made sure to emphasize how this program was all about *what the artist wanted to promote*, and what tracks were important to an artist in a given moment. But by the end of 2023, that was in question, as Spotify introduced "Pre-Campaign Insights" or PCI, an algorithm that would tell an artist or label which tracks were most likely to stream well in a Discovery Mode campaign—a scheme to "increase demand" and "drive retention." It was rolled out for "managed service" Discovery Mode customers, as opposed to "self-service" customers—terms from the advertising industry referring to whether a customer has a point-of-contact managing their campaign. For those eligible, the company claimed that, with roughly 85 percent accuracy, the PCI algorithm would recommend tracks "predicted to see a lift in streams" from a campaign: "Enabling more tracks that are more likely to achieve the customer goal of streams will create satisfied customers who retain," explained an employee, according to a review of a Slack message.

One independent record label manager said she had tried Discovery Mode campaigns for different artists on her indie rock label, but it was only the "folk-leaning artists" for whom it was most effective. "It serves passive listeners," she told me. She reflected on how frustrating it was that opting into Discovery Mode actually did lead to increased streams for her artists: "We did have someone reach out and be like, *Wow, I'm really hearing* insert song, *like, a lot, on Radio, did you pay for this?* And I'm like, *If it came from Radio, I guess maybe we did.*" The fact that someone would hear a promoted track and not know that it was promoted raised ethical concerns for her. "It is definitely sold to us like, this is just a kind of promo you can do in the digital world," she explained. "This, unfortunately, is the way that the future looks for us. And we have zero control over it."

"I don't like the idea of what Discovery Mode is," another independent label manager told me. "But unfortunately, with streaming, we're starting to get pushed up against this wall. It was a useful tool for us. And they're kind of making it so it's hard to say no to it, because it is helpful. All of our artists that we had running through the program did get a ton of new listeners, a ton of new followers . . ." He noted, at the time of our interview, that he was not sure yet what their royalty statements would look like. "Streaming is so difficult," he continued. "We're at a point in which we need to take every opportunity we can to make [up] the revenue that is missing. It's this vicious cycle where it's like, we're losing revenue, because of the age of streaming. And then the age of streaming is pushing these weird opportunities on us. And we need to take them in order to make up for that lost revenue. . . . It sadly is so desperate, because the industry just changes so consistently, and we are just constantly thinking of ways to keep up."

By late 2023, S4A was doubling down on its efforts to sell artists on Discovery Mode with an aggressive new marketing scheme. To soften its edges, the team recruited a workwear-clad Oregon singer-songwriter named Goth Babe. At some point during the early lockdown, he'd first crossed my feed, in a sponsored Instagram ad for the "POLLEN" playlist. "What's up guys. . . . Today I'm going to show you where I write my music, and a tour of the rest of my tiny house," he said into the camera, before panning around his miniature dwelling, like the millennial cozy-vibes version of MTV Cribs. This was Spotify's model artist: a solo creative entrepreneur, digital nomad, who posted as much about van life and his outdoorsy lifestyle as he did about his steady stream of singles and EPs. A cemented brand, cohesive storytelling, continuous engagement—when Daniel Ek talked about his ideal artist-entrepreneur, this was it. He was unsigned, but his management worked closely with "management services" company mTheory, which has maintained tight alliances with Spotify over the years. Flash forward to 2023, and both Goth Babe and mTheory were the faces of what Spotify was calling Campaign Kit.[6]

Discovery Mode wasn't Spotify's first go at paid promo. Since 2019, they had been trying to get artists to fork over cash in exchange for pop-up ads called "Marquees," which cost 50 cents per click, or 55 cents if the artist wanted to target "lapsed, casual, or recently interested listeners." An artist set a dollar amount for the campaign, which would then run for ten days, or until the budget was spent. "Our distributor has been very up front with us," one independent label owner told me. "They said, don't use this, you are going to lose money." In 2023, Spotify introduced another, similar ad product called Showcase, sort of like a sponsored shelf that sat right on the home page; those cost 40 cents per click, and lasted for fourteen days.[7]

Campaign Kit was Spotify's attempt to get artists to not just purchase Marquee ads, Showcase shelves, or to trade their royalties for algorithmic promotion—but to convince them that all of these tools worked best when purchased together. It was a four-part package, with the last component of the "kit" being Spotify's playlist pitching tool, the page within S4A where musicians or their labels could submit tracks, with descriptions and metadata, for editorial playlist consideration. Now the company was saying: *It's not enough to buy ads, be part of our payola scam, or pray at the altar of playlist pitching. You must actually do all of these things.*

Spotify liked to remind artists that playlist pitching was free, but it was also their way of continuing to sell the mythologies of playlisting that they'd been trying to instill for over a decade—especially at a time when many had started to question its relevance. At the same time, independent record label owners were growing wary of something else. Since the days of the peak playlist era, Spotify's curators had always been concerned with the broader story and promotion plan around a given artist or record—it was part of how they decided whether or not to get behind a track. And while paid tools like Discovery Mode and Marquee were part of Market-place—the team internally dedicated to selling creator tools—and playlists were part of Editorial, there was increasing overlap.

According to one independent label employee I spoke to, the paid tools started to get discussed by editors. "They do sort of come up in the curation conversations because the more that you are pulling all the different levers within the Spotify ecosystem, the more favorably things are seen overall," he explained. "So, you don't have to spend money on a Marquee, for instance, but if you don't do it, it gets looked at like, *Well, it can't be a priority then because you're not spending money there.* It's just that kind of *I'll scratch your back if you scratch mine.* That's always been the currency, though."

He compared it to the process of getting records stocked at big box stores: "If retailers are going to take your vinyl album, it's like, *Well, what are you doing to tell people it's on sale here? Are you doing street posters?* It's the same thing on digital services. It's not just *Ah yes, you've got a great record and we are going to support you. What's the campaign? What's the story? What can we expect? Have you got any festivals or TV appearances?* All of these things feed into whether people support the music or not. I'd love to think it's all about the music but it's really not. Clearly having great music helps. But there's actually a lot of great music out there."

In late 2023, a Showcase-related announcement hit the company Slack. "Writing you all to announce a massive milestone," an employee wrote. "In just 2 months since our launch, we have OFFICIALLY surpassed [1 million euro] booked in Showcase. This is a huge milestone for this group that worked so hard to launch this format. . . . From battling to get space on home, changing cost models, chasing down the *new* home, staying steady through that transition, introducing a brand new delivery optimization model, all the way to ONE MILLION booked. We should all be very proud of this moment. . . . As you go through the proverbial halls, don't forget to pat your local Native Ads Showcase drivers on the back."

Another employee pointed out that when Marquee and the artist-focused Native Ads business launched in 2019, the company's goal for the year was to prove that the business was viable. "We viewed reaching 1M in euro at the end of that year as a resounding success," they said. "To today be launching new products that hit that milestone in a fraction of the time is wild!" Spotify's pitches to the independent music industry seemed to be working.

These ambitions to monetize musicians were seriously concerning to many, though. The Artists Rights Alliance, in a *Rolling Stone* op-ed, called Discovery Mode "exploitative," "unfair," and a "money grab," noting the potential for the royalty cut to be "so steep that working artists and independent labels cannot even afford to pay it, clearing the field for major record labels and pop megastars to swallow up even more of the streaming pie." The group wrote that the biggest losers would be "working artists, independent labels, and above all music fans looking to expand and diversify their listening."[8]

In June of 2021, the United States House Judiciary Committee sent a letter to Daniel Ek, warning that the feature could establish a "race to the bottom" where artists feel required to accept lower royalties in order to be heard. The letter asserted that "at a time when the global pandemic has devastated incomes for musicians and other performers, without a clear path back to pre-pandemic levels, any plan that could ultimately lead to further cut pay for working artists and ultimately potentially less consumer choice raises significant policy issues."[9]

The authors of the House Judiciary letter outlined a series of questions directly for Daniel Ek: Would the pilot become permanent? What safeguards would protect artists from Discovery Mode boosts potentially canceling each other out? How would the "promotional" royalty rate be calculated and would it be the same for everyone? How could artists and labels measure the success of the program on their streams? And how would royalties be returned to artists if participating failed to increase streams?

Shortly after the Artists Rights Alliance op-ed was published in *Rolling Stone*, a staff member shared it in a Slack channel called the "ethics-club," where a group of Spotify employees would debate various ethical issues of the music streaming business. Some of these employees quickly agreed with the assertion that Discovery Mode was payola. One employee said that the article nicely summed up his "raised eyebrows" from a meeting earlier in the year when he'd first learned about the program.

"Controlling more of the listening experience via programming pretty clearly benefits us more than anybody else," one employee wrote. "That's exactly why we have goals to increase programmed share."

"This isn't just like selling a banner ad somewhere, the boosted plays come at the cost of other artists," said another. "And as the article correctly notes, the degenerate case is that artists stop benefitting at all from paying us."

Even Spotify's own employees could see that Discovery Mode was a deceptive practice. "I guess I'm not as concerned about the economics of offering artists the option of trading $ for exposure," someone else wrote on the Slack channel. "The part I feel worse about is not making it clear to consumers exactly where/when this is happening. Isn't a lack of transparency a part of what separates payola from 'marketplace'?"

As yet another employee in the ethics-club put it, Discovery Mode "moves money around from some artists to other artists, keeping more for ourselves in the process. Artists as a whole get less, we get more." The employee concerns kept coming: "It seems like a classic negative-sum game from an artist's perspective. Assuming promotional placement in fact is a desirable thing for them, they're individually incentivized to pay us for placement, but suffer in aggregate for doing so."

One former employee, who had worked on the Creator team, put it to me this way: "It's definitely a winner-take-all situation," he said. "They talk about how it's a win for Spotify, and it's a win for artists, and it's a win for listeners. But there's just no way that's mathematically possible. When you talk about the way that money is exchanged, that's not true. It is a win for Spotify, it is a win for labels, it is not a win for artists. And they continue to put themselves forward as if it's a win-win-win for everyone. But that whole concept is not possible."

Going into the second half of the 2020s, the record business seemed set on reducing payments to smaller artists by labeling them hobbyists and monetizing their experience—and in the process, returning higher margins to the platform and higher royalties to the musical 1 percent. The thinking seemed to be: some artists get paid for streams; some artists must pay for streams. Algorithmic playlists codify and automate the whole thing—and give Spotify the ability to push free or cheap content. It would benefit listeners and artists alike if Spotify would clearly label when tracks were part of the PFC program, or surfacing due to Discovery Mode or some other marketing partnership—even if doing so would detract from its long-running sham narrative that streaming is a democracy and whatever rises to the top is the will of the people.

In the early 1960s, in what became known as "the Payola Hearings," the U.S. government outlawed the practice of radio stations accepting under-the-table cash in exchange for airplay without disclosure. According to several accounts of the day's payola practices, sometimes DJs were handed stacks of cash, but other times they were offered fake songwriting credits or a percentage of royalties.

And while making payola illegal did not automatically make mainstream radio more fair—in fact, some say that now there exists just an "institutionalized" form of payola—outlawing it sent a message around the responsibility of regulators to take corporate deception of the public seriously. Payola was outlawed, in part, because regulators said accepting money in exchange for plays could artificially inflate popularity and mislead listeners.[10]

According to Kevin Erickson, the director of the Future of Music Coalition, there are important distinctions between the role of payola on radio and online. Payola has gone underground with radio, yes, but online, it is happening out in the open. Payola has "become integrated into the business model with programs like Discovery Mode," he told me. "It's explicitly a means of driving artist compensation down." On AM/FM radio, because musicians in the U.S. are not paid at all when they're played, there isn't the same sort of commercial incentive to use payola. "There's this whole other category of harm that happens on the digital side," he continued.

In Erickson's view, many of the issues artists face in the streaming era, including digital payola, are antitrust issues that both the Federal Communications Commission (FCC) and the Federal Trade Commission (FTC) have the power to take on as both unfair methods of competition (because they suppress wages and contribute to an anticompetitive market) and deceptive practices (because people don't have the ability to know whether they're listening to a song due to a curated recommendation or a business relationship). As he explained, the FTC especially has a "range of enforcement tools and investigative tools that give them a uniquely powerful position to be able to clamp down on this stuff and make an impact." And in particular, under the FTC Act, a "Section 5 rulemaking" banning digital payola on any service would be "a massive win for musicians, and could have implications for the sustainability of diverse online media providers across the board, which can include journalists, podcasters, authors, anybody who's trying to make a living from cultural production."

In addition to taking action on issues related to Discovery Mode, the FTC could also contribute to a more equitable streaming landscape by investigating the major record label contracts that are currently locked up by NDAs—as well as any contracts DSPs hold with aggregators and stock music providers, Erickson noted. In 2023, a study by the nonprofit Public Knowledge made a similar recommendation around the need for oversight when it comes to secret contracts, suggesting that the FTC subpoena documents and testimony to "pierce the NDA curtain" in order "to study this marketplace and determine just how bad things are."[11]

Fighting payola does not solve all of the problems that artists and listeners face with the current streaming model, but continuing to allow these abuses of power to play out unchecked is also a move in the wrong direction. As Erickson puts it: "Unaccountable power is the problem wherever it pops up. It's not about any particular technology. It's concentrated, unaccountable private power."

17

The Lobbyists

"So happy to have @POTUS on Spotify and with a cool, eclectic fun pair of playlists too!" tweeted Jonathan Prince, Spotify's then global head of communications and public policy, in the summer of 2015. "Worlds collide," he added, linking off to the first of President Barack Obama's now-infamous semiannual Spotify playlists. For Prince, this was indeed worlds colliding: just about a year earlier, he'd joined Spotify after years working in both the Obama and Clinton White Houses.[1]

One might reasonably wonder: Why was Spotify hiring former White House aides? And why were they lobbying the sitting United States president to make vacation playlists? This was the beginning of Spotify's long-game play to influence political power in DC. The strategy involved plenty of old-fashioned lobbying, taking a page from the corporate power playbook that had been established by the likes of Facebook and Amazon in the platform era. By the early 2020s, Facebook and Amazon had become the biggest corporate lobbying spenders in America, outspending both the oil and tobacco industries. Big tech's big lobbying power is part of why the U.S. has failed to pass general data privacy laws like the EU's GDPR.[2]

The Obamas had joined Spotify in 2012—announced on Tumblr, a sign of the times—but in 2015, their page got a refresh, seemingly in deeper collaboration with the platform: "Welcome to Spotify, Mr. President," @Spotify tweeted on launch day. Daniel Ek waded into the replies: "Some great tunes in there. Let me know if you need more! ;-)." The president even catered to the "moments" strategy that Spotify had been hyping for years, by releasing both daytime and nighttime versions of his summer playlist. It's not hard to imagine the Spotify reps on a call with a White House digital strategist: *People are just looking to soundtrack their lives!* [3]

"Give them both a listen and a subscribe—we think you're going to love it," wrote an Obama staffer on the official White House blog. "And make sure you follow the White House on Spotify—because we've got a lot more to come, from issue-specific playlists to songs selected by other people in the White House." An accompanying photo depicted President Obama working through his tracklist drafts on sheets of paper, while studiously reviewing songs on an iPad. (Interestingly, in the photo, he appears to be scrolling through iTunes, not Spotify.) [4]

Over the following year, the White House's official Spotify page would release the President's gym playlist, Vice President Biden's holiday soundtrack, and First Lady Michelle Obama's "International Day of the Girl"–themed mix. None of this was out of character: Obama was famously optimistic about technology. He was the first president to employ a chief technology officer, the first to attend South by Southwest's music and tech festivals, and was routinely called the first "social media president." His employees preached the empowering potential of tech, he built an in-house start-up, and even launched an innovation fellowship—conflating self-expression through the corporate platforms of modern technocracy with citizenship.

As 2016 came to a close, and Obama prepared to leave office, he was asked what he would be doing next. "I'm still waiting for my job at Spotify," he reportedly joked to a former Swedish ambassador. "'Cause I know y'all loved my playlist." This led Daniel Ek to tweet at Obama offering a job at Spotify, linking to a joke listing on the company's HR site for "President of Playlists." "As an organization we are full of hope, and always open to change," the posting read. Requirements: "At least eight years experience running a highly-regarded nation" and "experience in programming playlists at a federal level" such as a "celebratory, 'I just found my birth certificate' playlist." The applicant should have "good team spirit, excellent work ethic, a friendly and warm attitude, and a Nobel Peace Prize." [5]

The Obama playlists became a media phenomenon, covered by *Pitchfork* and *Good Morning America* alike. By 2019, Spotify had inked a multiyear podcast deal with the former president's production studio. Even as those contracts have expired, and the Obamas have left Spotify for Amazon, the summertime and year-end playlists have persisted, although not exclusive to any platform. And though it can all seem bizarre and humorous, this is part of how elected leaders culture-wash their reputations today. And part of Spotify's strategy for gaining political influence is indeed getting lawmakers and DC insiders onto the platform.

Case in point: in 2019, Spotify paid $240,000 to the DC lobbying firm Peck Madigan Jones, which has since rebranded to the Tiber Creek Group, hiring four of its lobbyists to meet with politicians and sway them on issues related to licensing, copyright, and music industry competition. Additionally, according to lobbying reports, they were to "inform Members of Congress how to use Anchor," referring to the podcast creation software Spotify had purchased that year, "to create podcasts to communicate with constituents and others." This was the year that Spotify made its big company-wide bets into podcasting, reimagining itself as not just the world's biggest music streaming service, but the world's biggest "audio first" service; they would eventually pay hundreds of millions to bring Joe Rogan and other big names exclusively to its platform. And while it is difficult to prove, for sure, whether all of this lobbying was successful, within a couple of years so many lawmakers had launched podcasts that the Capitol Hill publication *Roll Call* published a blog post about how "Congress wants to get into your earholes," and in 2022, *Politico* ran with the headline "Wow, Politicians Are Really Bad at Podcasting"—actually, not just bad, but "characterized by a crushing, mind-melting boredom." It makes sense that Spotify would want politicians to become playlisters and podcasters: by offering support, it could earn the company goodwill, and forge connections in DC.[6]

In 2023, Spotify made it onto a year-end top 10 list of its own: as of December 31, it was listed as one of the ten biggest spenders on lobbying fees in the "internet companies" category on the nonprofit-run database OpenSecrets.org. According to the website, which tracks money in politics, Spotify ranked ninth on the list, spending over $1.58 million. It paled in comparison to ByteDance's $8.74 million, Amazon's $19.2 million, and Meta's $19.3 million, but still, it was telling. Big technology companies have long aspired to buy political influence in order to normalize certain practices—around data collection, privacy, competition, tax evasion—and Spotify was among them.[7]

From 2015 to 2023, Spotify spent a total of $8,720,000 on lobbyists. Much of Spotify's political activity has focused on its battle against Apple, who, when Apple Music launched in 2015, had already been spending big in DC: the company had spent $4 million on lobbying in 2014. The following year, Spotify began catching up, hiring its first four lobbying firms: Peck Madigan Jones, along with Forbes-Tate, Gibson Group, and BakerHostetler. These firms represented a huge cross section of corporate interests, across finance, pharmaceuticals, airlines, oil, and beyond, including the likes of Facebook, eBay, and Pandora. At the time, *Politico* called it "an aggressive move" for Spotify, noting that the company was likely motivated, in part, by the Justice Department's then-looming considerations of changes to music licensing rules and copyright law.[8]

Spotify's fight against Apple has largely revolved around its App Store rules, with the former claiming that the latter unfairly restricts businesses by charging a 30 percent fee on in-app purchases, and prevents advertisement of cheaper deals outside the app. It's fascinating to watch play out: Spotify complains that Apple unfairly determines what users of its app marketplace can do. But the company, in turn, does the same to users and musicians on its own platform. In one video, Ek complained that Apple was making it impossible to communicate directly with his consumers—meanwhile, his app prevents artists from messaging their listeners, or reaching them directly without participating in its paid promotions. "Apple wants to tax us with 30 percent," Ek complains—the exact percentage of royalties that artists must give up in order to have their music surfaced by Discovery Mode. When Ek claims that Spotify is all about the open internet and leveling the playing field, at a certain point it starts to feel like what the musician Holly Herndon has called "platform gaslighting."[9]

Spotify repeatedly tells musicians that continuous storytelling is crucial to their brands—but the company, too, is in the business of selling stories about itself: to musicians, to users, to advertisers, and to lawmakers. One of the stories it has been most intent on shaping is an anti-Apple underdog narrative. And while Spotify is not wrong to push back against Apple's clear abuses of its power and position, the way in which it has invested in its David-and-Goliath story and framed itself as an antitrust hero confuses the reality that Spotify is also a platform giant guilty of exercising its outsized gatekeeper power.

The Apple App Store isn't the only issue that Spotify has tasked its lobbyists with tackling. In total, over forty different lobbyists have made the rounds in DC on Spotify's behalf over the years, and they have also attempted to sway decisions around various bills on consumer data privacy rights and regulating platform monopolies. Public lobbying reports do not include information about a company's exact stance on a given issue or bill, but other government forms can help paint a fuller picture. In its annual report to the Securities and Exchange Commission, for example, Spotify must detail its finances and current risks to its business, which can reveal what types of laws it might find harmful to its bottom line. For instance, several times in the annual report, Spotify states that the potential introduction of new data privacy laws could threaten its business: "Data security and privacy laws and regulations, and operating systems' practices and policies may impact our ability to collect user information and provide personalized content." And then later in the form, it specifically calls out the EU's GDPR and California's state-level data protection law, CCPA, pointing to "the evolution of privacy laws" as a potential risk to its advertising business.[10]

It hasn't only been outside lobbying firms working on Spotify's behalf. The first in-house lobbyist, Tom Manatos, was hired in February 2016, as vice president of government relations; he came from the lobbying group Internet Association after years working for Congresswoman Nancy Pelosi. "When I first started at Spotify my job was to make government officials aware of Spotify, and teach them what Spotify was," said Manatos, in a 2019 podcast interview, adding that it was a "big learning curve" to get all of those Congress members and senators up to speed, to sell them on "The Spotify Story." The company has also attempted to buy political influence by bringing former government employees into its fold, in the U.S. and beyond—and not just the one aforementioned former White House staffer. At the end of 2023, there were at least four former U.S. government employees working at Spotify, bringing experience and connections from the Department of Commerce, the Senate Judiciary Committee, the House, and the Senate.[11]

Spotify's SEC filings make clear that its broader government relations work is costly. At the end of the fiscal year 2023, one of Spotify's top executives, its chief public affairs officer Dustee Jenkins—a former George W. Bush White House appointee who now heads up Spotify's Government

Relations, Content Policy, and Communications teams—took home a base salary of $860,000. That's the high price of a master at corporate crisis PR. In a 2023 interview, Jenkins was asked about the most challenging things she'd tackled in her career, which also included several years managing communications for Target. "If you were to ask around, I probably am most well known for doing crisis communications," she said. "I wouldn't say it's my favorite part. But I feel like, over the years, I've gotten pretty good at it." Jenkins overviewed various crises she helped manage over the years: a high-profile Target data breach; conversations around "free speech and freedom of expression" on Spotify (likely referring to Joe Rogan's spread of COVID misinformation). "Then there are questions that linger about whether we pay artists enough," she continued. Jenkins then pointed to "Loud & Clear," Spotify's annual streaming economics report—where it selectively shares statistics about its artist payouts, attempting to brand itself as artist-friendly—a reminder that the report serves not just as a marketing campaign, but also a tool of crisis PR management.[12]

Spotify's other top execs take home similarly exorbitant sums, between salaries, bonuses, and stock awards. In 2023, Chief Financial Officer Paul Vogel was paid a base salary of $600,000, and cashed out 47,859 shares for $9.377 million. Notably, he cashed out the shares the day after Spotify laid off about fifteen hundred employees, which bumped the stock price—and then two days later, announced he was leaving the company. And then there are Spotify's two copresidents, Chief Product Officer Gustav Söderström and Chief Business Officer Alex Norström, who have been heavily rewarded for their loyalty to the company. Both have been with Spotify for over a decade, and in 2023 were paid base salaries in the range of $300,000 plus $1.6 million retention bonuses. In 2022, across their base salaries, option awards, and stock awards, Norström earned $9.2 million, and Söderström earned $14.16 million.[13]

It will seem unsurprising that the top executives of a $67 billion media conglomerate are all multimillionaires. Especially given the astronomical wealth of the conglomerate's owners. Ek has not taken a salary or a bonus since 2017, but as recently as 2023 he cashed out $100 million in stock options, bringing his net worth to over $4 billion. He and his cofounder, Martin Lorentzon, both landed on *Billboard*'s list of "Music's Top Money Makers" in 2023, which ranked individuals according to their 2022 fortunes in two categories: executives and stockholders. The latter list was topped by the Spotify cofounders, while the former included UMG president Lucian Grainge, whose compensation was $49.7 million for 2022, and reportedly $128 million for 2023.[14]

Lorentzon has avoided becoming a public figure to the same extent that Daniel Ek has, but he has become more wealthy from Spotify than anyone else, and maintains more voting power than any other shareholder. A 2023 profile in the Swedish men's magazine *King* called the fifty-four-year-old Sweden's richest tech billionaire. As of this writing, he is worth $7.7 billion. His days are spent exercising and eating lunches with inspiring people, the profile explained; he is invested in a new fragrance company and, with Ek, in a health-tech start-up, but has not actively contributed to Spotify's daily operations in over five years. When the journalist asked what he might do with all of his Spotify wealth, he was puzzled. "I don't have an answer yet," he said. But he proceeded to discuss how much money he had invested in his own bedroom: his mattress, the room temperature. The *King* interviewer followed up by asking if he had given any thought to what might happen to his money after he dies. His reply: "I don't want to die." He then clarified that he does believe in death, but that he aims to live until he is 120, under guidance from longevity experts.[15]

These are the real winners of the streaming revolution. And it is especially striking given that the company has barely ever turned a profit—only really beginning to do so in 2024—and that it is regularly cutting jobs, and remains so out of touch with the material realities of musicians' lives. This is wealth extracted from music. And it, as ever, is a reminder of whose interests are being served when Spotify spends millions lobbying lawmakers.

Lobbying, in general, is hidden to most of the public, because by and large, the practice works to serve the interests of the rich. It is a practice that ensures those with the most to spend have the biggest say in shaping policy. Some of the most pressing issues of the streaming era desperately require a political counterweight: at the very least, general data privacy laws to protect the public from surveillance, and regulation of ongoing payola practices. But when corporations are allowed to buy influence to shape political outcomes, artists and advocates are operating on the opposite of a level playing field.

18

The New Music Labor Movement

On a Saturday night in the summer of 2019, I rode the train to Times Square. It wasn't to check out someone's splashy Instagram-bait billboard, though; it was for a protest. A couple of musicians had organized a "Rally for Artists' Rights" inside the subway station, with the goal of providing, per their agenda, a "physical space to grieve." They wanted artists to reflect on the dire circumstances of the music economy, and to highlight the wealth gap between the majority of artists and Spotify's tech and marketing employees. It was part of a series of rallies they'd organized around the country, and the goal was to "bring artists into a worker's mindset," the agenda continued, and build solidarity for "the struggles of working-class independent artists."

The rally's lead organizer, Anjali, who makes music as Diaspoura, got on a mic and read their list of demands, including the need for algorithmic accountability, more open-sourcing of the recommendation systems, and a three-year plan to pay musicians a fair wage. It was a powerful message, but received by a sparse crowd: only six musicians, in total, showed up. The organizers were quickly outnumbered by nine NYPD officers, who confiscated their PA system and threatened arrests multiple times in the process. The event turned from a rally to a flyering mission, with participants passing out one-sheets and urging passersby to reconsider their relationships with corporate streaming services.

A few days later, I met up with Anjali for a coffee in downtown Manhattan, and they reflected on the low turnout. "I think it just calls attention to the disillusionment that people feel," they said. "And the stagnancy of the scene at the moment. But we passed out fifty leaflets, and there were some people that looked genuinely engaged, like they had never thought to question Spotify before."

"WHOSE STREAMS? OUR STREAMS!" In the spring of 2021, the United Musicians and Allied Workers (UMAW) held protests outside of Spotify offices around the world. Down the block from One World Trade Center, dozens of local indie rockers led chants in the streets, while brass and percussion players from another newly formed music labor group, the more jazz-adjacent Music Workers Alliance, backed them up. They paraded down to the NYC Spotify office and delivered a manila envelope addressed to Daniel Ek, containing the demands of UMAW's "Justice at Spotify" campaign: pay artists one penny per stream, end payola, make closed-door contracts with major labels transparent, credit all labor in recordings, adopt a user-centric payment model, and stop fighting songwriters in court. In thirty-one other cities, including Los Angeles, Paris, and São Paulo, similar protests were going down. Videos peppering social media captured crowds of musicians and supporters, some braving snow and rain, with an array of creative signs; "DANIEL EK WHERE'S MY CHECK?" and "MUSIC WORKER SOLIDARITY WITH BAMAZON UNION" were among them, the latter a message in support of the then-ongoing effort to organize Amazon workers in Bessemer, Alabama.[1]

UMAW had formed just a year earlier, a few weeks into the COVID-19 lockdown, when independent musicians, like many others, were feeling the strain on their already precarious livelihoods. For years, musicians had come to rely primarily on live shows for income, as the pro rata model funneled the biggest shares of streaming royalties to major labels. Now that the pandemic had shut down touring for the foreseeable future, the scam had been put into stark relief for working artists.

In 1941, on its instructional talking-blues style tune "Talkin' Union," the topical-folk Almanac Singers encouraged aggrieved workers to "pass out a leaflet and call a meeting / talk it over, speak your mind / decide to do something about it." In April 2020, members of protest-punk ensemble Downtown Boys did the pandemic-era equivalent: they started an email thread and scheduled a Zoom call with a few dozen musicians. "Very quickly, everyone had all of these different visions of what a different music industry could look like when it was being built collectively by the workers involved," the group's guitarist, Joey DeFrancesco, who is also a labor history scholar with a background organizing hotel workers, told me in a 2020 interview.[2]

During the first months of lockdown, UMAW's growing membership formed working groups on topics like venue relations, political education, police abolition, and streaming. From the start, the group zeroed in on the idea that music-related issues, such as debates over royalties and streaming models, don't exist in a political vacuum. Before even choosing a name, its first campaign focused on the expansion of pandemic unemployment benefits under the Coronavirus Aid, Relief, and Economic Security Act, mobilizing hundreds of musicians to circulate letters to Congress. "That was how we started—thinking, *How are music workers and gig workers going to be protected during this time?*" Josephine Shetty, one of the original UMAW musician-organizers, told me at the time. The letter advocated for immigrant access to relief programs, national rent and mortgage cancelation, Medicare for All, and funding for the Postal Service and the National Endowment for the Arts.[3]

UMAW wasn't the only group of newly activated musicians organizing during the pandemic. In fact, the group was part of a broader wave of music worker organizations to emerge in the early 2020s, which also included the more locally focused Music Workers Alliance (MWA), founded in response to "the lack of public discourse on the plight of working musicians and DJs in the local policy space" in New York City, according to their website. There is much overlap between the two organizations—they've worked together closely on a campaign pressuring South by Southwest music festival to raise artist payments, among other actions and petitions—but their priorities around streaming are different, which members of both groups are quick to remind me. MWA's belief is that taking on a streaming service like Spotify cannot happen until lawmakers deal with copyright infringement on YouTube, calling it "the leak in the bottom of the bucket" on their campaign website, that must be fixed to give artists leverage in streaming debates. It's logical: Spotify has long sold itself as "better than piracy," and as long as different forms of piracy exist, streaming services will double down on that narrative to justify paltry payouts. As MWA explains it, the only reason that free music on YouTube can legally exist is due to "safe harbor laws" included in a piece of late-nineties legislation called the Digital Millennium Copyright Act, which relieves giant companies like Google from being liable for the material that circulates on YouTube, and puts the responsibility of reporting copyright violations on the artists themselves. "Reforming DMCA Section 512 is the only way to fix the 'leak' and establish a fair functioning market for recorded music," MWA writes in its explainer. "Once this happens, we can organize and build leverage against streaming services, create viable alternatives, and raise the floor for royalty payouts."[4]

Both groups are doing something vital: encouraging musicians to become organizers, and pursue collective action, at a time when the centers of power in music only continue pushing atomization. Both groups also call attention to the difficulties that independent musicians—who are also largely freelancers—face in trying to form unions. "We define indie musicians not in terms of style of music but the fact that the bulk of working musicians in the United States are not represented by unions," Ty Citerman, a guitarist and chair of MWA's membership committee, told me. "We want to be public about standing with organized labor, but also the need for us to have a different organized labor structure for ourselves that actually serves us."

Musicians have long been organizing against the financial exploitations of new technologies—since at least the dawn of the commercial recorded music era. From the late 1920s onward, the American Federation of Musicians (AFM) protested how the rise of recordings was eliminating jobs for live musicians, especially those employed working in theaters and playing on radio broadcasts. In 1942, the president of AFM declared that musicians producing phonograph records were "playing for their own funerals" and called for a ban on all recording by AFM members. So the musicians went on strike. For two years, an estimated 136,000 union members refused to make any new records. The ban lasted until 1944, with the creation of the Recording Industries' Music Performance Trust Funds, founded on the idea that record producers should "share in the responsibility for the unemployment of musicians caused by recording by contributing royalties from record sales into a fund that would employ musicians for admission-free live public performances," according to the AFM. By the end of the strike, six hundred labels had signed agreements, and starting in 1947, thousands of AFM members were paid union rates to play free concerts at schools, parks, and other public places.[5]

DeFrancesco, the cofounder of UMAW, recounted this history in the pages of *Jacobin* in 2022, drawing connections to the ongoing fight for better streaming pay. "The AFM's successful strike offers key lessons about how to win a better deal for labor," he wrote. "After all, this radical change did not emerge from the actions of a few isolated celebrities, nor a disorganized consumer boycott, nor a tech utopian cure-all, but rather the flexing of strike power by an organized mass of music workers." As the new music labor organizers took on Spotify, they were building on a long history of musicians organizing to win.[6]

This is all despite the fact that UMAW and MWA are not actually unions: because independent artists are technically independent contractors, U.S. labor laws currently prohibit them from unionizing, instead making it so that musicians coordinating boycotts can be deemed illegal cartels. As of this writing, a piece of pending legislation, the Protect Working Musicians Act, aims to change that. Thus, the work of groups like UMAW and MWA is more comparable to efforts by the National Writers Union's Freelance Solidarity Project than, say, the work of the AFM, which today reportedly largely caters towards full-time musicians working in theaters and orchestras. "We're just trying to organize the unorganized, which is the vast majority of musicians right now," DeFrancesco told me in 2020. "There [are] so many similarities if you look at [efforts to] organize Uber, freelance writers, adjuncts. . . . It's the same problem, where it's so hard to organize because you have so many employers." Shetty agreed: "If musicians are the original gig workers . . . we have a responsibility to organize within that realm."[7]

UMAW's "Justice at Spotify" was just one of several campaigns it launched in its first few years, which also included the "Instruments into Prisons" gear drive, a collaboration between the police abolition working group and Die Jim Crow Records, and "#MyMerch," which raised awareness about the long-running practice of venues taking cuts from musicians' sales of T-shirts, vinyl records, and other merchandise. "Justice at Spotify" and its "penny per stream" demand were particularly wide-reaching, though. "We were thinking of it as education for other bands and our own fans,"

Damon Krukowski, of the groups Galaxie 500 and Damon & Naomi, and a founding UMAW organizer, told me. "Because people just don't understand the situation that streaming created for artists. Even other artists weren't understanding it," he recalled. "Demanding a penny per stream was a strategy to get people to say back, *Don't you already get more than that?* And then you get to say, *No, we make a third of that at best.* And even less if you're on a label. Many of us make zero. It did change the conversation. The message got through: we're being paid nothing."

By the end of its first year, over twenty thousand musicians had signed on to the campaign's demands, which were covered by every major music outlet. All of UMAW's press coverage also seemed to motivate Spotify's inaugural "Loud & Clear" report, which appeared in the spring of 2021, not long after those initial in-person protests.[8]

"Justice at Spotify" was part of a growing chorus of voices around the world calling for a major overhaul of the streaming system. In the UK, the Musicians' Union's popular "#BrokenRecord" campaign led to a parliamentary inquiry into streaming, which was announced in October 2020. Around that time, some UMAW streaming committee members started to wonder: Could the "Justice at Spotify" campaign help launch something similar in the U.S.?

As UMAW member Michael Abbey told me, this was the season when the group's streaming committee first started researching the various ways to potentially approach lawmakers. They started small. With guidance from some more experienced organizers, the committee put together email templates that members could use to reach out to the staffs of various Congress members. At that time, it was a relatively minor ask. "We didn't want to go in right away asking members of Congress to write a bill for us," said Abbey. "It was pretty much just asking for a meeting so we could discuss our efforts."

No one in UMAW had deep relationships with anyone in Washington. But Abbey had been volunteering for U.S. Congresswoman Rashida Tlaib for a while at that point, making calls for her reelection campaign and helping run phone banks. "When we were starting to reach out to legislative partners, I had thought, oh, well, maybe I could reach out to Rashida Tlaib," Abbey told me. "So I went on the volunteer Slack, and reached out to her data director at the time, who responded right away and put me in touch with the legislative director." According to Abbey, while Tlaib gets a lot of attention for national issues, she is very locally oriented, and so the fact that her hometown, Detroit, is the home of Motown, and has a rich music history, connected some dots: streaming justice was a local economic justice issue in her community.

Those initial messages to Tlaib's office were at the end of 2020, and an introductory phone call was set for January with Abbey and two other UMAW streaming committee members, Cody Fitzgerald of the band Stolen Jars and Mary Regalado of Downtown Boys. As Abbey recalled it: "It turned out that Andy [Goddeeris], the legislative director, is a big music fan. And he actually is a Downtown Boys fan. He was like, *Oh, I'm going to spin my Downtown Boys records after this call.*" At that point, again, UMAW was just looking to discuss the campaign with policymakers, in hopes they would maybe help amplify the then-upcoming in-person actions. If the result was Tlaib tweeting about the campaign, that would have been a success. "We were trying to keep it open-ended, but our ask was not really that big at that point."

At the meeting, Goddeeris suggested filming an interview between Tlaib and a local musician, which led to an online panel discussion featuring Tlaib alongside Detroit musician Shigeto, Los Angeles musician Julia Holter, mastering engineer Heba Kadry, and Joey DeFrancesco. It went live in August 2021: "Justice at Spotify: A Roundtable with Rep. Tlaib."

Throughout the course of the interview, the question of next steps came up, which opened the door to having another meeting with Tlaib's staff. The subject of a bill came up, Abbey recalled. "They did want to work on something, but the more of the legwork we could do for it, the faster things would move along. If we could find pro bono lawyers to work with, that would go a long way."

So UMAW's streaming committee got to work. The committee included about twenty different members over the years, and three-to-five core members as it shifted from a "momentum campaign to a legislative campaign," estimated Zack Nestel-Patt, an upright bass player and early UMAW member. It was a lot of musicians who had never organized before, let alone worked on writing new industry regulations into law.

"Everything started from zero," he told me. "We spent a year researching and discussing how to even approach this bill. That meant having a lot of conversations and reading a lot. And very slowly, we started putting these pieces together. But we're only meeting one hour once a week, so it's a very tedious and slow, slow process." The work ahead was twofold: they wanted to write a good bill, but they also had to think about the organizing work that would happen around the bill—how they could use the legislation to galvanize musicians to get involved in the organization, and hopefully stay for the long haul.

UMAW also had to decide how ambitious they wanted the bill to get. All of the members I spoke with seemed to agree that this bill was just one piece of a broader puzzle—that there's a broader vision for revaluing music socially and financially that involves new alternative platforms and public funding, for example. But, as an organization, they were deeply attuned to more immediate concerns: How would their musician members pay their rent and buy groceries? There was a consensus that they wanted to create a campaign that was less ideological and instead "deeply material," Nestel-Patt said, "as a way of galvanizing support across musicianship. . . . It felt like a very straightforward and simple way to seriously grow the rank and file and grassroots of an organization like UMAW. This is our minimum wage campaign. This is our 'Fight for $15' in the music space. In my personal organizing philosophy, that is the starting point of anything grander."

They also wanted to address something rather simple: "Every time there's a new, paradigm-shifting technology, there need to be new laws," said Abbey.

Once that framework was established, a pro bono legal team was put together, including legal scholar Rohan Grey, who had worked with Tlaib previously, and ended up writing the first version of what would become the bill; Henderson Cole, a music attorney who had been working for years on a proposal for a government-funded music streaming library; and the Harvard Law School Cyberlaw Clinic, which Krukowski had connected with during a past fellowship. Together, they worked on language that largely drew from a legal framework outlined in a 2021 UN report, arguing for the creation of a new, additional streaming royalty that bypasses record contracts and goes directly to artists.

With the law clinic, UMAW also studied two U.S. laws from the 1990s for further inspiration. First was the Audio Home Recording Act of 1992 (AHRA), a law that Congress passed to create a royalty fund drawn from companies manufacturing recordable digital media. It required that 2% of the price of CD-Rs and devices like CD recorders be diverted to a fund for songwriters and musicians. The second was the Digital Performance in Sound Recordings Act of 1995 (DPRA), a law passed to get artists paid directly from satellite radio and internet broadcast platforms, making sure funds from these platforms went directly to both recording rights-holders and recording musicians. Creating a new royalty that would pay musicians directly from streaming was not only possible, it had historic precedent.

The Living Wage for Musicians Act was announced in March 2024, aiming to "create a new royalty from streaming music that would bypass existing contracts, and go directly from platforms to artists," with the ultimate goal of paying artists an annual living wage. Against all odds, this group of scrappy, fed-up DIY musicians went from self-organized pandemic-era Zoom meetings to writing up legislation for the federal government. When we chatted shortly after its announcement, I asked Nestel-Patt how exactly he felt they'd been able to pull it off. "That's a question I ask myself every day," he said, with a laugh, on a video call. "It took a really long time." It had been three years since the in-person actions, which he estimated was a pretty long time to write a two-page bill.[9]

The centerpiece of the bill is the new royalty stream, paid directly from streaming services to the artists through a nonprofit administrator—added on top of the pre-existing streaming royalty system. The act would create an "Artist Compensation Royalty Fund" from a new additional fee paid by streaming subscribers, plus the streaming services would pay in 10 percent of their non-subscription revenue. Artists would then be paid directly from the fund according to their stream counts. The basic mechanisms are based on those pre-existing 1990s laws, the AHRA and the DPRA.

There are two other key provisions in the bill. The act includes a maximum payout per track, per month, mandating that after 1 million streams, money would go back into the pool to increase per-stream payouts for all other musicians. The bill also leaves open the possibility of state- and federal-level agencies directly contributing to the Artist Compensation Royalty Fund, leaving a door open for public music funding.

"A penny per stream, or this new royalty, isn't the horizon for our imagination of what the music industry could look like," clarified Abbey. "Or how music could be treated in society. There was talk about maybe having additional stuff in the bill that was maybe more radical. At least from my perspective, I thought it was really important for us to find some sort of emergency fix now, because the conditions we're seeing are so extreme. We didn't want to open up this really broad conversation of how America could completely change its attitude towards the arts, but obviously that is really important. It was just a realistic look at where we are culturally."

Just a few days after the bill was introduced in the spring of 2024, I spoke with Andy Goddeeris, Tlaib's senior policy counsel, who called the local response in Detroit "overwhelming," with "more positive outreach" than any bill he could recall in years. "It feels like everybody knows a musician in this town who is struggling," he said. "It's really an economic justice issue, and an issue of growing and supporting local businesses and our local economy. It dovetails with our other work."

"It speaks to how overdue something like this is, and also to how many musicians in our community don't have the same visibility as other workers," Goddeeris continued. "That's in part because, from what we keep hearing, they are all working two or three jobs in order to be a musician. They don't have as much time to organize or to get active politically."

To celebrate the introduction of the bill, Tlaib appeared at a UMAW-organized event raising awareness, featuring a DJ set from Shigeto, who was also part of that first Zoom roundtable. At the event, Goddeeris said musicians were profusely grateful, calling the bill potentially paradigm shifting—which he finds important, but also concerning. "I definitely understand that for artists this has a revolutionary potential," he said. "But to us, this is kind of the bare minimum. This is basic common decency and basic economic justice. This is not too much to ask."

For many listeners, the very idea of a stream, or even a song, has been abstracted and decontextualized, he said. "Part of what's so sinister about the streaming landscape now is how it's really devalued musicians' labor. When we listen to music on Spotify, we are not just listening to a song. We are consuming someone's labor at a really artificially reduced price. We're trying to get people thinking about consuming music in a different way, and to think about the ways in which artists are being exploited in that process."

While UMAW's musicians were drafting the Living Wage for Musicians Act, another group of workers creating value for Spotify were getting organized, too: its Swedish engineers. In November of 2022, they dropped a new podcast on Spotify. It was attributed to "Spotify Workers" and its first episode was titled "Why a collective agreement?" Within its first seconds, a software engineer named Henry Catalini Smith, who later served as the president of the Spotify Workers Union in 2023, spelled it out: "I work at one of the minority of companies in Sweden where we don't have a collective bargaining agreement yet." Sweden's labor market adheres to what's called the "Swedish Model"; citizens have a "right to association," or freedom to join a trade union, and 70 percent of workers are unionized. (In the U.S., the number is just over 10 percent.) "Collective agreements" are voluntary agreements between employer and employee regulating working conditions and rights. Camilla Frankelius of Sveriges Ingenjörer, the Swedish engineers union, told me that Spotify's aggressive opposition to a collective agreement was uncommon in Sweden.[10]

"A century of worker power has carved high expectations of working conditions into the bedrock of Swedish culture," Catalini Smith explained on the podcast. "There exist rare cases today where workers without collective agreements receive benefits like paid parental leave anyway," he continued, citing the six-month parental leave employee benefit that Spotify prides itself on. "Even then those workers are indirectly profiting from the strength of the labor movement, which made those benefits commonplace."

"Spotify was founded in Sweden but it has become quite an American company," Catalini Smith told me. "It's an American company with a union avoidance strategy, bought and paid for from one of the usual labor relations legal consulting companies."

In 2023, as the workers organized, Spotify passed pamphlets around its Stockholm offices discouraging the collective agreement. Under the headline "The Spotify Way," the company proclaimed that "it is in Spotify's DNA to challenge the status quo" and that Spotify "offers better terms and conditions" than union-won benefits. It provided a side-by-side analysis of Spotify's current benefits with those required by a standard collective bargaining agreement, implying that the latter could take away certain protections around pay, time off, remote work, and parental leave. Sveriges Ingenjörer, which had been helping Spotify workers in their fight for a collective agreement, offered a response debunking the pamphlet, line by line. "A collective agreement provides security," they wrote. "It is a solid foundation and not an obstacle that would prevent Spotify from continuing to offer its employees the same staff benefits they enjoy today."[11]

"Klarna did the same thing actually," said Frankelius, referring to the Swedish fintech giant. "The leaders of those companies, they are a little bit more like America than Sweden. They don't like unions. They don't like the Swedish way to work." According to Frankelius, the engineers union struggled to understand the resistance of these tech companies to collective agreements.

"We were actually really shocked when Spotify launched their campaign against unions and a collective agreement at the beginning of our negotiations," she told me. "It is not common, especially not for a Swedish company."

More collaboration between the disparate groups of workers organizing to hold streaming services accountable could be useful. Catalini Smith's advice for musician-organizers was to think bigger: "What does the picture look like if you include more international solidarity? . . . But the starting point is to build collective power."

Conclusion

When I spoke to members of UMAW about the Living Wage for Musicians Act, a common theme kept arising: advocating for streaming royalty regulation was a short-term goal, not the long-term vision. There are no silver bullets to achieve and sustain a more equitable and diverse music ecosystem: music is vast, and so ideas about how to make its digital economy more fair are always going to look different to artists from different scenes and practices. In fact, one of the biggest myths of the streaming era is that a one-size-fits-all solution could work for all artists, and so in imagining alternative tools and systems, challenging that very idea is vital.

For as long as musicians and journalists have publicly discussed the inequities of streaming, there has been no shortage of overeager tech entrepreneurs claiming their new apps will fix everything. And while the framing of their offerings tended to shift with tech hype, from the metaverse to NFTs, their promises were pretty consistent—things like "empowering" creators, "democratizing" access, streamlining and optimizing this or that. Some of their solutions could be intriguing, but it is, as ever, necessary to follow the money: start-ups were often just repackaged updates on the same old extractive model of attracting venture capital, scaling at all costs, and then squeezing artists and users for profit. Sometimes these start-ups were even the product of major label–run "innovation funds" or "accelerator networks" that are never all that innovative, and usually point back to upholding the record industry status quo.[1]

The problems created by venture capital are never going to be solved by more venture capital. There needs to be a political counterweight, but music needs alternatives, too. Rethinking the future of music also requires rethinking profit motives and power structures, and challenging a system where a small handful of entertainment and technology firms own so much of music. It requires investigating alternative models that are more cooperative, transparent, and artist-run, that support artists operating across diverse scales and practices, and that generally put people over profit.

Nati Linares, a longtime board member of the early streaming platform cooperative Resonate, once explained to me how music communities could learn from the environmental movement's "just transition" framework: "It's about fighting the bad and building the new," she explained. "It's a larger framework, but I love thinking about it like that. We have to be doing both at the same time." That means demanding artists get a better deal from Big Streaming, while also imagining alternative systems completely.

Linares is an advocate for what's called the solidarity economy—a deep-rooted international movement toward sustainable economic arrangements that value community ownership and democratic governance—and her ongoing work involves connecting the dots between those concepts and the arts. That could look like worker-owned cooperatives, participatory arts budgeting, or mutual aid networks, to name a few examples. "It's not just about what we're against," she once told me. "We also need to consider what we want to build."[2]

Imagining new futures for music requires collectivity, improvisation, and deep listening. These happen to be skills heavily ingrained in the musicians working on Catalytic Sound, a self-described creative music cooperative that has emerged as one of the more intriguing artist-run streaming projects of the post-Spotify era. In 2012, the improvising saxophonist Ken Vandermark looked around at his friend group and had a simple idea: Wouldn't running online merch be easier if they all did it together? Over the years, he'd watched his merch table sales decline at shows; he knew he had to do something to pick up more online orders, and figured some of his friends were probably in a similar position. The project was launched with the simple goal to create more income streams for a small collective of like-minded artists in the creative improvising scene.

Catalytic Sound has grown into a collective of thirty musicians who work together to run the online merch store as well as Catalytic Soundstream, a DIY streaming service launched in 2021 with a small-scale, artist-friendly economic model. And though it is called a cooperative, in practice it is something more singular: a bit more like a collective-run combination of digital merch table and community archive, with the time-tested independent payment model of a fifty-fifty split after expenses. Each month, half of the subscription revenues go to Catalytic, toward maintaining the site's infrastructure and paying for things like editorial copy, and the other half of the revenues go to the artists. And rather than tracking stream counts and paying musicians fractions of pennies per stream, Catalytic embraces a radical concept: the artist cut is just split thirty ways, with an equal share going to each member. Because Catalytic's offering is both streaming and directly purchasing music, artist fees reflect their Soundstream share as well as revenue from any direct purchases.[3]

The thirty-way even split provides an example for how artists and collectives could work together to break away from the per-stream valuation of music that fails so many artists. Not all music is meant to be played on repeat, and certainly not the type of avant-garde free-improvising music made by the members of the Catalytic collective.

Improvised musicians are particularly attuned to the type of work this collective experimentation requires, Vandermark told me, because "they almost always work in groups. And improvisers often work in many different bands at the same time. It's a unique way of making music. And so we've always worked that way. It's just natural to be yourself and cooperate in a group," he went on. "Some bands don't work, and they fall apart, because that cooperation doesn't happen, or the creative synergy doesn't happen. But we're used to doing that."

Listening to music on Catalytic Sound will not be for everyone, and that's the point. But for those who are already fans of one of the artists, or curious listeners who seek to learn more about this particular corner of improvised music, it is a wealth of recordings and information. The catalog is just a few hundred albums, which is minuscule compared to mainstream services, but because the selection rotates on a monthly basis, it's still a lot. Members are asked to contribute one exclusive record per year for Catalytic, so much of the catalog can't be found anywhere else. It's a place where you go to explore.

Perhaps the most compelling dimension of Catalytic Sound is that it is distinctly not a technological solution, but a social and economic one. It suggests that instead of thinking a revamped technology will fix the problems facing music, what needs to be reconsidered is the structures of power and money that surround said technology. It's just one type of blueprint for a group of musicians coming together to figure out what works best for themselves; a different way of thinking about pooling resources and digital infrastructure. "We made the decision that there's a limit in terms of time and money to what we can accomplish, and that limit is at thirty musicians," Vandermark told me. "But what we want to do is say that Catalytic is one model for a musicians' collective. It's not the one. The idea is to try to motivate other communities."

At a time when the music industry has insistently sold the idea of the hyper-individualistic solo creative entrepreneur as the model independent artist—where every artist is meant to act like the CEO of their own little media empire—there's power in collectives of artists pushing back, and asserting that true independence comes from working together with the people in your community to build an alternative. "The music industry is not going to help musicians," Vandermark concluded. "It's going to come down to us, but they'll do everything they can to break us."

Among Catalytic's thirty members is Luke Stewart, a DC composer, improviser, bassist, and multi-instrumentalist who plays with the revolutionary free jazz quintet Irreversible Entanglements and other groups. For Stewart, the collective decision-making of Catalytic is critical—it's what makes the project one that actually challenges the power structures of the music industry. "We're all running it together, which is a testament to the type of collectivity that we think is necessary for this," he told me, "and that I think is also implied in the music that we create, and the community that it serves. . . . We all have equal say."

"The music industry pushes the machine of celebrity, where it's all about one person doing everything, or one person's idea, which is never the case," Stewart continued. "Catalytic is all of our thing. And it truly operates in that fashion. Which I think is a powerful statement on the music and the community."

Stewart pointed out that the model of artists forming collectives in response to the exploitations of the commercial music world is not a new concept—specifically pointing to the legendary Association for the

Advancement of Creative Musicians, founded in 1965 in Chicago. One of Catalytic's long-term goals is to publish a book about different artist collectives and cooperatives, to show different models throughout history.

"One of the lies of streaming, of the modern-day music industry—and perhaps it goes along with the lie that's always been in place in certain aspects of the music industry—is that if you play the game in this way, then you should expect a certain result," Stewart told me. "If you take a deeper look, the people who have made the biggest impact are the ones who did not play the game the way it was supposed to be played."

Stewart points out that the value of a project like Catalytic is as much about streaming economics as it is the importance of musicians contextualizing and presenting their own music on their own terms—particularly when it comes to the jazz traditions that many Catalytic artists operate adjacent to—and taking power away from the type of listening encouraged by big streaming companies. The streaming giants, he said, are "ultimately just serving to perpetuate the idea that this specific art form, this specific approach to music and culture, is something to be in the background. Something for chilling, or wining and dining, or listening to while you're drinking coffee at Starbucks. Served to sell a product, to sell a mood and a lifestyle that goes along with mindless consumption of non-substantive things, like fast food. In a certain sense, it is chillin' music. But it's also, most importantly, vital music. The music itself is vital. Let alone the history, the tradition, the possibilities that have come out from this art form."

Part of the power of an artist-run platform, Stewart said, is encouraging listeners to dive in and learn about the records, the artists, and the communities—to invite people into the music in a deeper way. "I tell my students about the hip-hop method of digging in the crates and attuning your ear to samples, which is a way to exponentially raise your music IQ. And that method is gone in the streaming context. I'm not going to say it's all bad, because a lot of things are available at a moment's notice, and you can listen to almost anything. But ironically . . . we have so much opportunity, and so much information at our fingertips, but we also have a high level of ignorance about all sorts of things, and about culture and the arts especially."

Music today is at a crossroads, but the power of a project like Catalytic is a helpful orientation, contributing to an emerging constellation of road maps for alternate routes artists could take in working together to build sturdier and less extractive economic models for online music. Part of the model's simplicity is what makes it an interesting example to look toward; it invites interpolation and interpretation. It's exciting to think about how different regional scenes and independent labels could repurpose the basic framework and build on it.

And while Catalytic's model is relatively loose and improvising—a group of artists figuring out what works for them as they go—cooperatives generally do have more rigid structures. Typically, the word "cooperative" refers to a model of shared ownership. In a worker cooperative, the workers co-own the business, share the financial rewards, and democratically govern the operations. The post-platform era has ushered in a wave of interest in the model, including within media organizations, like the local NYC news blog *Hell Gate*, which launched in 2022 with a worker-owned model. In Canada, a group of music journalists have launched New Feeling, a unique cooperative model with three different types of stakeholders: worker-owners, member-owners, and community-owners.[4]

The latter is similar to the type of multi-stakeholder operation that governed Resonate, a long-running music streaming cooperative that emerged in the mid-2010s as part of the broader "platform cooperativism" movement—a whole sector of enterprises working to bring cooperative economics to digital platforms of all types—and owned by listeners, artists, and volunteers. By 2021, Resonate had seventeen hundred artist members. Listener-members could participate in its annual meeting—to, in theory, vote on how to direct its surplus income—or join the conversation on its online forum.[5]

When I checked in with Resonate's executive, brandon king, in early 2024, the project was on a hiatus, and he was reflecting on the challenges of trying to organize such a project primarily online. "How do we build a cooperative culture virtually? What does the cohesion look like? What does the accessibility look like? How are we making this accessible to communities who are generally not able to spend time online? Because it's overwhelmingly white cis male people who have time to invest in a co-op." King was clear about what lessons could be taken from the experiences, though, to imagine new paths forward. Later that same year, some former Resonate members were working on a new co-op vision.

When we spoke, king was excited about the idea of building local, place-based hubs, with artists collaborating in person, and then having an online space where the hubs are able to connect. And he was even clearer on why cooperative infrastructure in music is vital as ever. "I'm not interested in trying to change the music industry. I believe in delinking from harmful systems. The industry is broken. How are we setting up amongst ourselves networks of mutual aid and support and also figuring out how to grow a genuine community?" wondered king. "For me, in my horizontal principles, that seems like a much better infrastructure to try to create and build upon than trying to fix the music industry."

Solidarity can be hard to come by in the music world. On one hand, there's the winner-take-all celebrity model that encourages an every-person-for-themselves competitiveness. On the other hand, you have the precarious financial realities of the industry, which just make it hard to support projects involving lots of people. Nika Danilova, who makes music as Zola Jesus, once explained it to me this way: "I just don't respect the way the industry is set up at this current moment. It's extractive and exploitative. It's siloing musicians through this auteurism where we're all supposed to be these individual islands of artistic genius. So we're not being encouraged to collaborate."[6]

Like the burgeoning music labor movement, collectives and co-ops help contribute to a music world where there's more solidarity, a necessary ingredient to finding more sustainable ways forward. The problems with music streaming are problems more broadly of culture under capitalism—where decontextualization and historical amnesia make it so people do not look backward, forward, and around, but just flounder in their atomization. Collectives and cooperatives work to counter exactly that by creating the conditions for people to be in more direct collaboration with one another. It is hard work—the polar opposite of the frictionlessness that platform-optimized tech culture imposes. But friction is part of how real connections, and ultimately change, happen.

What would it look like if people actually had a say in helping shape the technologies they relied on in their everyday lives? And for those technologies to be governed in ways that were actually accountable to their communities? Those questions are good for music scenes, but they're also just good for communities in general.

If Catalytic Sound gives the appearance of a community-helmed music library, where each member's proverbial card affords access to hundreds of recordings and their context, the next best thing might be the public library itself offering this service.

In 2012, the year after Spotify launched in the U.S., a now-retired public librarian in Iowa City named John Hiett was in a bar listening live to a local singer-songwriter. He wasn't exactly thinking about how libraries could provide an alternative to technocratic platform monopolies that exploit musicians' labor and listeners' attention. He was thinking about his CD budget, and how not enough of it was being spent locally.[7]

As he later recalled in an NPR interview, he had thought to himself at the time: "How come we ship all of our music budget out of town? How come we don't do more with this?" Hiett pitched the idea of a locally focused music streaming offering to the library's webmaster. Then they went to the local city attorney, who wrote up a contract for local bands: $100 to distribute their recordings for two years. The Iowa City Local Music Project launched in June 2012 with 58 selections, and within a week 334 albums had been downloaded. For the scope of the project, it was a success.[8]

Since then, library-run streaming has taken off around the U.S. and Canada, providing a new type of digital resource to local music scenes, and a new vision for what locally-focused streaming could look like. Dozens of public libraries have launched community-driven local music streaming collections over the past decade: Seattle, Austin, Pittsburgh, Minneapolis, Eau Claire, Chapel Hill, Edmonton, Salt Lake City, and Denver among them. Library streaming raises a particularly radical idea: What if people participating in a local music scene could also be involved in helping to shape the digital tools people use in their everyday lives?

The majority of the projects in North America are run like this: Local musicians submit recordings for consideration once or twice a year, during an open-call period. Then a group of curators (typically five to ten locals deeply embedded in the town's music scene) or library staff choose forty to fifty albums to add to the collection, focusing on contemporary artists and material released in the past two to five years. Musicians are paid an up-front, onetime license fee, usually around $200 to $300 to license their record for two years. For musicians, this introduces crucial ideas for circulating digital music: acknowledging the importance of accessible, publicly available music, but also the material reality that artists should be paid, and not on a per-stream basis.

"It started out as something really rudimentary," said Jason Paulios, who now runs the Iowa City Local Music Project. "I took hard copy CDs to the webmaster, and he would rip them into FLAC, and then figure out a code." In more recent years, a new webmaster remade the library's website in a free, open-source content management system called Drupal, and then rebuilt the Local Music Project within that website. Paulios told me the backend is similar to publishing on Bandcamp, and in the spirit of sharing that seems to define public libraries, he was quick to mention their willingness to share their code with interested libraries.

Building out this infrastructure was "not insubstantial," Paulios explained. "We built three different versions of this thing. There's very few libraries, I think, that are interested in that, or have the capacity to do that. We've always had our own webmaster, which is kind of unique with city libraries, and such a gift."

Ann Arbor District Library was another of the first libraries to offer local streaming music—it has hosted a digital music collection since 2002. The concept of libraries providing free access to digital music downloads, or what some called "down-loans," was being explored in other countries in the early 2000s, as well. For example, Danish libraries in Copenhagen and Frederiksberg began offering legal, digital music files to patrons as early as November 2002, through a program called "Netmusik."

The Ann Arbor library began licensing local music for streaming starting in 2010, including a partnership with electronic label Ghostly International. According to Eli Neiburger, the library's deputy director, building the library's own streaming and mp3 downloads infrastructure directly into its website has been an important decision. A lot of the local music material—referred to as the Ann Arbor Music & Performance Server (AAMPS)—is stored in the library's own data center, in its basement. "It's really not that hard to serve an mp3 or other music file," he told me.

While many libraries turn to outside tech vendors to help run digital offerings, Neiburger feels strongly about the library controlling its own digital infrastructure—an ethos that extends beyond just music streaming—and it has to do with how commercial and streamlined the internet has become over the past two decades. "The early days of the web were ones where there was a lot more variety and a lot more opportunity," he went on. "As you've seen so much consolidation over the years, public libraries are one of the few forces resisting that. So I think it's all the more important that libraries are in control of their own infrastructure." Ann Arbor's library is in a uniquely flexible place: it's an independent government entity with its own elected board and tax, which has allowed the library to invest in its own IT team and code base, said Neiburger. "All of the stuff that we've built, we share freely, any other library can use it, but very few libraries are in the position infrastructurally to take advantage of it."

Many libraries without the resources to build their own streaming services have turned to an open-source software called MUSICat to power their local music collections. As of this writing, upwards of twenty libraries use the software, which grew out of the Madison Public Library's Yahara Music Library project, whose collaborators included Kelly Hiser, then a digital publishing researcher, and Preston Austin, a local tech vendor. Austin says the limitations of these as city-scale efforts are key: "How do you make a licensing system that's fair for all the artists in the world? I don't know. And with respect to city-scale licensing, I don't care. It's important that we don't care. . . . That's governance that says, actually people in Memphis know more about Memphis than people in California, and we don't need a generic solution for the whole world in order for people in Memphis to get paid."

Library streaming programs are more than collections: several librarians referred to them as "digital public spaces," a phrase that says as much about contemporary digital norms as it does about potential futures they're help-ing to build. To these librarians, creating a digital public space is as much about public-minded ownership—offering a space outside the incentives of multinational corporations and advertising businesses that define our digital lives today—as it is also about the governance of the space, and working in collaboration with local musicians and patrons to shape how it functions. Some libraries offer their cardholders access to non-locally focused music streaming services like Freegal and Hoopla. But in the eyes of many librarians, the local digital collections are not just about creating a pool of streamable music, but about the connections that get formed in the process and the activity that pops up around them.

The "digital public space" framework for an online music offering can partially be traced back to the Edmonton Public Library (EPL), which hosted a 2013 unconference attended by over fifty Edmonton musicians, to help design its streaming program, Capital City Records. Among its many takeaways, musicians expressed the importance of a collection that was regularly updated, interactive, and curated by the community—and of celebrating both history and the contemporary scene. The library has called the project's scope "local music history up to yesterday."

Raquel Mann, the digital public spaces librarian at Edmonton Public Library who oversees the Capital City Records streaming program, explained that its local music collection is important for all of the same reasons that its local author collection is important: local music is part of local history. "We started to realize that the traditional focus on famous authors, famous music—it doesn't really help us learn about ourselves, here," Mann explained. As part of her job at the library, Mann also helps to coordinate a digital space for local Indigenous storytelling, Voices of Amiskwaciy. "It really is the way we learn about our neighbors," she continued. "And really understand who lives with you, who lives in you. Where you live is really important, and local collections do that. You can't get that anywhere else."

In 2018, a group of Edmonton radio DJs approached the library with a large archive of interviews with local music legends. The library created a feature for community groups to work on their own projects and show-case them on the site, where the DJs can add profiles with audio, photos, and text. They're also working on preserving histories of shuttered local venues. "It's been quite emotional," Mann told me. "There was one radio host who broke down in tears when he saw it."

When Capital City Records was first launching, one of the local musicians who helped with early curation efforts was rapper, writer, and producer Rollie Pemberton, who performs as Cadence Weapon and previously served as Edmonton's poet laureate. For musicians like Pemberton, these types of local library projects sit at the intersection of multiple ongoing challenges in music: the disappearance of public space, and issues presented by the current music streaming status quo. "The way I think about engaging with streaming companies, it's like the Wizard of Oz to me," he explained. "You can't see them, you don't know who it is behind these playlists, you don't want to ruffle their feathers and then never end up on a playlist. It's this kind of fear involved with the anonymity of it. Whereas, if it's somebody from your community that you actually know, there's a certain level of trust there." Pemberton also pointed out how important it is that on Capital City Records, albums are presented without prominently listed play counts, which, on Spotify, tend to just reinforce a system where popular music becomes more popular.

When Zach Burba from then-Seattle-based band iji submitted music to the Seattle Public Library's Playback collection in 2016, the band was only making an average of $50 a year from streaming, and the $200 fee was helpful for scraping together rent. But for Burba, the value is more than financial. He's particularly interested in the library's role as an archive for local music, and how it can offer an alternative to "the impermanence of internet music and the way things kind of tend to disappear" as corporate platforms come and go.

Libraries, on the other hand, have strategies for preserving mp3s. Neiburger described the Ann Arbor District Library's approach as straight-forward: the files are backed up in multiple places, but ultimately it's approached "the same way as Excel files . . . backups are backups." A bigger question for him is what access will look like in the future: What happens if devices can no longer play mp3s? The library would likely need to transcode them into whatever the popular format of the day evolves into. Archiving is another reason he feels it's important for the library to own its digital infrastructure. While private companies might be thinking about the next quarter or the next year, libraries often think about how their collections will be useful in "five hundred years. . . . There's no one in the corporate world that has any incentive to think that way."

"I'm optimistic about this more than other things," Burba added. "There's a different expectation for library music. It's a place you go to discover or to learn something, instead of to find chill beats to study to, or background music for your party. It could be a really supportive thing for music scenes. I don't think it necessarily is that yet, but I think it could be."

Rollie Pemberton says we should look to expand the other types of resources that libraries provide music communities in addition to just local streaming. "I love this idea of libraries as venues, recording studios, and even just using the public space to hang out," he said. "Because our entire lives are just becoming overly policed, overly scrutinized. . . . This could just be the first step to something else. The really important thing about libraries is they're free public spaces that don't ask anything of you. We have fewer and fewer spaces like that. If people become more mindful of the connection there, we might be onto something cool for the future."

"We talk a lot about building with, not for," said Hiser, the MUSICat founder. "Partnering with communities and learning what their needs are. But on some level, people just need money. I would love to see a world in which more funding gets funneled through these projects so that license fees can be higher."

A statistic that librarians like to repeat is that there are more public libraries in America than there are McDonald's locations. That is a testament to the widespread perseverance of libraries as institutions, but also to the wide array of realities that libraries exist within. Libraries are not a monolith—they have different histories, structures, resources, capacities. To interact with a public library is to interact with an institution juggling countless issues of equity and access, not to mention budget cuts. Engaging with libraries as public spaces and local digital collections as public resources, we should make no assumptions about how a given library might conceptualize its relationship to the public. But the willingness of libraries to bring musicians into the process of governing these projects means there is an opportunity to help imagine and shape what they could be, and what future relationships between libraries and music scenes could exist.

For those interested in rallying support for the creation or increased funding of a local library streaming project, Hiser had this advice: find the names of the directors and board members of your local library, and create targeted campaigns. She also recommended opening up conversations with any known allies within the library, or librarians connected to local music. "People vote in local elections in pretty low numbers, but the impact of your local school board election or city council election is profound," she explained. "This is kind of the same thing. Those are the people who have the money at the library. And even though that money is declining right now in most places, it is all about strategies of local politics and demanding power in those places however you can." It helps expand the conversation about equitable music futures beyond corporate accountability and into the realm of civic engagement. As Hiser told me: "It can be so much more impactful than just yelling at Daniel Ek on the internet."

Like libraries, music benefits from solid positioning as a public good, and existing European models are evidence.

At a dark midsize rock club in Stockholm, I met with Dennis Lyxzén, singer of the long-running Swedish hardcore band Refused and post-punk band INVSN. I'd originally reached out to Lyxzén to discuss the early days of piracy in Sweden, and the long-term influence of streaming on independent musicians. Like a lot of people I spoke with during that trip to Sweden in the fall of 2023, though, Lyxzén was more eager to discuss something else threatening local music culture. Just a couple of weeks earlier, the right-wing government had finalized its plans to cut public funding to long-running adult education programs, including music classes that had long been a lifeline for musicians in Sweden. The government was also planning to slash funding for Sweden's long-running free cultural schools, *kulturskolans*, where children can take music lessons for free, and to which the country's successful music business has long been partially attributed to.[9]

"It's a huge conversation in Sweden right now," Lyxzén told me. "Adult education programs are like 90 percent of why Sweden has this great music scene, and they want to cut all that. They are saying, 'We should not pay for your hobbies.' It's once again, the same conversation. How do we [support] musicians making art? All of the musicians that you see on TV in Sweden, they all started in youth centers. There was an infrastructure to build from and become a popular musician—or not, you can also just play music because it's great. It starts as a hobby for everyone."

It was startling to hear the same rhetoric that was being peddled by the major label and streaming executives—about how tracks streaming under one thousand plays per month should be demonetized, because those musicians are unserious "hobbyists"—being used to justify cutting public funding for music, especially in Scandinavia. They were talking specifically about education programs, yes, but it was driven by the same anti-art argument: that music failing to ignite enough mass enthusiasm to achieve commercial success is not worth supporting. It's a toxic self-replicating system: create no infrastructure for supporting the arts, and then tell artists they are not worth supporting because they are unsuccessful.

"Piracy and streaming made it very, very, very difficult for people to do their art," Lyxzén continued. "A pandemic definitely did not help. It's been a rough go the last couple of years. I've been touring since '93. It's tougher and tougher to tour every year. Harder and harder to make a living playing music. It's diminishing returns."

The pandemic threw a wrench into the lives of touring musicians, but it also clarified some realities, for some artists. In the U.S., at least, there was a brief moment when some musicians receiving weekly unemployment felt not just relief, but a bit of a reality check: how even just this extra few hundred bucks a week was life-changing. They actually had time to work on their music. It was a glimpse into what a music practice could look like with even just a small bit of public funding or basic income. We saw it with our own eyes: it was possible.

Music is too important to be left solely to the marketplace. This subject has come up time and time again in my reporting: how brutal it is that there remains barely any public funding at all for music in the U.S. All around the world, though, there are examples of how to publicly fund music: grants, basic income, education programs.

Advocating for a universal basic income—where governments pay every citizen a fixed amount of money unconditionally every month—has been an official stance of the UK Musicians Union since 2021, alongside its "Fix Streaming" and "Composers Against Buyouts" campaigns. "Basic pay would mean some remuneration for those parts of a freelance musician's work that often go unpaid," writes the union. "The creativity, writing, development, everything that leads to the finished product. And it would empower freelancers who aren't eligible for sick pay to take time off to recover when they need to, instead of being forced to work through it to pay the bills. It's about musicians being paid something for all the work they do, in a way that enables every working musician to live with dignity and not in fear of what will happen during a crisis."[10]

The "universal" in universal basic income is, of course, essential—the point of these programs is that they are granted to everyone, not just some exceptional class of musicians and writers. But artists and cultural workers could make particularly good test subjects given how irregular and precarious their work tends to be. In 2022, the Irish government did just that, introducing a three-year Basic Income for the Arts pilot, granting 2,000 artists, including 584 musicians, a weekly payment of 325 euro. It's not a perfect system—out of 9,000 applications, fewer than one-quarter were selected randomly—but in the press, artists receiving the payments said they were life-changing.[11]

In late 2023, the Irish government published some early research on how the pilot was affecting artists, showing a decrease in anxiety and depression, and that recipients worked fewer hours at non-arts-related jobs, dedicating more hours to their arts practice. In a report at the *Irish Times*, music executive Angela Dorgan noted that music industry wealth disparities were part of why the program mattered: "I'm seeing report after report of how brilliantly the global music industry is doing, and how great the profits are, and yet the other reports on my desk show the low incomes and living conditions of the artists creating the work." One artist was quoted saying: "I feel the 2,000 people on the pilot have been given a taste of a better way to live and work. It's not one that removes all the difficulties of making art. But it removes some of the financial precarity around it, which is an extraordinarily freeing feeling. I hope the pilot is built upon, just so that more people get to experience that."[12]

The program, and the attendant freeing feeling, are not without precedent. In France, a somewhat similar program has existed since 1936. Once a musician clocks a certain number of hours as a performing artist—507 in a year—they become officially recognized as a working artist, and have access to a special unemployment system, known as *Intermittence de Spectacle*, that takes into consideration the irregular nature of working as an artist or technician. It's almost the same as Ireland's basic income, at around 1,300 euro per month, and serves hundreds of thousands of artists. Nicolas Dubourg, president of a French trade union for publicly funded cultural organizations, in a 2021 NPR interview, spoke to the strength of arts labor organizing in France: "They know how to demand an economic regime that works for them. They explained what it means to have irregular jobs and how a system of solidarity could work. And they got what they asked for."[13]

Jenny Hval, the Norwegian avant-garde musician and writer, told me about the various types of public funding made available to artists in her home country: some are project-oriented grants, while others are more like basic income, providing a salary for a period of time. She spoke to the level of trust and security that was granted by the basic income–type funding. "There are applications, and a lot of people never get [the income], and musicians hardly ever get them, but it allows for a completely different way to think about what creative work is. It allows for a practice that involves your whole being, instead of just the product, where you are a content creator. It's more integral. It has allowed me to think that I am a worker, and whether I am on tour, writing, participating in other people's projects, doing research, or just in a period of life where I am doing other things, that I am valued somehow. I am a citizen. It is creating worth at a deeper level."

Everyone wants an answer: What's the ethical alternative to Spotify? The one I often provide is, unfortunately, unsatisfying to many, because it is not simple. There is not one single answer. It's certainly not merely to download Apple or Amazon Music, or some other app that allows you to pay $10 a month for all of the music in the world. Rather than seek out another fix-all app, we should be honest with ourselves about the reality that this very model fails to meet the needs of most independent artists and listeners, and grapple with the complexity of that. Supporting art is a different equation.

Emphasizing individual habits, in general, can feel weak in the face of so much consolidation and financialization—and a musical surveillance apparatus with insidious influence on the world around us, whether we participate in it or not. Collective issues require collective solutions. But buying music directly from artists and independent record labels makes an actual difference; it is an important part of supporting the culture you'd like to see keep existing. That means tracking down where artists have their work on sale directly, whether online or at the local independent record shop. It also means keeping up, directly, with artists and labels, through communication channels that they control, which these days often means their email newsletters and personal websites, and being attuned to how they are asking for support. The easiest systems for accessing music from decades past are often not the best ones for discovering and supporting new independent music. An artist might say that the best way to support them and their work is buying a record from their label's website, a download through Bandcamp, or finding them on an emerging artist-run platform, for example.

Being a better individual consumer, of course, only gets us so far, and is surely not the only way to strengthen diverse cultural ecosystems. This also requires participating in alternative networks of communicating and contextualizing music: writing about the things that are exciting, sharing music with your friends, going to shows. I am energized by what feels like a real resurgence of interest in independent radio stations as community hubs, too. Independent radio offers something that hyper-personalized streaming can't: a sense of locality and shared listening experience. Against all odds, it feels like independent music journalism projects are rising from the ashes of corporate media collapse—newsletters, blogs, zines. That work is increasingly vital in the streaming era, and requires new funding models too.

At its most potent, music helps us give form to ideas and feelings that were previously inexpressible—fleeting moments where the ineffable becomes real, where loneliness dissipates, where the world briefly makes sense. And when music moves us in ways that we cannot fully fathom, it's the words of music writers that can help pull us closer toward understanding. Those are, in part, the stakes, if we keep letting music, as a whole, and its adjacent information ecology, get swept away in the crisis of media economics that we face today. Those are the stakes if we keep letting our musical landscape become ever more clogged with auto-generated repetitions of what's already come before, generic material that keeps the data machines rolling, mood metadata that limits our emotional horizons; if we keep giving too much power to corporations to shape our lives, and we don't protect working musicians' abilities to survive. We are foreclosing that possibility for music to evoke those ephemeral unknowns. We are losing a lot of music that will never be made. We are letting new expressions, emotional articulations, and points of connection slip away.

On a collective level, we have to be active participants in the cultural economies we want to see flourish; we have to validate the culture we want to see in the world. The corporate culture industry entrenches its power not just through controlling the marketplace but also by controlling the popular imagination, by convincing us that there are no alternatives. The alternatives are growing all around us, though.

To be sure, the broader equation for revaluing music also involves staying plugged into the organizing work, standing in solidarity with the new music labor movement groups, supporting the long political fights ahead. Streaming is not going away anytime soon, and some basic regulations are the bare minimum we can do to attempt clawing back the corporate stranglehold on culture, to try to get a bit more money into the pockets of working artists. Lawmakers should seriously consider new rules for digital payola. At the FTC, there should be more oversight of the major label licensing deals with all streaming services—not just Spotify. UMAW's Living Wage for Musicians Act would create a new, additional royalty stream paid directly to artists. The American Music Fairness Act aims to get artists in the U.S. paid when their music is played on AM and FM radio. And perhaps most important of all, the Protect Working Musicians Act would give artists the right to unionize and collectively bargain, thus giving them more negotiating power with not just streaming services, but the many other overly centralized powers in music, too.

And once more, we're not having a serious conversation about the future of music unless we're talking about public funding, cooperatives, unions, and international solidarity—and unless we realize that the fight for a more liberated and de-commodified cultural sphere is part of the broader struggle for a better world.

What musicians are dealing with today is also what working people everywhere are dealing with: precarious labor conditions, a lack of universal healthcare and affordable housing, a generally untenable rising cost of living. Musicians are being squeezed further and further, with an ever-growing gap between the wealthy and those living in poverty. Artists are either tremendously successful, or told they're worth nothing. We cannot stand for a world that says only the musicians with millions and billions of streams have value, just because the people running the pop labels have said so; just because keeping the major labels happy is how Daniel Ek and Martin Lorentzon stay growing their fortunes of billions.

Streaming claimed to solve piracy, but for many independent artists and listeners, the problems of the ultra-capitalist music business were never solved. The truth is that no technological intervention was ever going to easily solve such a complicated and ever-changing question: not piracy, not downloads, not streaming. There are no one-click solutions, and perhaps what music could benefit from most would be a wholesale rejection of technological solutionism. The problems faced by musicians, like those faced elsewhere in society, aren't technological problems: they're problems of power and labor.

Luckily, the future of music is not something that was unilaterally decided in 2008 when the major labels struck their first deals with Spotify, even though it can often feel that way. There was not one moment when they decided whether working artists would win or lose. Fairness and sustainability aren't buttons that just get permanently turned on or off; they are values that are continuously created and destroyed, negotiated and fought for and defended as technologies and formats come and go. It can be helpful to remember that there was a time when the very idea of streaming didn't feel so inevitable. And it was not very long ago.

When we think about repairing the broken world of music, we need to think bigger than just fixing the music industry. The way music has been reimagined by streaming is grim—but these problems are ultimately manifestations of a music industry that has been failing artists and the public for generations. To address the root causes of our ailing music culture, we need to have deeper conversations about why music matters, why universal access to music matters, and what systemic political and economic realities currently prevent so many people from engaging deeply with music. It is always worth remembering that our shared music cultures would be so much more compelling and diverse if so many did not need to abandon the arts for jobs with health insurance.

Ultimately, we can't just think about changing music, or changing music technology. That's not enough. We need to think about the world we want to live in, and where music fits into that vision.

A Note on Sources

To write *Mood Machine*, I interviewed over one hundred sources. Roughly one-third of them were former Spotify employees and industry insiders who preferred to remain anonymous for various reasons: some cited non-disclosure agreements, while others were worried about protecting their professional relationships. Other interviewees included musicians, label employees, journalists, researchers, and organizers. I meticulously reviewed Spotify company Slack messages and other internal communications and documents, which provided a close-up view of issues discussed in this book. For those wishing to hear more of Spotify's official corporate-sanctioned telling of its own origin story and other topics discussed here, there is ample information to be found on its website and blog, in many hours of media appearances by its top executives, and in company-created podcasts like *Spotify: A Product Story*. I have drawn from all of the above in piecing together this book, and also dug deep into music press archives, social media posts, YouTube videos of executives speaking at conferences, and beyond. Lastly, two books by Swedish authors were very helpful in grasping Spotify's early history: *Spotify Teardown*, coauthored by Maria Eriksson, Rasmus Fleischer, Anna Johansson, Pelle Snickars and Patrick Vonderau, and *The Spotify Play*, coauthored by Sven Carlsson and Jonas Leijonhufvud. Thank you to the authors of those books as well as all who took the time to speak with me.

Acknowledgments

Thank you, Jenn Pelly, for the meticulous notes on every page of this book (including probably this one), for helping me cross the finish line at a moment when it seemed unimaginable, and for answering a truly unfathomable number of questions any time I needed another perspective on a certain word, sentence structure, or life choice.

Jordan Lee, for being the first eyes to read every chapter in real time as they materialized, for your honest feedback and sharp thinking that have seeped into so many aspects of this project, and for simply believing in me.

Pier Harrison, for encouraging me to write that first article in 2016, being a great friend, and for always being down to help me figure out if I've described something about music licensing correctly.

Neon Mashurov, for extremely helpful notes on several chapters and years of friendship and co-working. Katie Alice Greer, Nathan Albert, and Jonathan Williger, for being the first people to read some of these chapters and for the supportive feedback.

Julia Dratel, for your collaboration and guidance with researching Spotify's lobbyists, navigating OpenSecrets, and for inspiring me to pursue the bigger political context.

Thank you to all of my editors past and present, including everyone at *The Baffler* over the years, especially Jonathon Sturgeon, for assigning and editing so much of my writing on this topic, and Zach Webb, for editing my more recent work. Some passages from chapters 3, 7, 18, and the conclusion are based on writing and reporting that originally appeared at *The Baffler*, the Pioneer Works *Broadcast*, and *In These Times*, and I am grateful to the editors who commissioned and edited those stories.

Thank you to David Turner for so many years of conversations on streaming, music, labor, and city politics. Thank you, Damon Krukowski, Kevin Erickson, Mat Dryhurst, and Holly Herndon, also, for all of the conversations on streaming over the years. You have all shaped my thinking.

Thank you to my agent, Ian Bonaparte, and my editor, Alessandra Bastagli, for all of your work to make this book come to life, as well as the rest of the team at One Signal. Thank you also to Danny Vazquez for helping this book find its way.

Thank you to everyone I met in Stockholm for taking the time to speak with me and generally pointing me in the right directions, especially Rasmus Fleischer, Sven Carlsson, Erik Mellin, Max Karlsson, Veronika Muchitsch, and everyone I met at the Mediations conference. Speaking of which, many ideas in this book began as talks or presentations given at various conferences over the years, and I'm grateful to the organizers of them all.

Thank you, again, to every single person who spoke with me, including many who are unnamed, for your honesty and trust. Thank you to Jason Leopold for an incredibly helpful conversation about investigative reporting at a critical juncture.

Thank you to all of the musicians who made time to speak for this book, including several interviews that are not included here for no reason other than lack of space, and many that were off the record. They all helped shape this project in one way or another. Thank you to UMAW, MWA, and everyone fighting to make music more fair.

I am immensely grateful to every person who made an introduction to a source, recommended an interviewee for this project, or sent me a reading recommendation—there were so many of you that I fear it would be impossible to make a list without forgetting someone. So many of the ideas and connections that helped create this book came from chance conversations with friends and acquaintances at shows, between bands, or outside a music venue. Thank you to anyone who has ever entertained a winding conversation about the digital music economy with me in the corner of a crowded gig when you could have been talking to anyone else about something more fun.

Thank you to all of my students at NYU, including those who expanded my knowledge of hyperpop and TikTok; everyone who took my "Topics:

What is Indie?" course in 2022 and helped me unpack some of the ideas explored in chapter 15; and to all of my colleagues, especially Dan Charnas for your words of wisdom around book writing. I have learned much from all of you.

Thank you to Maggie Vail for assigning me my first story on the music streaming economy in 2016. Thank you to Astra Taylor for being an early champion of my writing around this subject, and for writing books that have made such a profound impact on me.

Thank you to my group chats. Thank you to Chris Lee and Neon for a conversation in California that inspired me to write this book instead of applying to grad school (not sure if you remember). Thank you to Noah Klein and Jordan for driving three hours through LA traffic to get me to the music tech start-up carnival. To Faye Orlove, for the eleventh-hour design help and to Emily Reo, for tour help.

Thank you, Mom and Dad, for everything. Thank you for being the first ones to celebrate with me when I found out this book was happening, and for sending me every streaming-related article you came across for years. Thank you to my sister, Marissa, for being my friend as well as an inspiration.

Thank you to all the rest of my friends and family, including my grandmother Alice, who passed away while I was writing this book, and whose dry humor I deeply miss. During the last holiday gathering we spent together, she asked me a question in her thick Queens accent that shook me to the core. "What do ya think ya gonna say about the music business that hasn't been said arready?" I hope I answered it for you, Nanny.

Notes

Introduction

1 Astra Taylor, *The People's Platform* (Metropolitan Books, 2014).
2 At the end of 2023, the Recording Industry Association of America (RIAA), which serves as the lobbying arm for the three major record labels, reported that 84 percent of 2023 recorded music revenues came from streaming. It should be noted that while these statistics provide an overall look at the recorded music industry as a whole, they do not necessarily speak to the extremely vast spectrum of lived experiences felt by musicians and independent labels operating at different scales. For example, the RIAA also reports that in 2023, digital downloads accounted for only 3 percent of U.S. recorded music revenues, down 12 percent from the previous year. While that might be true at a macro scale, many vital independent record labels continue to report that the sale of digital downloads through their own websites and services like Bandcamp provide more sustainable income to their artists and operations than streaming revenues. For the RIAA report, see https://www.riaa.com/wp-content/uploads/2024/03 /2023-Year-End-Revenue-Statistics.pdf; for the 30 percent market share statistic, see Anne Steele, "Spotify Dominates Audio Streaming, but Where Are the Profits?," *Wall Street Journal*, January 19, 2024, https://www.wsj.com/business /media/spotify-streaming-music-podcasts-audiobooks-3e88180d; for Spotify's user and subscriber numbers, see newsroom.spotify.com/company-info.

1 The Bureau of Piracy

1 Quinn Norton, "Secrets of the Pirate Bay," *Wired*, August 16, 2006, https:// www.wired.com/2006/08/secrets-of-the-pirate-bay/; Jack Schofield, "Sweden's

Pirate Party Wins EU Seat," *Guardian*, June 7, 2009, https://www.theguardian
.com/technology/blog/2009/jun/08/elections-pirate-party-sweden.

2 Steve Knopper, *Appetite for Self-Destruction: The Spectacular Crash of the Record
Industry in the Digital Age* (Free Press, 2009); Alex Sayf Cummings, *Democracy
of Sound: Music Piracy and the Remaking of American Copyright in the Twentieth
Century* (Oxford University Press, 2013).

3 Knopper, *Appetite for Self-Destruction*.

4 Neil Strauss, "Record Labels' Answer to Napster Still Has Artists Feeling
Bypassed," *New York Times*, February 18, 2002, https://www.nytimes.com/2002
/02/18/arts/record-labels-answer-to-napster-still-has-artists-feeling-bypassed
.html.

5 Benny Evangelista, "Music Firms Open Online Services, but Will Fans Pay?"
SFGate, December 3, 2001, https://www.sfgate.com/business/article/music
-firms-open-online-services-but-will-fans-2845907.php; Michael Arrington,
"Troubles at imeem, but Company Says No Shutdown Imminent," *TechCrunch*,
March 25, 2009; Eric Eldon, "Music Startup imeem Making Money, Not Dying
Unless the Labels Kill It," *VentureBeat*, March 26, 2009.

6 Amanda Holpuch, "Minnesota Woman to Pay $220,000 Fine for 24 Illegally
Downloaded Songs," *Guardian*, September 11, 2012, https://www.theguardian
.com/technology/2012/sep/11/minnesota-woman-songs-illegally-downloaded;
John Seabrook, "Revenue Streams," *New Yorker*, November 17, 2014.

7 Dean Baker, "The Artistic Freedom Voucher: Internet Age Alternative to
Copyrights," Center for Economic and Policy Research, November 2003,
https://www.cepr.net/report/the-artistic-freedom-voucher-internet-age
-alternative-to-copyrights/.

8 Stephen Heyman, "Sweden's Notorious Distinction as a Haven for Online
Pirates," *New York Times*, June 17, 2015, https://www.nytimes.com/2015
/06/18/arts/international/swedens-notorious-distinction-as-a-haven-for
-online-pirates.html; Bruce Gain, "Europe Goes Gently on P2P Piracy,"
Wired, July 9, 2005, https://www.wired.com/2005/07/europe-goes-gently
-on-p2p-piracy/.

9 "US threatened Sweden with sanctions over piracy," *Local Sweden*, June 21,
2006, https://www.thelocal.se/20060621/4128.

10 Ernesto Van der Sar, "Pirate Bay Investigator to Cash in Temporarily at Warner Bros.,"
TorrentFreak, April 23, 2008, https://torrentfreak.com/pirate-bay-investigator
-to-cash-in-at-warner-bros-080423/.

11 Maria Eriksson, Rasmus Fleischer, Anna Johansson, Pelle Snickars, and Patrick
Vonderau, *Spotify Teardown: Inside the Black Box of Streaming Music* (The MIT
Press, 2019).

2 "Saving" the Music Industry

1 Sven Carlsson, Jonas Leijonhufvud, *The Spotify Play: How CEO and Founder Daniel Ek Beat Apple, Google, and Amazon in the Race for Audio Dominance* (Diversion Books, 2021).

2 Carlsson, Leijonhufvud, *The Spotify Play*.

3 Carlsson, Leijonhufvud, *The Spotify Play*.

4 Carlsson, Leijonhufvud, *The Spotify Play*; John Seabrook, "Revenue Streams," *New Yorker*, November 14, 2014.

5 Eriksson et al., *Spotify Teardown*; for Spotify's later rewritten version of its own history, see materials from its March 2018 Investor Day: https://investors.spotify.com/investor-day-2018-materials/default.aspx.

6 "STING Day 2015 Interview with Martin Lorentzon, Spotify," YouTube, uploaded by stingsthlm, May 18, 2015, https://www.youtube.com/watch?v=nOOMsSeKQg4&t=967s.

7 Tweet from Daniel Ek on April 23, 2023, saying that the company's "actual founding was on @MartinLorentzon's birthday dinner April 1st [2006]. And we moved into the office early August," https://x.com/eldsjal/status/1650304798023905280; Carlsson, Leijonhufvud, *The Spotify Play*, 2021.

8 "Andreas Ehn - Spotify - Keynote - Innovation Stage - BDL Accelerate 2016," YouTube, uploaded by BDLaccelerate, January 4, 2017, https://youtu.be/_RCE ZiAWRec?si=Gcq5LoLfhcIiVGwH.

9 To see versions of the official Spotify web page through the years, see https://web.archive.org/web/20240000000000*/spotify.com.

10 "Andreas Ehn," YouTube.

11 Ek's explanation of the first product can be found on Episode 01 of *Spotify: A Product Story*, a corporate history podcast made by Spotify itself in 2021, https://engineering.atspotify.com/podcasts/spotify-a-product-story/; Carlsson, Leijonhufvud, *The Spotify Play*.

12 Andy Maxwell, "Spotify's Beta Used 'Pirate' MP3 Files, Some from Pirate Bay," *TorrentFreak*, May 9, 2017, https://torrentfreak.com/spotifys-beta-used-pirate-mp3-files-some-from-pirate-bay-170509/.

13 "Daniel Ek: A Playlist for Entrepreneurs [Entire Talk]," YouTube, uploaded by Stanford eCorner, June 12, 2012, https://www.youtube.com/watch?v=Nps7hHoWVn8.

14 Dean Takahashi, "Sean Parker Says Spotify on Facebook Lives Up to Original Napster Vision (Video)," *VentureBeat*, September 23, 2011, https://venturebeat.com/media/sean-parker-says-spotify-on-facebook-lives-up-to-original-napster-vision-video/.

15 Stefanie Olsen, "Online Dolls Get $6 Million to Spend," *CNET*, June 28, 2006; Fred Goodman, "Meet Fred Davis, One of the Industry's Biggest Dealmakers (And, Yes, Clive's Son)," *Billboard*, April 11, 2019, https://www.billboard.com/music/music-news/fred-davis-the-raine-group-industry-dealmaker-interview-8506624/.

16 Goodman, "Meet Fred Davis."

17 Eliot Van Buskirk, "Study: Imeem Unseats Yahoo as Top U.S. Music-Streaming Site," *Wired*, May 13, 2008, https://www.wired.com/2008/05/imeem-unseats-y/.

18 Carlsson, Leijonhufvud, *The Spotify Play*; Knopper, *Appetite for Self-Destruction*.

19 Carlsson, Leijonhufvud, *The Spotify Play*.

20 Carlsson, Leijonhufvud, *The Spotify Play*; Micah Singleton, "This Was Sony Music's Contract with Spotify," *The Verge*, May 19, 2015, https://www.theverge.com/2015/5/19/8621581/sony-music-spotify-contract.

21 Carlsson, Leijonhufvud, *The Spotify Play*.

22 Merlin's current market share and number of members: merlinnetwork.org.

23 Helienne Lindvall, "Why MySpace Music Is Unfair on Indie Labels," *Guardian*, October 2, 2008, https://www.theguardian.com/music/musicblog/2008/oct/02/myspace.music.unfair.on.indies.

24 Merlin's 2008 press release, headlined "Merlin, the Virtual Fifth Major, To Join Spotify At Launch," https://merlinnetwork.org/merlin-the-virtual-fifth-major-to-join-spotify-at-launch/; "Spotify the Difference as Merlin Nets Licensing Deal," *Music Week*, October 18, 2008.

25 "Success of Online Market for Independent Artists," YouTube, posted by Future of Music Coalition, June 27, 2008, https://youtu.be/so28vuX6Ttc?si=aDd9GAu1KX9MlhHD.

26 Monica Anderson, "5 Facts About Alternative Weeklies," Pew Research Center, July 11, 2014, https://www.pewresearch.org/short-reads/2014/07/11/5-facts-about-alternative-weeklies/.

27 Sam Richards, "The Day the Music Evolved," *NME*, January 31, 2009.

28 For the *NME* quote, see the Richards article from 2009; for *Rolling Stone* calling Spotify the "slickest free legal music service we've ever seen," see "Free, Legal Music: A User's Guide" in its issue dated June 25, 2009; for *Rolling Stone* calling Spotify "the best argument yet for getting rid of your CDs," see a sidebar titled "Showdown: Spotify vs. iTunes" in its issue dated September 17, 2009; and for *Gawker* calling Spotify "everything iTunes should be," see a post dated August 20, 2009 titled "Spotify: Delicious Forbidden Fruit": https://www.gawkerarchives.com/5342064/spotify-delicious-forbidden-fruit.

29 Fredrik Soderling, "Spotify's Money Is Distributed Unevenly," *Dagens Nyheter*, December 9, 2010, http://www.dn.se/kultur-noje/nyheter/spotifys-pengar-fordelas-ojamnt.

30 Helienne Lindvall, "Spotify Should Give Indies a Fair Deal on Royalties," *Guardian*, February 1, 2011, https://www.theguardian.com/media/pda/2011/feb/01/spotify-royalties-independents.

3 Selling Lean-Back Listening

1 "In Conversation: Daniel Ek & Casey Rae-Hunter @ Summit09," YouTube, uploaded by Future of Music Coalition, February 1, 2012, https://www.youtube.com/watch?v=2qYIWbKbAkQ; "Engine Failure: Safiya Umoja Noble and Sarah T. Roberts on the Problems of Platform Capitalism," *Logic(s)*, December 1, 2017, https://logicmag.io/justice/safiya-umoja-noble-and-sarah-t-roberts/.

2 The quote about "new and exciting music experiences" can be found on the front page of Spotify at this time, accessed using the Internet Archive.

3 Nathan Ingraham, "Spotify Wants to Become 'the OS of Music' and Help Artists Earn More Along the Way," *The Verge*, March 7, 2012, https://www.theverge.com/2012/3/7/2851328/spotify-the-os-of-music.

4 Stuart Dredge, "Spotify's Daniel Ek: 'We want artists to be able to afford to create the music they want to create,'" *Guardian*, December 6, 2012, https://www.theguardian.com/technology/2012/dec/06/spotify-daniel-ek-interview; Josh Constine, "Spotify Launches Influencer Following Music Graph, Collection, and Instant Previews to Aid Discovery," *TechCrunch*, December 6, 2012, https://techcrunch.com/2012/12/06/spotify-following/.

5 Liz Pelly, "The Secret Lives of Playlists," *Watt*, June 2017, https://lizpelly.info/watt.

6 Stuart Dredge, "Spotify Introduces Browse Page to Help People Find Streaming Music Playlists," *Guardian*, August 5, 2013, https://www.theguardian.com/technology/appsblog/2013/aug/05/spotify-browse-music-ios-android; Ellis Hamburger, "Spotify's New Browse Feature Surfaces the Best of Its Billion Playlists," *The Verge*, August 5, 2013, https://www.theverge.com/2013/8/5/4589336/spotifys-browse-best-playlists.

7 Stuart Dredge, "Spotify Buys Tunigo: What Does It Mean for Rivals, Startups and Investors?" *Music Ally*, May 7, 2013, https://musically.com/2013/05/07/spotify-buys-tunigo-what-does-it-mean-for-rivals-startups-and-investors/.

8 A brief overview of the Snowfish service can be found on the personal website of designer Jakob Westman, who designed its visual identity, https://www.jakobwestman.com/design#/snowfish/; additional details were sourced through Internet Archive documentation of the Snowfish website.

9 "Tuning into Change: Exploring the Music Industry's Transformation with Nick Holmstén," *The Few With Boo* (podcast), December 6, 2023, 14:20, https://the-few-podcast-with-boo.simplecast.com/episodes/tuning-into-change-exploring-the-music-industrys-transformation-with-nick-holmsten-nqBeoYYN.

10 Darrell Etherington, "Spotify Acquires Music Discovery App Tunigo, a Spotify-Powered Songza Competitor," *TechCrunch*, May 3, 2013, https://techcrunch.com/2013/05/03/spotify-acquires-music-discovery-app-tunigo-a-spotify-powered-songza-competitor/.

11 Paul Sloan, "Spotify Tries to Go Mainstream, Launches Splashy Ad Campaign," *CNET*, March 25, 2013, cnet.com/tech/services-and-software/spotify-tries-to-go-mainstream-launches-splashy-ad-campaign/.

12 Lina Brion, Detlef Diederichsen, "Introduction: The Order of Playlists," *Listen to Lists* (Spector Books, 2021); Kristoffer Cornils, "On the History of the Playlist," *Listen to Lists* (Spector Books, 2021).

13 Jeremy Wade Morris, *Selling Digital Music, Formatting Culture* (University of California Press, 2015).

14 "Playlisting Plus (part 1 of 3) | Indie Week 2017," YouTube, uploaded by A2IM American Association of Independent Music, May 29, 2020, https://www.youtube.com/watch?v=NlVtdl8jEg8; "Playlisting Plus (part 2 of 3) | Indie Week 2017," YouTube, uploaded by A2IM American Association of Independent Music, May 29, 2020, https://www.youtube.com/watch?v=uoVtN8iNu54; "Playlisting Plus (part 3 of 3) | Indie Week 2017," YouTube, uploaded by A2IM American Association of Independent Music, May 29, 2020, https://www.youtube.com/watch?v=vqmYk_T1BXk.

15 "Playlisting Plus" on YouTube.

16 "Playlisting Plus" on YouTube.

17 Reggie Ugwu, "Inside the Playlist Factory," *BuzzFeed News*, July 12, 2016, https://www.buzzfeed.com/reggieugwu/the-unsung-heroes-of-the-music-streaming-boom; for the stat about there currently being 10,000 playlists on Spotify, see "The Spotify Effect (ft Sulinna Ong)," Youtube video, uploaded by NickyandCoco, Feb 2, 2024, https://www.youtube.com/watch?v=L4imZRY_Maw.

18 Ugwu, "Inside the Playlist Factory."

19 Spotify Charts website: https://charts.spotify.com/home.

20 "Playlisting Plus" on YouTube.

21 For a peak playlist era account of Spotify editors being obsessed with "leveling the playing field," see this Kaitlyn Tiffany piece from 2017: https://www.theverge.com/2017/11/13/16617900/spotify-playlist-curation-nyc-live-shows-fresh-finds-indie-latin-new-music.

22 David Pierce, "The Secret Hit-Making Power of the Spotify Playlist," *Wired*, May 3, 2017, https://www.wired.com/2017/05/secret-hit-making-power-spotify-playlist/.

23 "Quora Session with Daniel Ek," https://www.quora.com/profile/Daniel-Ek.

24 Pauline Oliveros, *Deep Listening: A Composer's Sound Practice* (Deep Listening Publications, 2005).

25 Tia DeNora, *Music in Everyday Life* (Cambridge University Press, 2000).

26 Stuart Dredge, "Spotify data reveals boom in sleep and relaxation albums," *Guardian*, September 7, 2015, https://www.theguardian.com/technology/2015/sep/07/spotify-data-sleep-relaxation-albums.

4 The Conquest of Chill

 1 Stuart Elliott, "Spotify, New to Advertising, Says 'I've Got the Music in Me,'" *New York Times*, March 25, 2013, https://archive.nytimes.com/mediadecoder.blogs.nytimes.com/2013/03/25/spotify-new-to-advertising-says-ive-got-the-music-in-me/.

 2 Julie Beck, "Hard Feelings: Science's Struggle to Define Emotions," *Atlantic*, February 25, 2014; Ned Carter Miles, "Are You 80% Angry and 2% Sad? Why 'Emotional AI' Is Fraught with Problems," *Guardian*, June 23, 2024, https://www.theguardian.com/technology/article/2024/jun/23/emotional-artificial-intelligence-chatgpt-4o-hume-algorithmic-bias.

 3 Michael Sherman article on "Edison Mood Music" published by the Discography of American Historical Recordings website, a project of the UC Santa Barbara Library, https://adp.library.ucsb.edu/index.php/resources/detail/434; Alexandra Hui, "Lost: Thomas Edison's Mood Music Found: New Ways of Listening," *Endeavour* 38 (2014): 139–142.

 4 Sherman, "Edison Mood Music"; Hui, "Lost: Thomas Edison's Mood Music Found."

 5 Hui, "Lost: Thomas Edison's Mood Music Found."

 6 Beverly Beyette, "Humming Right Along: It's a far cry from a haphazard menu of music. Muzak has a mission. On any given day, it offers 'stimulus progression' to 80 million American ears," *Los Angeles Times*, December 19, 1990; Benjamin Frisch, "That Seattle Muzak Sound," *Slate*, June 16, 2021, https://slate.com/podcasts/decoder-ring/2021/06/muzak-grunge-elevator-music; the official corporate history of Muzak per Mood Media's current website: https://us.moodmedia.com/blog/history-of-muzak/.

 7 From the moodmedia.com article.

 8 The history of *Music While You Work* is chronicled on the BBC website: https://www.bbc.com/historyofthebbc/anniversaries/june/music-while-you-work.

 9 David Owen, "The Soundtrack of Your Life," *New Yorker*, April 2, 2006, https://www.newyorker.com/magazine/2006/04/10/the-soundtrack-of-your-life.

10 To read Brian Eno's *Music for Airports* liner notes online, see http://music.hyperreal.org/artists/brian_eno/MFA-txt.html; "Endel App Creator on the Power of Endless Ambient Music," Apple, May 18, 2021, https://www.apple.com/newsroom/2021/05/endel-app-creator-on-the-power-of-endless-ambient-music/.

11 Lindsay Zoladz, "Brian Eno's Music for Anxious Times," *New York Times*, November 4, 2020, https://www.nytimes.com/2020/11/04/arts/music/brian-eno-film-music.html.

12 Nick Shave, "Erik Satie: Prepare yourself . . . ," *Guardian*, June 25, 2016, https://www.theguardian.com/music/2016/jun/25/erik-satie-vexations-furniture-music; Spencer Doran, *Kankyō Ongaku: Japanese Ambient, Environmental & New Age Music 1980–1990*, liner notes, Light in the Attic (2019); "Composing for Space: The Meticulous Design of Japanese Environmental Sounds," *The Vinyl Factory*, https://thevinylfactory.com/features/kankyo-ongaku-japanese-environmental-sounds-spencer-doran/.

13 Philip Sherburne, "A Conversation with Brian Eno About Ambient Music," *Pitchfork*, February 16, 2017, https://pitchfork.com/features/interview/10023-a-conversation-with-brian-eno-about-ambient-music/.

14 "Spotify CEO Daniel Ek on earnings, changes in consumption patterns and more," *Squawk on the Street*, CNBC (video), https://www.cnbc.com/video/2020/04/29/spotify-ceo-daniel-ek-earnings-full-interview-squawk-street.html.

5   Ghost Artists for Hire

1 "'How Music Got Free' tells the story of record profits to online pirates," *WBUR*, June 11, 2024.

2 John McDuling, "The Music Industry Has Hit Its Rock Bottom," *Quartz*, April 14, 2015, https://qz.com/383109/the-music-industry-has-hit-its-rock-bottom.

3 Tim Ingham, "Spotify Is Making Its Own Records . . . and Putting Them on Playlists," *Music Business Worldwide*, August 31, 2016, https://www.musicbusinessworldwide.com/spotify-is-creating-its-own-recordings-and-putting-them-on-playlists/.

4 Linus Larsson, Hugo Lindkvist, Hugo Ewald Hurinsky, "*DN avslöjar: Svenska fejkartisterna som tog över på Spotify—större än Robyn*" ("DN Reveals: The Swedish Fake Artists Who Took Over Spotify—Bigger Than Robyn"), https://www.dn.se/kultur/dn-avslojar-svenska-fejkartisterna-som-tog-over-pa-spotify-storre-an-robyn/.

5 Tobias Lightning, "Queenstreet Is Ridiculously Profitable—Now Harald Mix (and Max Martin!) Has Bought In," *Breakit*, July 20, 2022, https://www.breakit.se/artikel/33758/queenstreet-ar-lojligt-lonsamma-nu-har-harald-mix-och-max-martin-kopt-in-sig.

6   The Background Music Makers

1 Daniel Tencer, "Epidemic Sound Has Courted Controversy over Its 'Buy-Out Deals.' Here's Exactly How the Company Pays Artists . . . ," *Music Business*

Worldwide, April 25, 2024, https://www.musicbusinessworldwide.com/epidemic
-sound-has-courted-controversy-over-its-buy-out-deals-heres-exactly-how-the
-company-pays-artists/.

2 Kathryn Kranhold, "TV and Film Composers Say Netflix, Other Streaming
Services Insist on Buying Out Their Music Rights," *Billboard*, December 11,
2019, https://www.billboard.com/pro/tv-film-composers-say-netflix-insisting
-on-music-rights-buyouts/.

3 Ingrid Lunden, "Epidemic Sound Raises $450M at a $1.4B Valuation to 'Soundtrack
the Internet,'" *TechCrunch*, March 11, 2011, https://techcrunch.com/2021/03/11
/epidemic-sound-raises-450m-at-a-1-4b-valuation-to-soundtrack-the-internet/.

4 "David Bowie 'Inspirations,'" YouTube, uploaded by @BoWIElover, May 15,
2011, 13:22, https://www.youtube.com/watch?v=pDmb_aR_OnY.

7 Streambait Pop

1 The Spotify artist-facing marketing initiative was called "Spotify Artists" upon
launch, and rebranded "Spotify for Artists" later on; "Welcome to The Game
Plan," YouTube, uploaded by Spotify for Artists, May 23, 2018, https://youtu
.be/nB0orl5B70I?si=S9qnGZITO2ic6Aeb.

2 "How to Read Your Data," YouTube, posted by Spotify for Artists, May 23,
2018, https://www.youtube.com/watch?v=686CoVucG54.

3 Rob Horning, "Three Things: Datafication, More Ozempic, AI Phones," *Internal Exile*, October 16, 2023, https://robhorning.substack.com/p/three-things.

4 Anytime an individual track's playlist history is chronicled, those details were
sourced from the website spotontrack.com, through which subscribers can
search any track and view a history of the playlists that track has appeared on,
the date it was added, the date it was removed, and other information.

5 Lyndsey Havens, "Why All Eyes Are on Billie Eilish, the New Model for
Streaming Era Success," *Billboard*, May 9, 2019, https://www.billboard.com
/music/pop/billie-eilish-billboard-cover-story-2019-8510552/.

6 David Turner, "Billie Eilish: The Exception That Proves the Rule," *Penny Fractions*,
October 23, 2019, https://pennyfractions.ghost.io/billie-eilish-the-exception-that
-proves-the-rule/; U.S. Securities and Exchange Commission, "Form F-1 Registra-
tion Statement Under the Securities Act of 1933: Spotify Technology S.A.," https://
www.sec.gov/Archives/edgar/data/1639920/000119312518063434/d494294df1.htm.

7 Eric Drott, *Streaming Music, Streaming Capital*, Duke University Press, 2024.

8 Charlie Taylor, "Spotify Holds Its First Songwriting Camp in Dublin," *Irish
Times*, March 5, 2020, https://www.irishtimes.com/business/technology/spotify
-holds-its-first-songwriting-camp-in-dublin-1.4192697; "Head of Songwriter
and Publishing Relations Jules Parker Explains How Spotify Is Bringing

Behind-the-Scenes Creators into the Spotlight," *Spotify for the Record*, July 8, 2020, https://newsroom.spotify.com/2020-07-08/head-of-songwriter-and -publishing-relations-jules-parker-explains-how-spotify-is-bringing-behind -the-scenes-creators-into-the-spotlight/.

9 Playlist history sourced via spotontrack.com.

10 Brittney McKenna, "Spotify, Amazon Among Streaming Platforms Fighting Songwriters Royalty Increase," *American Songwriter*, 2019, https://american songwriter.com/spotify-amazon-among-streaming-platforms-fighting-song writers-royalty-increase/.

11 Kristin Robinson, "TikTok Is Testing Ground for New Singles—Why Labels Love It (and Some Artists & Writers Don't)," *Billboard*, May 27, 2022, https:// www.billboard.com/pro/tiktok-song-promo-campaigns-teasers-marketing-song writer-splits/.

12 Elias Leight, "With Sped-Up Songs Taking Over, Artists Feel the Need for Speed," *Billboard*, March 13, 2023, https://www.billboard.com/pro/sped-up -songs-taking-over-labels-tiktok/

13 @gaylecantspell, TikTok, July 29, 2021, https://www.tiktok.com/@gaylecantspell /video/6990510290978786566; @danielswall, TikTok, January 6, 2022, https:// www.tiktok.com/@danielswall/video/7050208352160435503?lang=en.

14 Mark Katz, *Capturing Sound: How Technology Has Changed Music* (University of California Press, 2010); Jeremy Wade Morris, "Music Platforms and the Optimization of Culture," *Social Media + Society*, 2020, https://doi.org/10.1177 /2056305120940690.

15 Dane Wesolko, "The Theory of Affordances," Medium, June 14, 2016.

16 "Data and the Future of the Music Business | Warner Music Group," You-Tube, uploaded by Snowflake Inc., October 26, 2021, https://www.youtube .com/watch?v=UeX85ZAo-NM; "Warner Music Group Acquires Sodatone," Warner Music Group website, March 28, 2018, https://www.wmg.com/news /warner-music-group-acquires-sodatone-33396.

8 Listen to Yourself

1 Eriksson et al., *Spotify Teardown*.

2 Nick Seaver, *Computing Taste: Algorithms and the Makers of Music Recommen- dation* (University of Chicago Press, 2022).

3 Tim Ingham, "Turns Out Spotify Acquired the Echo Nest for Just 50M," *Music Business Worldwide*, May, 10, 2015, https://www.musicbusinessworldwide.com /spotify-acquired-echo-nest-just-e50m/; Rob Matheson, "Finding Harmony with Big Data," *MIT News*, July 10, 2013, https://news.mit.edu/2013/echo -nest-harmony-with-big-data-0710.

4 "Rethink Music 2012 - Hackers Results and Ken Parks (Spotify)," YouTube, uploaded by RethinkMusic2011, May 30, 2012, https://www.youtube.com /watch?v=LCMxGL24P5M.

5 To access Spotify's public API: https://developer.spotify.com/documentation /web-api.

6 Spotify's explanation of "taste profiles": https://support.spotify.com/us/article /your-taste-profile/.

7 Stuart Dredge, "Spotify launches Discover Weekly personalised 'mixtape' play-list," *Music Ally*, July 20, 2015, https://musically.com/2015/07/20/spotify-discover -weekly-personalised-mixtape-playlist/; Victor Luckerson, "Here's the Story Behind Spotify's Coolest Feature," *Time*, December 1, 2015, https://time.com /4131520/spotify-discover-weekly-playlists/.

8 "Learn More About the Audio Aura in Your Spotify 2021 Wrapped with Aura Reader Mystic Michaela," *Spotify for the Record*, December 1, 2021, https:// newsroom.spotify.com/2021-12-01/learn-more-about-the-audio-aura-in-your -spotify-2021-wrapped-with-aura-reader-mystic-michaela/.

9 Walter Benjamin, *The Work of Art in the Age of Mechanical Reproduction*, trans-lated by J. A. Underwood (Penguin Books, 2008).

10 "Your Music, Your World | Playlists Made for You on Spotify," YouTube, uploaded by Spotify, August 23, 2023, https://www.youtube.com/watch?v =93eeorv2e3M.

11 "Farmers Market," playlist on Spotify, https://open.spotify.com/playlist /37i9dQZF1DX9pryhDLql25; "aesthetic," playlist on Spotify, https://open .spotify.com/playlist/37i9dQZF1DX8uc99H0ZBLU; "sad girl country," playlist on Spotify, https://open.spotify.com/playlist/37i9dQZF1DWU4lunzhQdRx; "sad girl sh*t," playlist on Spotify, https://open.spotify.com/playlist/37i9dQZF 1DWYfVqUciU2jI; "sad girl starter pack," playlist on Spotify, https://open .spotify.com/playlist/37i9dQZF1DWW2hj3ZtMbuO.

9 Self-Driving Music

1 "Tunigo Serves Up A Music-To-Life Mentality," Arctic Startup, March 18, 2013, https://arcticstartup.com/tunigo-serves-up-a-music-to-life-mentality/; Cherie Hu, "Why Spotify Thinks Its 'Self-Driving Music' Strategy Will Benefit Creators," *Billboard*, March 19, 2018, https://www.billboard.com/pro/why-spotify -thinks-self-driving-music-strategy-will-benefit-creators.

2 "Spotify CTO Gustav Söderström: TikTok's Music; How Olivia Rodrigo Gamed the Algo | 20VC #936," YouTube video, posted by @20VC with Harry Stebbings, October 12, 2022, https://www.youtube.com/watch?v=P jUR2gW4BMM.

3 Glenn McDonald's tweet about how "Every Noise at Once" was a way of helping musical knowledge "self-organize" is at https://x.com/glenn_mcdonald /status/1733887827400614250; Cherie Hu, "What Is 'Escape Room' and Why Is It One of My Top Genres on Spotify?" *Medium*, December 15, 2016, https:// festivalpeak.com/what-is-escape-room-and-why-is-it-one-of-my-top-genres -on-spotify-a886372f003f.

4 Maura Johnston, "How Spotify Discovers the Genres of Tomorrow," *Spotify for Artists* blog, June 7, 2018, https://artists.spotify.com/en/blog/how-spotify -discovers-the-genres-of-tomorrow.

5 Kieran Press-Reynolds, "Can a Streaming Platform Create a Niche Music Genre?" *No Bells*, April 18, 2022, https://nobells.blog/webcore-hyperpop-phonk-playlist/.

6 Noah Simon, "Hyperpop Origins (Part 1): Definitions (?) & Aesthetic Influences," YouTube video, May 20, 2021, https://www.youtube.com/ watch?v=VbAr_5G8yik; Noah Simon, "Hyperpop Origins (Pt. 2): Net Labels and Internet Community," YouTube video, May 27, 2021, https://www.you tube.com/watch?v=J6kAauWNUkc&t=86s; Noah Simon, "Hyperpop Origins (Pt. 3): The New School," YouTube video, June 3, 2021, https://www.youtube .com/watch?v=8w6LgSMoX_c; Noah Simon, "Hyperpop Origins (Pt. 4): Spo- tify & Where To Go From Here," YouTube video, June 10, 2021, https://www .youtube.com/watch?v=vJbiDkNGUL4.

7 Ben Dandridge-Lemco, "How Hyperpop, a Small Spotify Playlist, Grew into a Big Deal," *New York Times*, November 10, 2020, https://www.nytimes.com /2020/11/10/arts/music/hyperpop-spotify.html.

8 Maria Eriksson, "Close Reading Big Data: The Echo Nest and the Production of (Rotten) Music Metadata," *First Monday* 21(7) (2016), https://doi.org/10.5210 /fm.v21i7.6303.

9 Simon, "Hyperpop Origins."

10 Press-Reynolds, "Can a Streaming Platform Create."

11 The Iglooghost Twitter post: https://x.com/IGLOOGHOST/status /714487790659088384.

12 Glenn McDonald, "bemused complicated partial credit layoff friday morning," *furialog*, January 26, 2024, https://www.furia.com/page.cgi?type=log&id=475.

13 The strategy behind the "POLLEN" playlist is described on the website of its designer: https://portorocha.com/pollen.

14 Jacob Moore, "What Is Lorem? Inside One of Spotify's Best New Playlists," *Complex*, December 11, 2019, https://www.complex.com/pigeons-and-planes /a/jacob-moore/lorem-spotify-playlist; Stuart Dredge, "Lorem, Pollen and Oyster: How Spotify's Genreless Playlists Are 'Driven by Culture,'" *Music Ally*, September 23, 2020, https://musically.com/2020/09/23/lorem-pollen-and-oyster -how-spotifys-genreless-playlists-are-driven-by-culture/.

10 Fandom as Data

1 The "oddly specific playlists" Facebook group: https://www.facebook.com/ groups/757415814732620.

2 Robin James, "What is a vibe?" *It's Her Factory*, January 29, 2021, https:// itsherfactory.substack.com/p/what-is-a-vibe; "Philosophy and Vibes with Robin James," *Sound Expertise* podcast, https://soundexpertise.org/philosophy-and- vibes-with-robin-james/.

3 Jacques Attali, *Noise: The Political Economy of Music* (University of Minnesota Press, 1985).

11 Sounds for Self-Optimization

1 Daniel Tencer, "AI Music App Boomy Has Created 14.4m Tracks to Date. Spotify Just Deleted a Bunch of Its Uploads After Detecting 'Stream Manipu- lation,'" *Music Business Worldwide*, May 3, 2023, https://www.musicbusiness- worldwide.com/ai-music-app-boomy-spotify-stream-manipulation/.

2 For the Boomy CEO quote, see: https://x.com/MusicAlly/status /1650852184819376128; for the Boomy press release announcing its partnership with Warner, see: https://www.wmg.com/news/boomy-partners-with-ada-worldwide -on-global-distribution-deal.

3 "Spotify Ejects Thousands of AI-Made Songs in Purge of Fake Streams," *Finan- cial Times*, May 8, 2023, https://www.ft.com/content/b6802c8f-50e7-4df8-8682 -cca794881e30.

4 Elizabeth Dilts Marshall, "Spotify's Daniel Ek Praises AI's Potential to Boost Music Creation—and the Company's Bottom Line," *Billboard*, April 25, 2023, https://www.billboard.com/pro/spotify-ceo-daniel-ek-praises-artificial -intelligence/.

5 "Music AI Ethics Tracker," *Water & Music*, https://www.waterandmusic.com /data/ai-ethics-tracker.

6 Joe Coscarelli, "Capitol Drops 'Virtual Rapper' FN Meka After Backlash over Stereotypes," *New York Times*, August 23, 2022, https://www.nytimes.com /2022/08/23/arts/music/fn-meka-dropped-capitol-records.html; "AI rapper FN Meka dropped by Capitol over racial stereotyping," *BBC*, August 24, 2022, https://www.bbc.com/news/newsbeat-62659741; Enongo Lumum- ba-Kasongo, "(A)I, Rapper: Who Voices Hip-Hop's Future?," *Public Books*, April 21, 2022, https://www.publicbooks.org/ai-rap-synthesis-tools-black -hip-hop/.

7 Marshall, "Spotify's Daniel Ek Praises AI's Potential"; "The Guy Behind the Viral A.I. Drake Song," YouTube video uploaded by @yokai, May 21, 2023.

8 Cory Doctorow, "The 'Enshittification' of TikTok or How, Exactly, Platforms Die," *Wired*, January 23, 2023, https://www.wired.com/story/tiktok-platforms -cory-doctorow/.

9 For a basic overview of Endel, see https://endel.io/about.

10 Websites for other "personalized background music" apps: notboring.software/ product/vibes, wiredvibeapp.com, lifescoremusic.com/; Mike Powell, "Natural Selection: How a New Age Hustler Sold the Sound of the World," *Pitchfork*, November 2, 2016, https://pitchfork.com/features/cover-story/9971-natural -selection-how-a-new-age-hustler-sold-the-sound-of-the-world/.

11 "Passive Mindfulness with Oleg Stavitsky, CEO & Co-Founder of Endel," *The Look Up! Podcast*, July 8, 2020, https://www.thelookuppodcast.com/episodes/ passive-mindfulness-with-oleg-stavitsky-ceo-amp-co-founder-of-endel; for the Endel "manifesto," see https://manifesto.endel.io/.

12 Chris Deville, "Algorithm Gets Major-Label Distribution Deal," *Stereogum*, March 22, 2019, https://www.stereogum.com/2036887/endel-algorithm -warners-bros-record-deal/news/; UMG press release, "Endel and Universal Music Group to Create AI-Powered, Artist-Driven Functional Music, Designed to Support Listener Wellness," May 23, 2023, https://www.universalmusic.com/ endel-and-universal-music-group-to-create-ai-powered-artist-driven-functional -music-designed-to-support-listener-wellness/; Aisha Malik, "Endel raises $15M to further develop Its AI-Powered Sound Wellness Technology," *TechCrunch*, April 5, 2022, https://techcrunch.com/2022/04/05/endel-raises-15m-to-further-develop -its-ai-powered-sound-wellness-technology/; Mandy Dalugdug, "Amazon Music Strikes Playlist Partnership with Generative AI Music Company Endel," *Music Business Worldwide*, February 20, 2023, https://www.musicbusinessworldwide .com/amazon-music-strikes-playlist-partnership-with-generative-ai-music -company-endel12/.

13 Sheldon Pearce, "James Blake & Endel: 'Wind Down,'" *New Yorker*, June 3, 2022, https://www.newyorker.com/goings-on-about-town/night-life/james -blake-and-endel-wind-down; "Generative AI Can Be a Co-Songwriter, Not a Copycat: Guest Post by Endel CEO Oleg Stavitsky," *Variety*, March 29, 2023, https://variety.com/2023/music/opinion/generative-ai-csongwriter-endel -oleg-stavitsky-artificial-intelligence-1235568233/.

14 Bob Wilson, "The Science behind Focus," Endel, June 28, 2022, https://endel .io/blog/the-science-behind-focus; "Modeling The Effect of Background Sounds on Human Focus Using Brain Decoding Technology," Arctop, https://arctop .com/deep-dives/modeling-focus.

15 UMG press release for "MUSIC + HEALTH" summit, https://www.universalmusic .com/universal-music-group-and-thrive-global-launch-music-health-summit/.

12 Streaming as Surveillance

1 Tim Peterson, "Spotify to use playlists as proxy for targeting ads to activities, moods," AdAge, April, 16, 2015, https://adage.com/article/digital/spotify -playlists-gauge-moods-ad-targeting/298066; Zach Rodgers, "Podcast: How Spotify Blazed a Trail in Audio Ads," *AdExchanger Talks*, June 8, 2017, https:// www.adexchanger.com/ad-exchange-news/podcast-spotify-blazed-trail-audio -ads/.

2 Spotify Advertising Team, "How Listeners See Video Ads on Spotify," August 2, 2020, https://ads.spotify.com/en-US/news-and-insights/how-listeners-see -video-ads-on-spotify/.

3 See Spotify's annual report for advertising revenue: https://investors.spotify.com /financials/default.aspx; Gen Z trend report: https://ads.spotify.com/en-US/ culture-next/gen-z-trends-report/

4 Natasha Singer, "Making Ads That Whisper to the Brain," *New York Times*, November 13, 2010, https://www.nytimes.com/2010/11/14/business/14stream .html/; Matt Wall, "What Are Neuromarketers Really Selling?," *Slate*, July 16, 2013, https://slate.com/technology/2013/07/does-neuromarketing -work-poor-data-secret-analysis-and-logical-errors.html; "Brain scam?" *Nature Neuroscience*, July 2004, https://www.nature.com/articles/nn0704-683.

5 Spotify neuromarketing campaign: https://ads.spotify.com/en-US/news-and -insights/wpp-neuro-insight-digital-audio-report/.

6 Eric Drott, *Streaming Music, Streaming Capital*, Duke University Press, 2024.

7 Justin Sherman, "Data Brokers Are a Threat to Democracy," *Wired*, April 13, 2021, https://www.wired.com/story/opinion-data-brokers-are-a-threat-to -democracy; Spotify Cookies Vendor List: https://www.spotify.com/us/legal /cookies-vendor-list/; Liz Pelly, "Big Mood Machine," The Baffler, June 10, 2019, https://thebaffler.com/downstream/big-mood-machine-pelly; for details on WPP and Spotify's renewed partnership announced in 2023, see this press release: https://www.wpp.com/en/news/2023/08/wpp-spotify-announce-first -of-its-kind-global-partnership.

8 Devin Coldewey, "Signal's Meredith Whittaker: AI is fundamentally 'a sur- veillance technology'," Tech Crunch, September 25, 2023, https://techcrunch. com/2023/09/25/signals-meredith-whittaker-ai-is-fundamentally-a-s urveil- lance-technology/

9 Mark Savage, "Spotify wants to suggest songs based on your emotions," BBC, January 28, 2021, https://www.bbc.com/news/entertainment-arts-55839655; Murray Stassen, "Spotify has a patent for personality tracking technology— and it's pretty creepy stuff," Music Business Worldwide, October 7, 2020,

https://www.musicbusinessworldwide.com/spotify-has-a-patent-for-personality
-trackin g-technology-and-its-pretty-creepy/; Ashley King, "Spotify Patents
Technology to Target Listeners Based on 'Nostalgia Metrics,'" *Digital Music
News*, September 30, 2020, https://www.digitalmusicnews.com/2020/09/30/
spotify-nostalgia-patent-2020/.

10 For the AI Now Institute's 2019 Report: https://ainowinstitute.org/wp-content/
uploads/2023/04/AI_Now_2019_Report.pdf; for a press release regarding a
consulting firm's claims about the present and future of the "emotion detection
and recognition market": https://www.prnewswire.co.uk/news-releases/emotion
-detection-and-recognition-mark et-is-expected-to-generate-a-revenue-of-usd
-60-86-billion-by-2030--globally-at-13-ca gr-verified-market-research-301730403
.html.

11 The Privacy International explanation of why privacy matters: https://privacy
international.org/learning-resources/privacy-matters

12 Sarah Perez, "Spotify will now let brands sponsor its Discover Weekly playlist," *Tech Crunch*, January 7, 2019, https://techcrunch.com/2019/01/07/spotify
-will-let-now-brands-sponsor-its-discover- weekly-weekly-playlist/; To see the
Microsoft AI commercial featuring Common: https://www.ispot.tv/ad/Ijcr/
microsoft-ai-inspiring-possibility-featuring-common; David E. Sanger, "Microsoft Says It Will Sell Pentagon Artificial Intelligence and Other Advanced
Technology," *New York Times*, October 26, 2018, https://www.nytimes
.com/2018/10/26/us/politics/ai-microsoft-pentagon.html

13 Morgan Meaker, "A battlefield AI company says it's one of the good guys,"
Wired, July 20, 2023, https://www.wired.com/story/helsing-ai-military-defense
-tech/; Daniel Ek and Tom Enders, "Europe's need to catch up with soft-
ware-led New Defense," *Politico*, June 10, 2022, https://www.politico.eu/article/
europes-need-to-catch-up-with-software-led-new-defe nse/; Abigail Velez,
"Musicians protest at SXSW, demanding 'no ties' with military contractors,"
CBS Austin, March 15, 2024, https://cbsaustin.com/news/local/musicians
-boycotting-sxsw-host-protest-and-rally.

14 "The Future of Digital Experiences in the Smart City | BlackBerry Summit
2023," YouTube video posted by BlackBerry, January 6, 2024, https://www
.youtube.com/watch?v=Rdd3_TCLmC8.

13   The First .0035 Is the Hardest

1 Don Giovanni Records tweet: https://x.com/DonGiovanniRecs/status
/1050488619247591424.

2 Spotify's own explanation of how it pays artists: https://support.spotify.com
/us/artists/article/royalties/.

3 For a summary of the UN music streaming report: https://weareumaw.org
/un-report.

4 Howie Singer and Bill Rosenblatt, *Key Changes: The Ten Times Technology Trans-
formed the Music Industry* (Oxford, 2023).

5 Chris Cooke, *Dissecting the Digital Dollar: Third Edition* (Music Managers
Forum, 2020).

6 Cooke, *Dissecting the Digital Dollar*; Meredith Rose, "Streaming in the Dark:
Where Music Listeners' Money Goes—and Doesn't," Public Knowledge, May
2023, https://publicknowledge.org/policy/streaming-in-the-dark-where-music
-listeners-money-goes-and-doesnt/.

7 Damon Krukowski, "Making Cents," *Pitchfork*, November 14, 2012, https://
pitchfork.com/features/article/8993-the-cloud/.

8 Larry Fitzmaurice, "How Indie Artists Actually Make Money in 2019," *Vulture*,
April 8, 2019, https://www.vulture.com/2019/04/how-indie-artists-actually
-make-money-in-2019.html.

9 "The First Ever Musicians' Census Report Launched," September 11, 2023,
https://www.helpmusicians.org.uk/about-us/news/the-first-ever-musicians
-census-report-launched.

10 "Inaugural Music Industry Research Association (MIRA) Survey of Musicians
Executive Summary" press release, https://psrc.princeton.edu/sites/g/files/
toruqf1971/files/resource-links/report_on_mira_musician_survey.pdf.

11 "Modernizing Our Royalty System to Drive an Additional $1 Billion Toward
Emerging and Professional Artists," *Spotify for Artists* blog, November 21, 2023,
https://artists.spotify.com/en/blog/modernizing-our-royalty-system; for the
86% stat, see: instagram.com/weareumaw/p/C5T7yIduStW/.

12 Dan Rys, "Lucian Grainge Calls for 'Updated Model' for Music Industry:
Read His Memo to UMG Staff," *Billboard*, January 11, 2023, https://www.
billboard.com/pro/lucian-grainge-umg-full-staff-memo-2023-read-message/;
Anna Nicolaou, "The Incredible Resilience of the Music Industry," *Financial
Times*, September 8, 2023, https://www.ft.com/content/b85ab5af-bd03-4da8
-971a-316e7c7897dc.

13 Stuart Dredge, "UMG Boss Slams Artist-Centric Critics as 'Merchants of
Garbage,'" *Music Ally*, October 27, 2023, https://musically.com/2023/10/27
/umg-boss-slams-artist-centric-critics-as-merchants-of-garbage/.

14 Paul Resnikoff, "Spotify Executive Calls Artist 'Entitled' for Requesting Payment of One Penny Per Stream," *Digital Music News*, June 29, 2021, https://
www.digitalmusicnews.com/2021/06/29/spotify-executive-entitled-pay-penny
-per-stream/.

15 Spotify Investor Day 2018: https://investors.spotify.com/investor-day-2018
-materials/default.aspx.

16 These numbers come from Spotify's "Loud & Clear" report, https://loudand
clear.byspotify.com/.

14   An App for a Boss

1 Taylor Swift, "For Taylor Swift, the Future of Music Is a Love Story," *Wall Street
Journal*, July 7, 2014, https://www.wsj.com/articles/for-taylor-swift-the-future
-of-music-is-a-love-story-1404763219; Daniel Ek, "$2 Billion and Counting,"
Spotify for Artists blog, November 12, 2014, https://artists.spotify.com/en/blog
/2-billion-and-counting.
2 The Third Bridge Creative website includes the *Spotify for Artists* blog as a case
study: https://www.thirdbridgecreative.com/strategy/b2c-content-marketing
-for-creators.
3 Taylor Lorenz, "The Real Difference Between Creators and Influencers," *Atlantic*, May 31, 2019, https://www.theatlantic.com/technology/archive/2019/05/
how-creators-became-influencers/590725/.
4 Amanda Perelli, "The Creator Economy Is a $250 Billion Industry and It's Here
To Stay," *Business Insider*, November 16, 2023, https://www.businessinsider.
com/creator-economy-250-billion-market-and-here-to-stay-2023-11; Chris-
tine Muhlke, "For Content Creators, It's the Wild West," *New York Times*,
December 6, 2023, https://www.nytimes.com/2023/12/06/business/dealbook
/content-creator-economy.html.
5 Liz Pelly, "Playing in the Social Factory: An Interview with Astra Taylor," *The
Media*, September 11, 2015, http://www.fvckthemedia.com/issue61/astra-taylor.
6 Chris Anderson, *The Long Tail: Why the Future of Business Is Selling Less of More*
(Hachette Books, 2006); Rupert Neate, "Daniel Ek profile: 'Spotify will be
worth tens of billions,'" *Telegraph*, February 17, 2010, https://www.telegraph.
co.uk/finance/newsbysector/mediatechnologyandtelecoms/media/7259509/
Daniel-Ek-profile-Spotify-will-be-worth-tens-of-billions.html; for the "one million artists making a living off of their music" quote, see Ek's remarks at Spotify's
2018 Investor Day: https://www.youtube.com/watch?v=6QxA5qBRZxM.
7 Stuart Dredge, "Spotify CEO Talks Covid-19, Artist Incomes and Podcasting
(Interview)," *Music Ally*, July 30, 2020, https://musically.com/2020/07/30
/spotify-ceo-talks-covid-19-artist-incomes-and-podcasting-interview/.

15   Indie Vibes

1 Stuart Berman, "Lance Allen and the New Secrets of DIY Success," *Spotify for
Artists* blog, May 1, 2018, https://artists.spotify.com/en/blog/lance-allen-and
-the-new-secrets-of-diy-success.

2 "Indie Music and the Web | Maggie Vail at MozFest," YouTube video posted by Mozilla, February 9, 2017, https://www.youtube.com/watch?v=RyAdgOoJm_E.

3 Chris Eggertsen, "Spotify Paid Out a Record \$4.5B to Independent Labels & Publishers in 2023," *Billboard*, February 27, 2024, https://www.billboard.com/business/streaming/spotify-paid-indie-music-labels-publishers-2023-1235615863.

4 See this press release from when AWAL was owned by Kobalt, who called it their "streaming label for independent artists," https://www.kobaltmusic.com/press/awal-demystifies-streaming-data-for-independent-artists/, and this press release on the Sony Music Entertainment website regarding its purchase of AWAL, https://www.sonymusic.com/sonymusic/cma-clears-awal-neighbouring-rights-acquisition/.

5 Tim Ingham, "'I look at AWAL as the best artist development company in the business,'" *Music Business Worldwide*, August 1, 2023, https://www.musicbusinessworldwide.com/i-look-at-awal-as-the-best-artist-development-company-in-the-business/.

6 A copy of the press release about AWAL's data app: https://www.globenewswire.com/news-release/2017/03/28/1115065/0/en/AWAL-De-Mystifies-Streaming-Data-for-Independent-Artists.html.

7 See AWAL's website for an in-depth description of its model: https://www.awal.com/how-it-works/.

8 Joe Coscarelli, "A Teenager, Her Ukulele and a Bedroom Pop Empire in the Making," *New York Times*, October 11, 2019, https://www.nytimes.com/2019/10/11/arts/music/mxmtoon.html; Thania Garcia, "Music Industry Moves: Laufey Reaffirms Global Record Deal with AWAL," *Variety*, November 15, 2023, https://variety.com/2023/music/news/hybe-expands-latin-market-exile-music-acquisition-1235790435/.

9 Stuart Dredge, "CMA Provisionally Clears Sony Music's Acquisition of AWAL," *Music Ally*, February 11, 2022, https://musically.com/2022/02/11/cma-sony-music-awal-acquisition-decision/; Tim Ingham, "Why Did Sony Music Just Spend \$430 Million on Indie Label AWAL?," *Rolling Stone*, February 2, 2021, https://www.rollingstone.com/pro/features/why-did-sony-music-just-spend-430-million-on-kobalt-indie-label-awal-1122350/; David Turner, "What's Lost If Sony Owns AWAL," *Penny Fractions*, February 23, 2022, https://pennyfractions.ghost.io/are-major-labels-too-big-in-2022/.

10 For the personal website of one of the strategists who helped develop Lorem, see https://ceciliaazcarate.com/lorem-spotify; "#Lorem," YouTube, posted by Spotify, October 21, 2020, https://www.youtube.com/watch?v=cPiKwHZ3NdY.

11 Michael Dominguez, "Inside Spotify's Gen-Z Hub, Lorem," *Hits Daily Double*, October 22, 2020, https://hitsdailydouble.com/news&id=323718&title=INSIDE-SPOTIFYS-GEN-Z-ALT-HUB-LOREM.

12 Samantha Hissong, "Distrokid Will Act Like a Dating App for Artists Seeking Labels," *Rolling Stone*, January 28, 2021, https://www.rollingstone.com/pro/news/distrokid-music-dating-app-republic-records-1119521/; Murray Stassen, "Universal Acquires Mtheory's Label Division," *Music Business Worldwide*, September 13, 2022, https://www.musicbusinessworldwide.com/universal-acquires-mtheorys-label-division-jt-myers-and-nat-pastor-to-run-umgs-global-artist-services-business/; Warner Music Group press release regarding the Boomy partnership, https://www.wmg.com/news/boomy-partners-with-ada-worldwide-on-global-distribution-deal; Tim Ingham, "Confirmed: Warner Music Group Won't Be Making a Bid for Believe," *Music Business Worldwide*, April 6, 2024, https://www.musicbusinessworldwide.com/after-all-that-warner-music-group-wont-be-making-a-bid-for-believe/.

16   This Is . . . Payola?

1 "Podcasts as a Source of News and Information," Pew Research Center, April 18, 2023, https://www.pewresearch.org/journalism/2023/04/18/podcasts-as-a-source-of-news-and-information/; Sara Fischer, "Americans mostly believe news they hear on podcasts," April 18, 2023, Axios, https://www.axios.com/2023/04/18/podcasts-news-trust-pew-study.

2 "Amplifying Artist Input in Your Personalized Recommendations," *Spotify for the Record* blog, November 2, 2020, https://newsroom.spotify.com/2020-11-02/amplifying-artist-input-in-your-personalized-recommendations/.

3 Murray Stassen, "3 Things to Know About Spotify's Controversial New 'Pay for Influence' Tool, Discovery Mode," *Music Business Worldwide*, November 4, 2020, https://www.musicbusinessworldwide.com/3-things-to-know-about-spotifys-controversial-new-pay-for-influence-tool-discovery-mode.

4 For Spotify's current description of Discovery Mode, including the cost and the playlists that feature its discounted tracks: https://artists.spotify.com/en/discovery-mode.

5 Stassen, *Music Business Worldwide*, 2020.

6 "How Goth Babe Amplified New Releases and Gave New Life to His Catalog with Campaign Kit," *Spotify for Artists* blog, January 15, 2024, https://artists.spotify.com/en/blog/how-goth-babe-used-campaign-kit-to-amplify-his-music.

7 Some basic information about how Spotify charges for Marquees and Showcases can be found at https://support.spotify.com/us/artists/article/campaign-payment-and-budget/; my source for the per-click prices was a Spotify email forwarded to me by a source.

8 The Artist Rights Alliance, "Op-Ed: Spotify's New 'Discovery Mode' Is Just Payola," *Rolling Stone*, May 18, 2021, https://www.rollingstone.com/pro/music-biz-commentary/spotify-payola-artist-rights-alliance-1170544/.

9 Madison Bloom, "Spotify Facing House Judiciary Committee Probe Over Discovery Mode," *Pitchfork*, June 3, 2021, https://pitchfork.com/news/spotify-facing-house-judiciary-committee-probe-over-discovery-mode/.

10 Fredric Dannen, *Hit Men: Power Brokers and Fast Money Inside the Music Business* (Vintage, 1991).

11 Meredith Rose, "Streaming in the Dark: Where Music Listeners' Money Goes—and Doesn't," Public Knowledge, May 2023, https://publicknowledge.org/policy/streaming-in-the-dark-where-music-listeners-money-goes-and-doesnt/.

17   The Lobbyists Working Against Musicians in DC

1 For the Jonathan Prince tweet, see: https://x.com/jonathanmprince/status/632289141527552000; Greg Hazley, "Prince Shuffles to Spotify to Head Comms," O'Dwyer's, September 25, 2014, https://www.odwyerpr.com/story/public/3207/2014-09-25/prince-shuffles-spotify-head-comms.html.

2 Tony Romm, "Tech Giants Led by Amazon, Facebook and Google Spent Nearly Half a Billion on Lobbying over the Past Decade, New Data Shows," *Washington Post*, January 22, 2020, https://www.washingtonpost.com/technology/2020/01/22/amazon-facebook-google-lobbying-2019/; Fatma Khaled, "Facebook and Amazon are now the top lobbying spenders in the US," *Business Insider*, Mar 25, 2021, https://www.businessinsider.com/facebook-and-amazon-are-countrys-top-lobbying-spenders-report-2021-3; Max Kortlander, Marleen Stikker, "Democracy Threatens Big Tech's Business Model," *Tech Policy Press*, March 6, 2024, https://www.techpolicy.press/democracy-threatens-big-techs-business-model/.

3 Noreen Malone, "Barack Obama Just Joined Spotify," *New York*, https://nymag.com/intelligencer/2012/02/barack-obama-just-joined-spotify.html.

4 Kori Schulman, "The White House Just Joined Spotify: Listen to the President's Summer Playlist," *The White House Blog*, August 14, 2015, https://obamawhitehouse.archives.gov/blog/2015/08/14/white-house-just-joined-spotify-listen-presidents-summer-playlist.

5 Marissa G. Muller, "Barack Obama Has a Job Waiting for Him at Spotify," *Teen Vogue*, January 9, 2017, https://www.teenvogue.com/story/barack-obama-job-offer-spotify-president-playlists.

6 All information regarding Spotify's lobbying efforts was retrieved via OpenSecrets.org; Kathryn Lyons, "Everyone Has a Podcast Now, Including Rep. Dan Crenshaw," *Roll Call*, February 12, 2020, https://rollcall.com/2020/02/12/everyone-has-a-podcast-now-including-rep-dan-crenshaw/; Derek Robertson, "Wow, Politicians Are Really Bad at Podcasting," *Politico*, August 19, 2022, https://www.politico.com/news/magazine/2022/08/19/boring-podcasts-00052659.

7 See this OpenSecrets page: https://www.opensecrets.org/federal-lobbying/industries/summary?cycle=2023&id=B13.

8 Anna Palmer and Tony Romm, "Spotify Turns Up Volume in D.C.," *Politico*, April 15, 2015, https://www.politico.com/story/2015/04/spotify-washington-lobbying-firms-117001.

9 Emma Roth, "Why Spotify Is Still Fighting with Apple in Europe," *The Verge*, May 9, 2024, https://www.theverge.com/2024/5/9/24152380/spotify-apple-fight-european-union-dma; the video mentioned here was posted by Daniel Ek on his LinkedIn page in 2024: https://www.linkedin.com/posts/daniel-ek-1b52093a_the-european-commission-finally-ruled-against-activity-7170430331504746497-0QcI/.

10 United States Securities and Exchange Commission Form 20-F for Spotify Technology S.A., https://s29.q4cdn.com/175625835/files/doc_financials/2023/ar/26aaaf29-7cd9-4a5d-ab1f-b06277f5f2a5.pdf.

11 "Working for Speaker Pelosi, Spotify, and More with Tom Manatos," *The Lobbying Show*, April 22, 2019, https://thelobbyingshow.libsyn.com/working-for-speaker-pelosi-spotify-and-more-with-tom-manatos.

12 Mary Huber, "A deep dive with Spotify's chief public affairs officer," The University of Austin at Texas Moody College of Communication, November 30, 2024, https://moody.utexas.edu/news/deep-dive-spotifys-chief-public-affairs-officer.

13 Tim Ingham, "On Tuesday, Paul Vogel, CFO of Spotify, Cashed $9.3M In Shares—24 Hours After His Company Confirmed 1,500 Layoffs. Tonight, Daniel Ek Has Announced Vogel Is Out," *Music Business Worldwide*, December 7, 2023, https://www.musicbusinessworldwide.com/this-week-paul-vogel-cfo-of-spotify-cashed-out-9m-in-shares-as-his-company-announced-1500-layoffs-tonight-daniel-ek-announced-vogel-is-out/.

14 Glenn Peoples, "Music's Top Money Makers: The Highest-Paid Executives and Stockholders at Publicly Traded Companies," *Billboard*, Sept. 26, 2023, https://www.billboard.com/pro/best-paid-music-executives-stockholders-publicly-traded-companies/; Elizabeth Dilts Marshall, "UMG CEO Lucian Grainge's $128M 2023 Pay Package Approved by Shareholders," *Billboard*, May 16, 2024.

15 Henrik Huldschiner, "Spotify Founder Martin Lorentzon in Exclusive Interview: 'My goal is to be 120 years old,'" *King*, October 5, 2023, https://www.kingmagazine.se/martin-lorentzon-intervju-2023/.

18   The New Music Labor Movement

1 For an overview of the UMAW "Justice at Spotify" campaign: https://weare umaw.org/justice-at-spotify.

2 Liz Pelly, "With Gigs Canceled and No Relief, Musicians Form a Nationwide Union," *In These Times*, December 7, 2020, https://inthesetimes.com/article /union-of-musicians-and-allied-workers-organize-during-covid-musicians -gig-workers-rights.

3 Pelly, "With Gigs Canceled."

4 For an overview of Music Workers Alliance as an organization and its streaming justice work, see https://musicworkersalliance.org/about-page; https://musicwork-ersalliance.org/streaming-justice, and for more on its origins, see https:// www.openskyjazz.com/2024/01/jerome-harris-advocating-for-independent -musicians/.

5 David Turner, "Stars and Strikes: Why Musicians Need Unions," *Real Life Magazine*, December 13, 2018, https://reallifemag.com/stars-and-strikes/.

6 Joey La Neve DeFrancesco, "Musicians Can and Should Organize to Improve Their Pay and Working Conditions," *Jacobin*, February 1, 2020, https://jacobin .com/2020/02/musicians-working-conditions-afm-amazon-sxsw-nomusicforice.

7 Pelly, "With Gigs Canceled."

8 "#JusticeAtSpotify: A Year in Review," UMAW, https://weareumaw.org/news /justiceatspotify-a-year-in-review.

9 For the Living Wage for Musicians Act details: "Make Streaming Pay," https:// weareumaw.org/news/make-streaming-pay.

10 "Why a collective agreement?" Posted by Spotify Workers, https://open.spotify .com/episode/o8vKk6N8bkrWhco6wTgUzG.

11 "Information to members of Engineers of Sweden employed at Spotify regarding the value of collective agreements," April 26, 2023, shared with me by the Sveriges Ingenjörer.

Conclusion

1 Capitol Music Group press release: https://www.prnewswire.com/news -releases/capitol-music-group-launches-capitol-innovation-center-to-be-based -at-companys-iconic-tower-and-state-of-the-art-recording-studios-300627088 .html; UMG press release: https://www.universalmusic.com/universal -music-group-launches-accelerator-engagement-network/; Sony Innovation Fund: https://www.sonyinnovationfund.com/; WMG press release: https:// www.wmg.com/news/warner-music-group-and-polygon-labs-launch-music -accelerator-program-to-power-the-next-great-evolution-of-the-music-industry -through-blockchain-technology.

2 For a deeper dive on the solidarity economy, see https://neweconomy.net/ solidarity-economy/ & for connections between the solidarity economy and artists: https://art.coop/.

3 https://www.catalyticsound.com/about/.

4 https://hellgatenyc.com/about/ & https://newfeeling.ca/about-the-co-op/.

5 "An Alternative Model for Music Streaming," Written evidence submitted by Resonate Co-operative to the UK Parliament Digital, Culture, Media and Sport Select Committee inquiry into the Economics of Music Streaming, https://committees.parliament.uk/writtenevidence/15377/pdf/.

6 Liz Pelly, "Zola Jesus Finds Purpose in the Process," NPR Music, June 21, 2002, https://www.npr.org/2022/06/21/1104432916/zola-jesus-finds-purpose-in-the-process.

7 Liz Pelly, "Library Music: In the age of streaming, public libraries offer small-scale alternatives for local archiving," Pioneer Works *Broadcast*, September 10, 2021, https://pioneerworks.org/broadcast/library-music-liz-pelly.

8 Clay Masters, "A Unique Digital Music Service, For Locals Only," *NPR Music*, August 22, 2013, https://www.npr.org/sections/therecord/2013/08/22/213863138/a-unique-digital-music-service-for-locals-only.

9 For an archive of the Danish Netmusik project, see: https://web.archive.org/web/20040402180038/http://www.netmusik.dk/default.asp?funk=OmNetmus&tId=Nyt.

10 Orla Barry, "The changing landscape for Sweden's successful music industry," *The World*, August 3, 2023, https://theworld.org/stories/2023/08/03/changing-landscape-sweden-s-successful-music-industry.

11 "#KeepMusicAlive: Let's Talk About Universal Basic Income," Musicians Union, https://musiciansunion.org.uk/all-campaigns/let-s-talk-about-universal-basic-income.

12 Ronan McGreevy, "Basic Income Support for Artists Described as a 'Seismic Leap Forward,'" *Irish Times*, September 8, 2022, https://www.irishtimes.com/culture/2022/09/08/basic-income-support-for-artists-described-as-a-seismic-leap-forward/.

13 Emmet Malone, "'Life Changing' Income Scheme for Artists Means More Spend Time on Work and Fewer Suffer from Depression," *Irish Times*, May 27, 2024, https://www.irishtimes.com/culture/art/2024/05/27/life-changing-income-scheme-for-artists-means-more-spend-time-on-work-and-fewer-suffer-from-depression/.

14 Eleanor Beardsley and Katie Kheriji-Watts, "In France, Performing Artists Are Guaranteed Unemployment Income," *All Things Considered*, NPR, January 11, 2021, https://www.npr.org/2021/01/11/954994402/how-france-is-helping-its-artists-during-the-pandemic.

Index

Abbey, Michael, 209–12
AI (artificial intelligence)
 AI DJ, 97, 106–8, 116
 Boomy, 125–28, 183
 ethics of, 130–31
 to identify new talent, 90–91
 military use of, 146–47
 mood data collected by, 144–45
 music generated by, 66, 75, 125–36
 training of, 94–96, 126
Akiyama, Kuniharu, 46
algorithms, viii, ix, 92–94, 96–104,
  115–16, 120, 122–23
Allen, Lance, 172–73, 184
Almanac Singers, 205
Amazon, 4, 65, 133–34, 170–71, 197, 198–99
American Federation of Musicians
  (AFM), 207–8
American Music Fairness Act, 234
Andasun, Mat, 72–73
Anderson, Chris, 166–67
Anderson, Jim, 158–9
Anjali, 204–5
Ann Arbor District Library, 225–26, 228
Anohni, 54
Antipiratbyrån, 2

Apple, 4, 200–201
 See also iTunes
Arctop, 135
Arm, Mark, 43
artist-centric payment system, 156–57,
  187–88, 194
Artist Compensation Royalty Fund, 212
Artistic Freedom Voucher, 7–8
Artists Rights Alliance, 192–93
Ashikawa, Satoshi, 46
Association for the Advancement of
  Creative Musicians, 220–21
Attali, Jacques, 30, 123–24
Audio Auras, 102–3
Audio Home Recording Act (AHRA),
  211–12
Austin, Preston, 224
Autoplay, 98–99, 186–88
AWAL, 131–32, 178–80, 183, 261nn4–5

background music, 26, 35–38, 41–2,
  57–58, 68–78
 See also chill music; Muzak/muzak;
  PFC; stock music
Bandcamp, 20, 225, 243n2
Basic Income for the Arts, 231–32

About the Author

Liz Pelly is a contributing editor at *The Baffler*. Her byline has appeared in the *Guardian*, *Pitchfork*, *Rolling Stone*, and other outlets, and she frequently discusses music streaming on radio and podcasts spanning music, culture, and technology, including appearances on the *New York Times Popcast*, NPR *Morning Edition*, *Resident Advisor*'s *The Hour*, *Feminist Internet*, *Tech Won't Save Us*, and many others. Pelly has spoken about the effects of music streaming and platform capitalism internationally at music festivals and academic conferences alike. She's spent over a decade involved in all-ages show booking and helping run community art spaces.